MY FARE CITY

Kelly,

For all you do
Thanks for you!

Bud

MY FARE CITY

A CABBY'S DIARY AFTER DARK
AND LETTERS TO BUD

BUD CARSON

15781

For the San Francisco Taxi Drivers who have been
murdered on duty, may you not be forgotten.
Earnest A. Pinataro, 1947, Bluebird Cab, Newcomb near Quint
John K. Dearth, 1948, 25th Street and Capp
Samuel Bergman, 1963, Yellow Cab, near Park Merced
Victor J. Zarchinski, 1967, Luxor Cab, near 122 19th Avenue
Paul Stine, 1969, Yellow Cab, Washington and Cherry
Charles Jarman, 1970, Yellow Cab, Jackson Street in Pacific Heights
Fred J. Hooper, 1971, Yellow Cab, Newcomb near Lane
Roland J. Canfield, 1973, Yellow Cab, Noe and 27th Street
Gene DiLabbio, 1974, Yellow Cab, Chestnut and Kearny
John Dadian, 1975, DeSoto Cab, near Seal Rock Inn
Robert Duran, 1976, Eagle Cab, 18th Street and Linda
Michael Albert, 1977, Veterans Cab, Watchman Way
Albert H. Hohl, 1981, Luxor Cab, Eddy and Scott
George Ring, 1984, Yellow Cab, Scott and Grove
Leonard Smith, 1986, Allied Cab, Western Addition
George Oppenlander, 1988, Yellow Cab, Barneveld and Sweeny
John B. Coleman, 1989, Yellow Cab, Farragut Street
Andrew Lee Scott, 1991, Yellow Cab, Maddux and Quint
Parminder Singh, 1992, Yellow Cab, Funston and Lake
Richard Harcos, 1992, Luxor Cab, 200 block of Blythedale
David Hayes, 1993, City Cab, City of Richmond
Daljeet Singh Ghotra, 1997, Yellow Cab, Laguna and Ellis
Gennady Penskoy, 1998, United Cab, Sunnydale and Sawyer
Munther Salman, 1999, Yellow Cab, City of Richmond
Sukhpal Singh Sodhi, 2002, United Cab, 24th Street and Folsom

CONTENTS

"Bud Carson's *My Fare City* is intelligent, poetic, gritty, and gives us middle-class play-it-safers a fascinating look at the darker side of society."
San Francisco Chronicle

"Exploring the depths of American Reality as few have before . . . unique perspectives on life and how to live it."
YAHOO!'s Picks of the Week

"Four Stars . . . a gritty portrayal . . . real life in the home of the brave."
Simpatico Netlife

"Bud Carson takes you on a wild taxi ride free of charge through San Francisco. You'll never be a tight tipper again! He takes risks to bring you the inside story, from admitting to smoking dope in the cab to getting laid on the job, with lively descriptions of passengers and rides. Apparently, 'in this business you have to be careful not to get a full-time girl because you end up wasting your nights servicing her instead of the vehicle.' This is uncensored reality and one of the best examples of journal work"
Netsurfer Digest

"Driving a cab is very dreamlike, and if you don't record the beautiful and horrific things you see immediately, it gets lost in a haze of faces and places that eventually fade away."
Bud Carson from *Yahoo! Internet Life* feature "How America Uses the Net"

Keep the Sunny Side Up and the Greasy Side Down
Please don't drink and drive.
MyFareCity.com

Foreword

I moved to San Francisco just before the 1989 earthquake. Since that time I have worked a variety of jobs, some legal and some not so legal, but never in my wildest dreams or scariest nightmares did I ever expect to find myself driving a taxicab from dusk 'til dawn. That's what makes life so grand, all of those blind corners can lead to almost anything. Most guys move on to their other interests by the end of the first year; then there are the chosen few, who the longer we keep driving, the harder it is to get out. I was just never interested in what the establishment had to offer me. Like all "underachievers," I was intelligent enough to get by with little or no effort while putting the majority of my energy into self-medication. That's the politically correct way of saying I grew up smoking pot, eating acid, and doing whatever else whenever possible to escape the reality of a world I wanted to be as far away from as possible. I must say I did a damn good job of that, until I became a San Francisco Taxi Driver.

Chapter One

LIFE IS A TEST

Taxicab Regulations Section E, Part 3, subset 3
A Taxicab driver shall, if requested, reasonably assist a handicapped, disabled or elderly person to get in and out of the taxicab vehicle if within the physical capacity of the driver. If unable to assist, the driver shall notify their dispatch and request a driver or other appropriate service capable of handling the request. The driver shall record the request and results on the waybill. The taxicab driver shall remain with the passenger until assistance from another driver or appropriate service has arrived.

I left the yard this Tuesday ready to work. I mean I'm always ready to work, I just don't always feel like pulling a ten-hour shift. Still, I do, mainly because money is a huge motivator. In this business, making lots of money, or the prospect of making lots of money drives the cabbie like a worker bee. I thought about deadheading south to the airport for my first plan of attack but before I could get on the highway, the dispatcher was howling for a night driver over the radio. Spear and Folsom, the Financial District. I pounced on it like a clairvoyant, hoping I had my mojo. Upon arrival at the pickup address on Spear St., I found the day driver with the fare in the back seat waiting for me. He helped the fare out of his cab, and then I took over. The fare appeared to be about 100 years old, or if not 100, then very old. He walked slowly with the aid of crutches, the kind that wrap around your forearm. I walked next to him, offering to assist. I opened my back door, at which he politely demanded to sit in the front seat. When I say demanded it was in the way a grandparent might tell you, not ask you to do something. I quickly opened the front door, rearranged my office and slid the seat back.

His hair was very sparse, but still there. The years had not been kind to him physically but he had lived to tell about them, which does count for something. He had a hearing aid in his left ear and although his face was wrinkled and worn, he spoke with confidence and authority. The old bird glanced over and told me, "Do you know we are going to Tiburon?" I said, "No, but I do now." I was pleased to figure out at this point why the day driver couldn't take the fare. The reason was the fare was going further than the day driver had time for. The shifts change from about 2 P.M. until 6 P.M. New York does this too. By the look on his face, the day driver musta been pretty late; I imagined he's not looking forward to seeing the window guy, or the night driver for that matter. He smoked the tires real good as he headed southbound on Harrison St.

So I was off for a ride north across the Golden Gate Bridge to bring the old man home. He introduced himself as Sam, and was very chatty as we left downtown. He mentioned that he had recently turned 94 years old. Wow, 94 years old, almost Willard Scott material. I wondered how long he had been working in the Financial, doing the daily grind. As we traversed our way toward the bridge, I told him I hope I've got the moxy at 94 that he does. He smiled, and kept talking, not to me, but with me. He spoke of his life, and I of mine. It was nice to communicate with a man well my senior with the greatest of ease. I mean this guy was just a pleasure to be with, his body was failing, but his mind was as sharp as anybody's I've ever met.

As we neared the bridge, I spoke of my many miles, and the

variety of people I meet. I told him that the youngest passenger in my back seat had been a 2-day-old baby coming home from the hospital with her mother. He asked for details. The newborn was in a child seat faced to the rear, so I couldn't see her. Her mother told me the baby's fat little cheeks were bouncing up and down. The mom was glowing, and the baby was as well behaved as any fare could be. No crying, farting, or funky smell which is more than I can say for the majority of my fares. So I had a 2-day-old rider, now a 94-year-old man, and I think it's safe to say, everybody in between.

Sam, like the newborn's mom, was kind of glowing himself now. I asked him why he was feeling so good today. He casually mentioned he had just finished his last day of work for Hills Bros. Coffee, after 74 years of loyal service. I doubt this will ever happen again unless you happen to be in a serious family business where retirement comes with a marble block instead of a Rolex and a lifetime guarantee. This was hard for me to believe, so I called him on it. He said, "Don't believe me, eh?" He handed me the Bay Area section of the daily newspaper, with his picture on the front page.

After he turned sixty, he was kept on as a consultant, and then several years ago Nestle bought them out. Sam was asked to head up all the archiving of the company. It sounded kind of like archiving his life. He said some stuff goes to the national archive, other stuff to private interests. I asked him what the fate of the huge neon Hills Bros. Coffee sign you see approaching My Fare City on the Bay Bridge was. He assured me it is here to stay.

As I drove, he told me of his family, his wife who had passed away, but sons, daughters, and grandchildren were spread around the Bay Area. His travels, both vast and beautiful, sounded great, but even more so just listening to the man was captivating. It seemed he was in a pretty good mood. He was still the loyal, friendly, warm person he had been through life to bring him to this point. Still, no more 365 Spear, nothing left to archive, just the memories. It seemed like uncharted territory for a man with a 74-year routine. Maybe I was wrong and he was ready to kick his feet up and relax. He sure couldn't do much more physically.

I wanted to pull something out of the hat I had done of some importance, and was scratching my head hoping it would help. Then I remembered. "So Sam, ya know I'm in a documentary on America's haunted houses," I said. I appeared in a reenactment scene at a haunted house near Santa Cruz, in a small town called Brookdale. The Brookdale Lodge is about it for the town. You could blink going down highway 9 to Santa Cruz and never know you passed it. Sam lifted his finger up as if to tell me to stop talking after I said the place was built in the '20s. It came as no shock when Sam casually told me he used to drink martinis there in the '30s. No way. Prehaunting! I had not mentioned that the deep end of the pool is glass overlooking the bar; I didn't need to. Sam told me back in the '20s/'30s the ladies would swim topless in the pool wearing mermaid bottoms, while the gents sipped their martinis. Too cool. The cosmic string once again.

When we arrived at Sam's place in Tiburon, I helped him out of the vehicle and asked if I could assist him further. Frankly I was curious as to how he lived. I fetched his mail (he had a lot), and followed him inside. It wasn't what I expected. Real sterile, everything in place and easy to get to. I guess I expected to see more old stuff, memories and the like. I had to remember that they were all there, inside Sam, the man with the mind as sharp as the ginsu knife. What I saw was a place that would be easy to transform once Sam passed on. The whole idea of him never going back to the financial district to work, or consult, or even archive was a bit depressing. It appeared that, along with his company, he had archived his life, had all his affairs in order. I could never be ready or prepared to die, at least not like this. I wondered what Sam would do now. Working nights I can say that daytime TV gets old pretty quick. Though I will give Bob Barker credit for still letting us know which price is right and who should come on down.

I asked Sam if I could use the bathroom after setting his mail down where he asked me to. The bathroom was clean, and geared for use by an old person. After I took a whiz and washed my hands, I entered the living room trying to take in the whole situation. His age, his real retirement, and what his plan would be now. There were ups and downs going through my mind and I tried to stay upbeat. I asked Sam if there was anything else I could do for him. He just smiled a warm and sincere smile, not the fake Southern California thing, and said no, that would do it. As I turned to leave he asked if I wanted a lemonade juice squeeze. I graciously accepted as he said that was about all he could handle these days. I hope I'm as fortunate when I am 94, that is if I even make it to 94. I felt like his last link in the chain of business and what he could associate with it. After I grabbed the lemonade I could have just left, but being an independent contractor (I lease the cab by the day), I can do what I want to do. I figured traffic would be real slow going back to the city so a short break in the action wouldn't be a bad idea. I stayed to chat with Sam as I drank the lemonade. I felt like I was in God's waiting room. I figured when would I have a chance to learn a bit of wisdom from a man like Sam. Shit, he was in his prime when I was still a twinkle in my mother's eye.

As I left his place I wondered what he would do now, after 74 years of conformity. I did not want to accept that Sam's next big move in life would be his exit. It saddened me but at the same time filled me with joy that this man had affected his own and other people's lives for almost a century. Wanting to do more, but knowing I had done all I could, I bid Sam farewell. I shut the door behind me as Sam had planted himself firmly on his couch for the evening news. On the way back to the city I thought about Sam, his life, and his commitment to go on as long as his body would let him. His mind was as sharp as could be, but his body failing, and now a new direction seemed quite a cross to bear, at least to me. I will never forget the old man, and probably won't chance upon him again. It's meeting people like Sam that make this job worth it. The money is always a good thing, I won't ever argue this, but it's the random meetings with people like today that really make me rich. It's that warm fuzzy feeling again.

On the way back over the Golden Gate Bridge I thought about the two-day-old baby, Sam, and everybody in between, and wondered who I would chance upon next. The cosmic string never breaks in my life. There is some rhyme and reason that is directly related to driving the night shift in San Francisco. I never know who I'll meet or where I'll go. This might drive some people crazy, but I love it. So I will continue to drive and if you flag I'll stop. The only folks I will pass have the crack pipe still in hand. It's almost impossible to be prejudicial in San Francisco. So many lives and so many different people all making it work the best they can. In my eyes, as with many who live here, you can be in a business suit or you can personify grunge and you will get the same respect from me. As long as your money is green and you don't insult me, everything will be fine. As far as Sam goes, I figure the next time he will be in print will be in the obituary column. Nonetheless, he will live on in my mind. I will never forget him. I am glad my job served as a tool in life this fine day.

After midnight, life got real, real strange. I had been deep in thought, feelin' mighty good 'til I got a call on my cell phone from Vanessa, another working girl. She took a round trip to the Westin St. Francis at Union Square. I dropped her with instructions to return in 45 minutes. This way, my time wasn't wrapped up waiting. If she needs me sooner she can call me on my cell and let me know. She has the time thing down pretty good. Five minutes less than psychotherapy.

On the way back to her place in the Mission District, she got a page. She asked to make a call on my cell phone. No problem because more business for her means more business for me.

It was a call from a couple of guys looking to get horizontal. She was firm that two guys are $250.00 a head. She only counts one per person, the little one I'm sure as that's what most of us guys think with. A-OK and we are off to the Marina, the night stays alive. I dropped her and went to the 24-hour Kinkos to make some copies. Free copies if it's late enough, system maintenance happens after midnight. No sooner had I made one copy than she called me to come get her. I zipped down Van Ness like a bat outta hell, and made it in about five minutes. She was out front with the two guys. She got in and said the joker's only had $100.00. This won't do it, although Vanessa will on occasion give a half-hour for a Franklin. I kinda wanted her to make some money so in turn I would get a better tip. It's hard enough to get a decent tip, if any, from the working girls, but if they don't finalize their transactions, forget it. Skirting the gray line of pandering, I weighed my options. I then told Vanessa that we were on the other side of town and maybe she could work something out. I am just a driver, not a pimp. I just wished that whatever was supposed to happen, would. She agreed to fuck one of the two if I came up to the room to make sure nothing went wrong. Great, another task not mentioned in the job description. I parked, went up to the guy's room, and surveyed the situation. One guy was passed out on the bed with beer cans strewn about. Basically there was nothing out of the ordinary. Kurt, the one who was gonna get some, went to the bathroom with Vanessa while I watched TV with the third guy, Jim. Too bad for Jim. His buddy with a hooker bent over in the john while he watched TV with yours truly. I would never fuck Vanessa. Thankfully she ain't my type.

Oh well. She finished, I mean he finished, and we went on our merry way. I carry mace and brass knuckles in case of emergency. So far I have not had to use either while on duty, and I stress while on duty. Vanessa is also a heroin addict, I have not met a hooker who isn't a junkie as a second profession, or vice versa. I like Vanessa; she gives me plenty of business and is a good person. I don't make judgments on anybody's lifestyle as long as it doesn't interfere with mine. A fine line I assure you.

Chapter Two

DEAD AHEAD

Taxicab Regulations: Section VI, Part G, subset 4
No driver shall operate a taxicab or continue to operate a taxicab while using any controlled substance, except when it is pursuant to the instruction of a licensed medical practitioner, who advised the driver that the substance will not adversely affect the driver's ability to operate a taxicab.

Sundays are always slow, and the hardest day to get off work. I figured that I would work the airport, as I have had some good luck there lately. The airport is a crapshoot, no doubt about it. I got my cab and deadheaded down. I had three shorts and ended up spending several hours there, a helluva lot more time than I expected, but then I did say it was a crapshoot. I felt like a shuttle bus to the outer parking lots, and grew tired of the bartertown of cabbies waiting for fares.

I then got a Mill Valley fare out of the south terminal and was glad to say good-bye to the airport for the day. The lady was a few years older than me, but she looked hot, and smelled nice too. I chatted it up with her as she talked about her family in Switzerland.

She kept going on about the difficulty of caring for people when they get old. Her mom was very old. Frankly, so was the conversation at this point. We never made it to Swedish massage or any other hot topics, oh well. Since she was cute, I naturally carried her bags from the cab to her front door and wished her well.

Feeling a tad reflective I smoked a joint driving back over the Golden Gate Bridge to celebrate cracking the nightly nut. Though the airport dealt me a few shorts I could have done without, I was descending back to the city with my gates 'n gas in the bag. After I got off the bridge some young gal flagged me at Lombard and Baker, in the Marina. She asked how my night had been; also commenting on how the car reeked of pot. I thought the cab was refreshed. Did my 440 air conditioning fail me? (four windows down, forty m.p.h.). I don't go for the Christmas tree hanging from the rear-view. I mentioned to the little cupcake in the back that my last fare to Marin was smokin' en route. I went on to say the lady sure did look like she was enjoying the ride. As we arrived at her destination I pointed out that if someone asks to smoke in my cab I don't ask what, I just say yes.

Chapter Three

THEY CALL IT STORMY MONDAY

Taxicab Regulations: Section VI, Part I, subset 1
No taxicab driver shall refuse, or direct or permit the refusal, of prospective passengers in any area or district of the City and County of San Francisco for transportation to any place in said City and County, or to the San Francisco International Airport, at rates authorized by law, if said prospective passenger presents themselves for transportation in a clean, sober, and orderly manner and for a lawful purpose.

Mondays are usually the shits, but at least the majority of people are back at work. I mean the rats are back in the financial district nibbling at the old chunk of cheese, and they will no doubt leave a few crumbs for us cabbies.

I was busy most of the night, on autopilot, but couldn't manage to get any long fares. I kept thinking of this National Geographic special I had seen recently. It was on rats. Now I was already privy to the fact the rats outnumbered humans in ess eff back when Feinstein was mayor in the '70s. I love those kind of funky facts.

Funky, not trivial. What I was not aware of was that if a rat does not constantly chew then its fangs will push up through his brain, killing him. So as much as I felt like I was spinning my wheels trying to get lucky, I knew I was surviving. I think ten dollars with a tip was my high fare. I did a helluva lot of running around. For the most part I had a lot of not-so-seasoned tourists and the like. Blurry, but like one long stroke of a brush across the picture of My Fare City, a masterpiece was hiding in there somewhere.

I wasn't quite sure what convention was in town this week, usually I can tell. Sometimes it makes a difference knowing, more often not. The Direct Marketers will rock, cab everywhere and tip well. The mayor's convention, obviously a different matter entirely. I did bag a mayor last year, dropped him off at the side door of the Fairmont, laying low I guess.

So up and down I went for the better part of the night. I was feelin' like Jack who was lookin' for Jill, racing up, and down Nob Hill. Hell, it took until almost midnight to make my gate and it seemed like I should have made more; it always does. The service industry was still keeping me busy well after midnight when I got a call on my cell phone from a regular rider, Brenda. She needed a ride out of town. I waited an hour for her and then took her home. An important business meeting I'm sure . . . It was a quick sixty bucks for about an hour and twenty minutes work, a sound decision on my part. She is a nice girl, but there are more than enough Jodie Fosters to go around. I can't let myself get personally involved with them, it's just business I guess. I came in an hour early on a stormy Monday that went well financially, in the end . . .

Chapter Four

BUT TUESDAY'S JUST AS BAD

Taxicab Regulations: Section VI, Part E, subset 7.
Every driver must be able to provide change for a minimum of Twenty Dollars to any passenger.

"triple five cal"

I didn't feel like working today, but I needed the money. The Financial District was back in full swing, and the rainy rush hour ran later than usual. As I pulled up to the intersection of California and Kearney, I noticed no cabs were at the BofA. Before I could go around the corner some idiot with a three-piece suit jumped in the back, catching me with my doors unlocked. As we drove by the line of people waiting at the BofA, an old man shook his umbrella at us; I guess he was scolding the guy who skipped the queue. Too early in my night to worry 'bout it as slippery streets and worn out radials were on my mind.

The rider answered a call on his cell phone, and I raised an eyebrow when he kept calling the person on the other line a heeb, a racial slur I hadn't heard in a while. He saved face though by getting off the phone and telling me a Jewish joke (with the disclaimer that he was a Jewish lawyer). I had to subscribe to the school of "it's OK to insult your own." This was fine by me. I'm personally equal opportunity in the insult department, or so I'm told.

Still in character I suppose, he asked for a blank receipt, then handed me three bucks. He made a point to let me know I could keep the change (all ten cents). What a cheap bastard. I gave him the blank receipt, kept my mouth shut, and moved on to greener pastures. Although, I have to admit, the joke wasn't bad:

Q—What did the dyslexic Rabbi say?
A—Yo! (Quick and short, like the ride.)

Into the evening, the local bars were a good supply of particularly bad-smelling drunks. The weather contributed to this no doubt, adding that special kind of odor only rain-soaked clothes can get. It's quite noxious, and can overpower the smell of everything else within a yard or two. Though my cab got that aroma that wouldn't leave, at least nobody puked. I did end up with a sleeper around midnight, later than usual for this kind of ride. I had to count out the drunk's money for him, which is at least better than a runner. The guy handed me his cash and told me to make sure I got a good tip. After uncrumpling his wad of bills, I collected the fare, and a few bucks tip. I wanted to make sure the fare made it all the way into his residence; he was weaving on the way to the door. A lady, his wife I imagine, answered the door while he was making sense of his keys, and pulled his drunken ass inside. I slipped back into the night. A textbook Tuesday ended as I rode my bicycle home from the boneyard, and got soaked.

Chapter Five

HUMP DAY

Taxicab Regulations: Section VI, Part E, subset 2
A Taxicab Driver shall comply with all reasonable requests of any passenger.

Wednesday wasn't great financially, but I did get laid. In this business you have to be careful not to have a full-time girl because you end up wasting your nights servicing her instead of the vehicle. Sounds cold, I know, but it's all about timing and the money you can bring in during the next ten hours. Any time wasted had better be worth it in some way. Cab driving is an experiment in time and motion, or so says the SF Taxi Commission.

After the usual line of ants left the Financial District, I received a call from Brenda. It was around midnight, and she needed a ride in twenty minutes, chop chop! I got to her apartment building in about five, but could not buzz her because the management turns the system off at 10 P.M. I used my cell phone to ring her, after which she came to the door. Across the street, the pool hall's neon light buzzed, as it always does 'til they lock up at 4 A.M. She told me to come in, as she was not quite ready yet. Following, I scurried in the door, noticing her heart shaped ass all the way down the hall.

Her place was completely trashed. The first thing I said to her as I do to all hookers was, "You look beautiful." I don't know why, it's just a line I guess. The picture before me I was processing was perfect, or so it felt. Like a cubic zirconia in the rough stood Brenda, wearing a small black nightie. She had several candles lit throughout the messy room. I don't think she had any of this prepared, but I was hoping my timing was right. I am a sucker for a pretty face. She caught me off guard by saying I'm an angel and she wanted me to come closer. No problem. My clothes were off as fast as I could untie my high top Chuck Taylor's. They don't teach you about this kind of Bingo in Cab College, though putting a condom in your accident kit was mentioned. We're not in Kansas anymore, Toto.

We spent an hour of power and passion before I knew what hit me. This was the first time I had fucked her, and the best. She was beautiful, but her soul was lost. Things would have been perfect except for the cold, hard reality of the situation. I'm just a toy to her, and vice versa. Thankfully hookers are horny outside of turning tricks. The tricks are strictly business. I guess I was just monkey business.

After we got dressed I had to watch Brenda do her daily heroin fix, then we were both back at work. I never bothered to ask about the twenty-minute timetable, as everything seemed to go exactly as planned in some strange way.

I arrived back at the garage a few hours later with only a couple of fares scribbled on my waybill. The window guy commented on how I had lipstick smeared all over my cheek and neck, smiling for a change as well. I hadn't bothered to check myself, so I just smiled back. My gross rides were only about $20.00 for the night. He said I was having too much fun at this job as I threw him his nightly kickback. I told him I was unable to document all my rides for the evening. "Tied up" was the explanation I used. He knocked twice on the counter, acknowledging my tip, followed by a wave good-bye.

Chapter Six

THURSDAY'S MY FRIDAY

Taxicab Regulations: Section VI, Part C, subset 7
The driver is to remain in service at all times during a shift, with
the exception of meal/and or rest breaks.

My scheduled days off are Friday and Saturday. You might ask
me why I have the busy days off? Two reasons: mental health, and
that's just the way it worked out. Today the day driver was late and
I didn't get out until after 6 P.M. I managed to stay occupied the
entire night, mostly because of more rain, and let us not forget
that Thursday is the unspoken start of the weekend in My Fare
City.

On this Thursday, I met a man from France who wanted a good
steak. After making sure no translation errors were occurring, I
had the information we needed. Best pepper steak in the city, full
dinners served 'til 1 A.M, and they only accept cash. It could mean
only one place, The Brazenhead. It's hard to find, as it has no sign
out front. I would never have known about the restaurant myself
were it not for word of mouth.

When he asked me if I would like to join him, I said that would
be fine, taking into account that the money for food outweighed

32

any earnings I could make in the next hour. I had also worked myself into being very hungry just talking about the place. The guy was not gay, thankfully, and was very nice. He treated me like an ambassador, and rightly so. We ate, he drank, I gave him a free ride back to his hotel and wished him well, as he did me. I learned a bit about his culture, and he about mine. I couldn't pronounce his name so I just called him Frenchy. I regained much faith in people doing nice things for each other, for whatever reason, more commonly known as random acts of kindness. As much fog as there is over the dark side of the city, a few beams of light shine through every now and then.

As I bid him farewell outside of his hotel, Frenchy smiled and went along to his life. I made less money than I would have without the free dinner, but it was worth it. If you have ever had the pleasure of dining at the Brazenhead you would know exactly what I mean. Those impromptu breaks always are worth it if you can afford them. I'm someone who will always be in it for the experience as well as the money. Both hold value in my life, as did this Thursday.

Chapter Seven

GOLDEN GATE

Taxicab regulations: Section V, Part 11, subset 11
Drivers shall, at the beginning of a trip, inform passenger(s) whose announced destination requires the crossing of a toll bridge, the amount of the toll charged and that the toll charge is to be paid by the passenger(s) regardless of the direction in which the toll is collected.

I couldn't decide what mode of transportation, public or otherwise, to take to work this afternoon. I ended up waiting for and taking the bus. The bus driver was kind enough to teach me the trick of folding your one-dollar bill longways so it will feed in to the machine. Only those with the shakiest of hands or worn-out bills get this lesson. Ironic, I thought, because it was foreshadowing more indecision. I picked up my cab and decided to play the city, hoping to find that diamond in the rough. Instead, I meandered across town on a lot of short hops, not bad if people tip well. I went from the Financial District to the Castro, then south of Market, and on and on.

Until I actually got behind the wheel of a taxi, I thought I knew the city inside and out. What I really knew were my local haunts.

Force feeding would be an understatement describing my first few months as a taxi driver. Not anymore, as I'm a seasoned veteran of all the hoods now.

I took a south-of-Market radio call at BMW, where I picked up a lady from the body shop. Appropriate cause she had a very fine body. It's the first 10 seconds that a man sees a woman that he decides if he wants to have sex with her. It took me about five, but no matter, this one was out of my league, and was wearing a ring. BMW gives their customers our company's vouchers for a limit of $10.00. I guess they figure if ten bucks won't get ya home, it will at least get you close. Well, this lady had the right idea. After leaving BMW, she asked if we went over the ten-dollar mark if she could pay the remainder. Damn straight she can. So off I went with her to the mini-market, the dry cleaners, Walgreens, her bank, the fucking post office, and then home. The meter running, she ran up $17.50. Though I had to wait a bit (cab drivers hate to wait), she bid me farewell and handed me a $20.00 bill and the voucher, which I made out for $10.00. No more coffee talk; see ya, wouldn't wanna be ya.

Five minutes later, I answered a radio call in the Marina and picked up an old lady who, before I could figure her out, directed me to drive to Sausalito, which is over the Golden Gate Bridge. "Nice fare," I'm thinkin' to myself. You need at least one out-of-town fare to make some good cash, and keep your sanity. About halfway over the Golden Gate Bridge she asks what brand of credit card do I take. I calmly explained that we do not take credit cards as a form of payment. She mumbled something I couldn't understand and said that a personal check would have to do. Who am I to refuse a check from a kind old lady? "No problem, lady," I told her regarding the check, though I don't think she was talking to me. Upon arriving in Sausalito, the meter read $13.40: This plus the $3.00 charge for the bridge (rider pays) made her total $16.40 for those of you who don't like to add. She handed over a check made out for $16.50. I never would have pegged the hag to stiff me on the tip. So, I politely asked her if there was anything wrong with the service, and said to her that she was the first person not to add any tip as far back as I could remember. I was trying not to remember too hard. She fished out a buck from the bottom of her gunnysack just to shut me up. Bridge toll takes its toll; the Golden Gate Bridge raised its toll from $2.00 to $3.00, which nobody much appreciated. I noticed at the end of the night that the only ID on her check was her name, that's it. Not an address or anything else. I hope she doesn't turn out to be a grandmother of the Freemen.

"golden gate bridge"

On the way back to San Francisco, I pulled up to a bus stop in Sausalito and gave a girl a free ride back to civilization, illegal but chivalrous. She was cute and said she had never had a free cab ride before. As we crossed the bridge back I noticed I was very low on petrol. The Golden Gate Bridge is the only place in the state of California where you can actually get a ticket for running out of gas. No shit. I dropped her by the Palace of Fine Arts in front of a beautiful home. I wondered who was keepin' her warm at night but was more concerned I might run out of gas, a bummer on or off the

Golden Gate. I didn't ask her for a phone number, I figured the experience was unique enough already.

I got some gas, and then took an untimely break at Clown Alley for a burger and some fries. As I went back in service, the radio was hot, but I was not. I fucked up. I broke the rhyme and meter of the cosmic string. After I got back on the road, I never really got "it" back. Every radio call I would check in for, someone else would always be a block closer. The dispatcher said at the end of the night that he had never seen someone try so hard and have such bad luck to boot. Hell, even Austin Powers lost his mojo for a spell, little consolation at this point. At least I had made my gates, gas, kickbacks, etc., so anything else was gravy, even though mine was quite lumpy.

As I kept missing various orders throughout the Financial, I did find two other drivers from my company at separate places and arranged to meet up at a 101 California, in the Financial. After we met, which was well after midnight, we could hear cross-streets given out in the Financial followed by the screeching of tires on route to the location. We had a good time gossiping about the industry, the management, and whatever else came to mind. Most disturbing, no doubt, was that one of our drivers, a black guy, was with a fare at a red light that was broken and would not change. After some time, the driver proceeds through, gets pulled over, and is issued a ticket. I could understand the cabbie trying to protect himself, but he and the passengers never saw that light change the entire time it took to issue the ticket, which was at least ten to fifteen minutes. When dealing with the SFPD it's you against them, end of story. And, if it's someone else dealing with 'em that's better than you. Unfortunately, that is true even if it's a fellow driver. I hope he beats the ticket or at least is eligible for traffic school.

After I finally got a fare and bid farewell to my friends and fellow drivers, I got a flag that took me back to the Marina. It was time to go fishin'. No, not for fish, but for fares. I did manage to get a radio call at Lombard and Baker. The bartender from the Final Final went across town, and tipped well. I stumbled through the last hour or so and was on my way to turn in a half hour early when a guy flagged me down and asked if I would go to the East Bay. I only said to him, "East bay . . . Pre-pay." He gave me forty dollars as I noticed the pierced nose. Nonetheless, there ain't much to class distinctions in My Fare City, so it was no big deal. I took a forty-five minute round-trip drive, trimmed it into thirty-three minutes and was $35.00 richer upon arrival back at the garage. No regulars tonight, I guess they need some rest too.

Chapter Eight

FAT TUESDAY

Taxicab Regulations: Section VI, Part D, subset 5
No driver may smoke, drink, or eat while passenger(s) are in the taxicab

After the usual exodus from the Financial District to the Marina, the Fat Tuesday crowd started to come alive. The Fillmore was buzzing with deadheads still in denial that Jerry is dead. As long as they are happy, I'm happy for them. Usually, deadheads ask if they can smoke, this being the polite thing to do. Well these young, and very cute, deadheads in the back seat, going to the Fillmore Auditorium, just lit up a bowl of kind bud and started smoking away. Halfway to the Fillmore, I pulled over and asked the girls if they know what happens if they get caught smoking pot in a San Francisco cab. I made sure to turn on the super bright overhead light for effect. Both of them, being stoned, were at a loss for words. I explained to them that it's best to ask the driver if they are allowed to smoke, no matter what it is they smoke. After they finally nodded that no, they don't know what happens if you get caught smokin' kind bud in my cab, I replied. The answer is simple,

I told 'em: "Gotta load the driver a fresh bowl" After a brief moment of silence, I then said, "Make it so" And so it was, sooo good.

Before I started driving a cab, I always would sneak beers on the way to my destination. I found out in Cab College that it's legal to drink alcohol in a cab. Anybody can drink booze in a cab, moving or not, except the driver obviously. Booze and red light running are in my top-ten list of things not to do while driving a cab. Fate is already nipping at your heels; don't let it catch up by doing something too reckless.

In California, we don't have many places to smoke anything these days. It's illegal to smoke in bars or where food is served. The smoking ban in bars is the biggest joke. You can go purchase the last legal drug, booze, but are denied smoking a cig' at the same time. A new subculture has risen of people forced outside to do smoke, kind of a hassle for me as they all end up looking like prospective riders. I don't smoke cigarettes, I never have, but I do believe in personal freedom and the government has gone too far into people's lives this time. Smoke 'em if ya got 'em in my cab.

I seem to get people flying in from New York lately at SFO. After the six-hour flight and only that seedy smoking room at the airport, they really enjoy the right to enjoy a cig' on the cab ride to the city. Heck, I'll even carry a pack of smokes in the glove box in case one is needed for my fare. One smoke can be an extra couple bucks tip. Not a bad deal if you think about it. So I try to give the best service to get a good tip, without which I would suffer financially.

After midnight, I heard on the radio that it was Abe Vigoda's birthday. About the same time, a strange moment, I thought, I received a call on my cell phone from Brenda. She got a call and needed to go to a hotel down by the airport. She would pay me sixty dollars round trip, but I would be stuck for an hour down by the airport. Still a good deal for after midnight. An airport run costs around $30.00 so my waiting time would be justified by taking a break and catching up on some reading. Hookers, Brenda included, are a strange lot. They all have the same laugh. Kinda like the

Wicked Witch of the West mixed with a sea lion. At least they are one small step off the street. This is why they call themselves escorts instead of what they really are. Heck, I can relate with the working girls being a whore myself, and a cheaper one than them. I'm not selling sex, just myself.

If you are an escort, you get your business by people calling your agency, and then the agency pages you. An escort charges from $200.00 to $350.00 depending on what they can arrange with their client. Brenda's buzzer was off so I called her on my cell phone when I arrived, SOP (standard operating procedure) so far. She wasn't ready and asked if I would come in and wait, not a problem. I must admit to still being a bit smitten by the raw level of honesty we have together. Forget Las Vegas, how about "Leaving My Fare City"? I had been in her place before, but tonight it looked worse than usual. Clothes were strewn about everywhere; her frameless bed in the corner had no sheets or blankets on it. I sat on the floor and watched cable while she finished getting ready in the bathroom. A friend of hers, and neighbor, came to the door and I knew Brenda was waiting to see her.

Brenda is in the mid-stages of heroin addiction. She will snort it or have her friend and neighbor inject her since she can't do it on her own yet. I will say, when Brenda came out of the bathroom and answered the door, she did look beautiful. She looked like a college girl, not a whore. I sat patiently while her friend shot her up and then left. Looks like just business tonight I thought to myself.

After a few minutes, Brenda was nodding out, and I suggested we had better go, as the trip would take fifteen or twenty minutes at least. She was pretty fucked up, but she did hear me and grabbed her Coke. She always drinks Coke, not Pepsi. Then digging through her purse, she dug out a bindle with some white powder in it, crystal meth, I found out later. She poured it in to her Coke and took a gulp. She managed to stand up. I helped her out the door to the cab waiting out front, flashers on. She likes sitting in the front seat, which is fine with me. I think its part of her idea that she isn't a whore, just an escort. If you get paid for sex you can call yourself what you want, the reality is still the same. By sitting in the front seat she is a friend rather than just another fare. People from Australia tend to go for the front seat as well, but for different reasons I would imagine. Friend or fare, it's OK, as long as I get paid. I do kinda sound like a whore, don't I? Halfway to her destination, the speed started to take effect and this was comforting to me simply for the fact that I don't get paid until she does. She was in no condition to turn a trick when we left her apartment, but the speed balanced her buzz enough so I figured she would make it through. The makeup on her arms did a pretty good job of covering the track marks, and upon arrival at the hotel she was actually pretty coherent.

About an hour later, I drove her back to the City. My night was sixty dollars better than it was. My relationship with Brenda and other working girls is ongoing, and I've been exposed to a very seedy and depressing side of life. Still, it can be slim pickin's for a night driver during the week. I try to stay philosophical, but it's hard not to be cynical on this shift. I hope to take the sum of my experiences to help me in my life, though I'll admit, it's hard not to get personal. Real life isn't like the movies: You can't just save someone from themselves if they don't want help, and who am I to judge what is right and what is wrong? This was supposed to be a spectator sport. Wanting to save hookers from themselves wasn't in the job description, only in the movie.

Chapter Nine

THE BANK FOR BANK

Taxicab Regulations: Section VI, Part C, subset 4
Every Taxicab Driver is to start and end the shift at the color scheme's principal place of business and make the change of shift to another taxicab operator at the color scheme's principal place of business on the private property of the color scheme holder. (Start and end your shift at the boneyard.)

Last night the fog had turned into a light drizzle, and not wanting to get wet I opted to take public transport to work. As I entered the bus, I realized the smell of all those people was going to be worse than a little drizzle, but it was too late because the machine had just taken my dollar. I got a transfer even though I had no need for it. I figured somebody down on their luck might need a free bus ride, but I never found any takers.

Strangely enough the bus was running on time and got me to work about forty-five minutes before my car was due in. I was actually looking forward to hanging around the garage with the new guys. New drivers are always waiting around since they do not have an assigned cab yet. The new drivers always give me a boost because they have not lost that twinkle in their eye or that spring in their step. However, eventually their light will fade in time just as mine has recently.

I also like to get to work early because the garage has a couple of arcade machines and a pool table. The management actually popped for some repairs and replaced the rails on the pool table, which surprised me because they usually have several dead spots. I could tell right away that the new rails really made a difference. When we play pool at the garage, it's always for honor, there is no cash involved. If I feel the need to gamble with other cab drivers then I go to the airport.

I have been employed for some time now and I have spent many an afternoon shooting pool at the garage. This always pays off when I play at bars because I usually win, unless I am being hustled, which does occasionally happen. Last evening when I got to the garage, a little Mexican day driver had had the table for some time when I put my quarters down. At that time he was on a roll and I think he thought he would beat me. Unfortunately for him, I had other plans and bumped him off the table with a vengeance (he usually beats me). After knocking off a few more drivers, it was time for me to hit the road because I could see my cab in the gas line. Even though I did not win any money, I had the honor of winning tucked gracefully in my back pocket. I would pull this victory out sooner or later in the evening because I would inevitably need that good luck.

Competition from the other drivers runs from the pool table to the road and just can't be avoided. Worst part being the drivers from your team working against you. In the Financial District it is especially cutthroat. A call will come over the radio and three or four of your guys will race toward it. Even though the dispatcher gives the call to a certain cab, it really comes down to who gets there first. Driving in the Financial can be dangerous practice but that is just the nature of the beast.

My first fare of the night was out of triple-five California (BofA building) where a young lady got in the back on the passenger side. I like it when the fare sits on the passenger side because it is easier to speak with them on a more personal basis. The rear view can be frustrating as well, though that does seem like the next level. As you all know by now, I like to chat and I was hoping this gal did as well. When I spoke to her, I called her Sharon and she was a bit freaked out about it because we were strangers at this point. But before she got too miffed I pointed to her nametag and repeated the name on it to her. Nametags are a great way to freak out unsuspecting tourists; I have had some fun with this one. She was relieved that I knew her name only by her tag, which she promptly ripped off to avoid any further ill communications. Other than a pretty face and a great figure she was not much fun to talk to. In fact, she really did not have much substance to her, but then again ours was such a short-term relationship that it did not matter. She gave me a ten spot for a $7.40 ride. Not a bad start in retrospect.

I had a good feeling about triple-five Cal and I decided to play it throughout the evening. Some fares were short ones while others were decent. I went to Ocean Beach as well as the deep Mission. I made myself a promise to stay away from the airport unless I actually got a ride down, which never happened last night. Mixing up my plan of attack keeps things fresh.

Cab driving is ninety percent luck, so with this in mind I was on a mission to pick up from the BofA as many fares as I could with the hope that the elusive diamond in the rough would show itself. Lately it seems I get the rough. After a blur of tourists, drunks, business people, and monkey business people I found myself back at triple-five Cal trying to shake off the weirdness of the hours that had passed. A few cabs were in line ahead so I had a few minutes to read and relax. As you can probably imagine, I chose to relax instead of read. I tilted my seat back and tuned into my favorite college radio station. They happened to be playing some light techno that fit the mood. I took a few deep breaths and closed my eyes.

A tapping on my window woke me and I opened up the door locks before my head had a chance to clear. Some bozo got in the back and while the car remained in park he gave me a fifteen-minute pitch for $16.50 that he needed supposedly to get his Saab out of a parking lot nearby. Among other things, he claimed to be a millionaire and would gladly give me a cashier's check for one hundred thousand dollars for my trouble. This guy had obviously used the scam for years because he had the story down pat. I kicked him out of the cab after snapping a picture of him—a real Kodak moment, I assure you.

I spoke with a cabbie later who explained to me that he got the same pitch. The guy was workin' it, but with no results from the drivers on the night shift. The funny thing is, cab drivers are so money hungry that they will actually listen to this guy if there is not a paying fare around. When I returned to the BofA to look for my last fare of the night, the millionaire who had no money was gone. I was surprised to see a couple of cabs still hanging out. I pulled behind them shifted the gear into park and was almost instantly asleep.

I was rudely awakened when some cab driver behind me in line got a little too excessive with his horning. I was about to get angry at the fool to my rear, but when I saw what time it was I realized I didn't have time; I was late returning the cab. Fortunately, I hit all the green lights as I drove down Mission Street and, lucky for me, the cab didn't turn into a pumpkin. After a slap on the wrist from the window guy, I mounted my bicycle and headed home eager to end my nightly journey. I got to sleep before the sunrise and thus had a decent six-hour night of rest. I had dreams about cab driving and they were much more boring than real life.

Chapter Ten

FOGDOG

Taxicab Regulations Section I, Part 1077a Municipal Police Code
These Taxicab regulations are promulgated under Appendix F of
the Charter of the City and County of San Francisco and Article 16
of the San Francisco Municipal Police Code. The Chief of Police or
Designee may suspend or exempt any or all of these rules and
regulations when implementing special studies and or projects to
service needs relating to the Public Convenience and Necessity.

The fog, which I used to consider a sorry-ass excuse for rain,
was heavy today. The weathermen here will call it rain if your
windows mist up, certainly not what I consider rain. It's feast or
famine with the rain here. I remember it rained for 42 days, and
nights, no shit. I was convinced I would see Noah and his Ark floating
in under the Golden Gate. I think Noah wouldn't be too happy about
the domestic partners law, as the Salvation Army was already
defeated here on that one. This was a city thing where all companies
doing business with the city had to comply with this law, which
affords benefits to same-sex partners in a relationship. When the
mighty refused to comply with the domestic partners law, they
were left with the choice of being in compliance with the city or

with their beliefs. I think everybody has hummed the famous tune, "Do You Know the Way to San Jose" but none better than my bell ringing buddies at the Salvation Army as they didn't move the programs that help people out of the city, but moved their administration offices there, to remain in compliance with both of their authorities. I left a few lost souls to be inducted into "The Army", and figure to have rung enough bells at Christmas myself to give many an angel their wings (including myself).

Business was not that great and it turned out to be one of those "be in the right place at the right time" kind of nights. I meandered through the city like a laboratory rat seeking out a chunk of cheese, with my maze eventually ending in front of the window guy's bulletproof glass. After I got close to the Financial, I saw a flag, and skidded to a stop right in front of the guy. The fare got in and commented on how comfortable he was. Neil Young was crooning away on the radio and provided the mood and feel. Free and easy like it was way back when.

My fare directed me to 6th and Market, a nefarious corner, and within a block of Brenda's place. I asked the fare how long he would be and he assured me that it would be no longer than five minutes. I told him that was OK with me because it was a round trip. So, just for kicks I asked him what he was going to that location for. He told me he had to pick up a friend. I then wondered why I had even bothered to ask. While I waited for him I parked by a fire hydrant and the steam from a manhole cover swirled around my cab as I kept the motor running, and in neutral. I had my wheels turned away from the curb just in case. If any riffraff reared its ugly head I would be able to exit stage left. I tuned in some fusion jazz, and the scene looked surreal to put it mildly. It felt as if I was in a Clint Eastwood movie, until 10 minutes had gone by, then it felt like Ferris Bueller's day off meets the Bad Lieutenant. I put the car in park, and popped around the corner to House of Fascination.

The House of Fascination is a trip. It's a cheap gambling game you play by rolling a ball onto a square of holes, the object being to get a row. Kind of a tic-tac-toe for crack heads. Everyone competes against one another, and the clientele is a mixed bag o' nuts. Maybe you will see a transvestite, a brother, a gangbanger, a washed-up hooker, a dirty old man, or occasionally even a taxi driver. Get the pic? To win you gotta be quick, like a cabbie driving through the Tenderloin. Tube steaks that have been turning on the rollers for days provide one of the many curious smells in this parallel universe. It is a true Bud enigma and the highlight of the rough and tumble intersection of 6th and Market. After 15 minutes I went back to my cab, with the buck fifty I won in The House of Fascination.

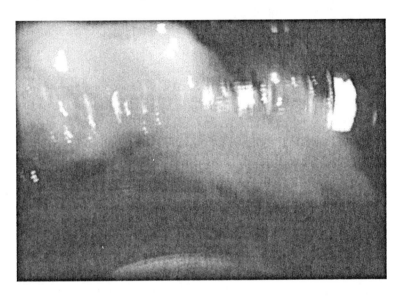

"steam"

The fare casually came out of the house alone, lookin' like he was feeling irie. We had a pleasant ride on the way back, for different reasons I imagine. Funny thing is, an hour later I heard the same address in the Haight called out by dispatch for another pickup. Another run maybe? I don't know and I shouldn't pry when it comes to felons in the rear. Tweekers love the anonymity of a taxicab, junkies less often. See the junkies have the all-city-delivery service, run by the south-of-the-border types from the Mission. Yeah, you call, and the heroin gets delivered. Seems like the tweekers would benefit from this, but they gotta go out and get it themselves. I will never really know who my rider's friend was, but I have a pretty good idea. I think his name is Mr. Brownstone. Guess he didn't have the number for delivery.

I saw two babes flag me at a bus stop, and was wondering if they were partners. I then took a mental snapshot of where I was. Smack dab center of the Castro District, gay flag flying proudly at the corner. Personal freedom is OK by me, that's why I drive a cab. As they were running across the street, I could not help but check 'em out. They were beautiful, but unfortunately on the other team I suspected. They directed me to Clipper Street in the Upper Market area. As we ascended the hills, I got the twenty-question thing from them. How old are you? Where are you from? Etc. etc. I even got asked if I was straight or gay. A question like that can either be a good sign or a bad sign. I have a pal who is a homosexual cabbie and he gets more propositions than flies on shit or white on rice. There are plenty of gay cabbies out there and it seems like they have more of an opportunity to kick boots than the straight ones like me do. Just the lay of the land I guess.

I was feeling really lazy and had some reading to catch up on so I decided to play the airport. I deadheaded south. The dispatcher who works the early evening shift takes orders for airport runs for the next day and calls his buddies to give them out. I ain't one of 'em. I did have a prearranged fare that turned into a no go prior to my empty ride to SFO. This really fucked the rhyme and meter of the night. No need driving when you got a chip on your shoulder, so cooling my heels was not a bad idea in retrospect.

All the long runs I have got off the radio did not tell the dispatcher where their destination was. Go figure. I know a lot more now than I used to, but I am still not a seasoned career cabbie, either. We drivers who are not a part of the good old boy network have to work that much harder for our money. Having an ace up my sleeve for an airport run can be good since I have not gotten too deep in this racket, yet. Too bad my ace was a deuce this day.

Finally, late night, I found it, or it found me, the elusive diamond in the rough. The graveyard dispatcher comes on at 11 P.M., and gives me a radio call that went over the bay bridge east to Fremont. Translated, that is $110.00 in cabbie language, and money like that talks loud.

By the time I descended back over the Bay Bridge into the city, my mood had lightened, as my wallet got a bit heavier. The skyline was electric. The streets were mean and the lights were green. I should not complain about the money because the experience of driving through the Financial District after 3 A.M. is borderline religious. It's like the world went out for a while and left me all alone with My Fare City to patrol. I wished it did not have to end, but could hear the fat lady faintly in the distance warming up to sing her tune, for her Bud.

Chapter Eleven

TRUE MEN

Taxicab Regulations Section XVI, Part B, subset 8
All drivers must know how to speak the following phrase in English
"Good morning. And if I don't see ya; good afternoon, good evening,
and good night." This requirement under the future City Charter is
to be included on the verbal section of the city's A-card exam.

The movie *The Truman Show* was fucking hilarious and I often
feel like old Truman. Someday I should be able to break through
the walls that surround me as well. But alas, not today. Last night
was another scripted hodgepodge of faces, places, and a variety of
different cases. Hard cases, that is, were the common theme of
the night. I bopped around early in the evening and picked up some
cool bartenders from the Highball Lounge in North Beach. Spencer
and his buddy were a bit ragged, but isn't everybody in the service
industry at some point during the evening. They were not much for
conversation either because they had just finished their shift.
However, they did offer me a beer. I think I will take them up on
that beer if I ever get a night off. We all laughed when I
ceremoniously honked the horn two times for good luck as I passed
through the Broadway Tunnel. I am sure I've been cursed by many

a pedestrian during my two-horn salute. Sometimes, when I am feeling more musical I will honk a few bars of my favorite car tune from the movie *The Car*. The evil devil car honk is, "Da, Da, Da, Daaa!!!" Only once has my fare not approved of the ritual honking. After further inquiry I found out it was because they have to walk through the tunnel everyday to get to work.

Too bad, so sad. That's what I have to say to any working stiff that has to brave the noise, the pollution, and the claustrophobia of walking through the Broadway Tunnel. For those of you who have done it (most locals have), you know what I mean. If you have to do it at all, make sure you are stinking drunk and coming from the North Beach side. I think of the Broadway Tunnel as one long dirty bathroom because it has tile walls and smells real bad.

For some reason, no one obeys any speed limit in the tunnel and this is especially true when two cabs enter at the same time. I know that as soon as I am in the tunnel, it's off to the races. I have personally peaked my speed at well over ninety miles per hour during one race. The guy I had in the back seat told me to cool it, this wasn't *Ben Hur*.

Before dark I passed by a skateboarder in the Financial District. We caught each other's eyes and I could tell he was a bit fearful of me. I rolled down my passenger window because I did not have a fare and told the kid to grab on to the back bumper. As I increased my speed I told him to let go when I said to. I made it up to over thirty miles per hour and saw a green light at the intersection up ahead, then I yelled back for the skater to let go. He let go and I slowed down to watch him rocket over Kearney Street at close to thirty miles per hour. I took a hard left on Kearney and in the distance I could hear him screaming, "YA HOO!" My own little version of *Breaking Away* . . . I often freak skaters out by offering them a "power boost." So far, no one has refused and I have not been cited by the Man. When I am at the wheel, skateboarders never know what they are going to get in the heart of My Fare City. A free ride is better than a poke in the eye, so says Bud.

The fog was rolling in over Twin Peaks. At one time I had a theory that the fog would keep people indoors, but I was proven wrong. It is a little easier to have theories about which nights of the week are best for business. While Sundays are a flip of the coin, Mondays and Tuesdays are always the pits. There just isn't much going on late at night early in the week. Remember, not being able to legally purchase alcohol after 2 A.M. makes business slow considerably after the bars close. After-hours clubs are few and far between and you can forget about those early in the week. The only real after hours are the bars that lock up and do, how shall I say . . . a little quality control.

Chapter Twelve

CHURCH LADY

Taxicab Regulations: Section V, Part B, subset 3
Seats, upholstery and rugs shall match the vehicle's interior colors
and must be kept in good repair. They must not be torn, separated
or ripped. Seat springs may not be broken nor may they protrude
through the upholstery. Seats shall be firm and comfortable and
the tension of the seat springs shall be evenly distributed. Seat
covers may not be used to replace upholstery (unless the colors
match the vehicle's interior colors and they are sufficiently padded).

Thursdays are always the unspoken start of the weekend. People
in the Financial District are cramming to make their Friday coast,
and the party crowd is in full force with the Marina and North Beach
being the popular points of destination. It dawned on me early in the
shift that my cab has approximately 300,000 more miles on it than
my car. Yes, I do own one.

I was very glad the cab was a junker for this run, a round trip
to Twin Peaks. The couple that flagged me down from the Lower
Haight seemed pretty tame, at first. Standard operating procedure
in this case is turn the motor off, remove the key, leave the meter

running, and tell the riders to give the horn a toot when they are done with their personal business, whatever that may be.

"scenic viewpoint"

I enjoyed the fifteen minutes to gaze over My Fare City. It looked so beautiful. It was the best view of the city without a doubt, at least at the moment. The night was clear and a bit cold, but anytime the meter is running, I get that warm fuzzy feeling. I must say, they were both glowing on the way back down to the Haight. I got the distinct feeling they were tripping, but no matter, their money is as green as anybody else's. They were well behaved and happy to have flagged me down, which is not always easy in San Francisco. They were good tippers, needless to say. So, my Twin Peaks break gave my late evening a nice boost financially and it gave me a nice break. It never ceases to amaze me all the kinds of weird sexual fantasies in this town. The downside is I often end up mighty horny, usually with no prospects in sight. Then again, I am almost always horny. Having sex with your lover in a cab does not seem strange to me now, as it would have when I first came to the Golden State. At least these folks let me leave the cab during the deed. Yes, I have had a couple do it while I was driving them around. I gave them the green light; man did we get a few looks from other drivers. Glad my mom lives in another state. So many different agendas walk among each other in the city, that tolerance is the norm. If you have a problem with different lifestyles, especially alternative ones, think about moving. People don't think about when the next earthquake will hit, but more so on how to live life to the fullest so when the big one does hit, you won't have any regrets if your number is up.

No working girls tonight, but on the other end of the scale, I took a lady who flagged me down out to the Sunset district. I gave her my cell phone number for personal service, and then she quickly asked if she could pass it on to her coworkers. No problem, networking makes the world go round. After I said this I glanced at the card she gave me. She works for the Christian Science Church. Shit, forget casual sex.

I was feeling the pressure of driving, of the gate fee, kickbacks, a broken tail light, and all the other shit that weighs me down. Then the church lady shined a little light on me. As I went on with her about the long hours and the struggle for making money, she reminded me how being in an office all day would suck by comparison. She reminded me of the personal freedom I was granted by having my A-card. And not only freedom, you can get some unusual perks if you play your hand right. I've never paid a cover charge since receiving my A-card. The bums won't hit me up for change, cause they know better. From concerts to strip clubs, my hack license has worked for me, not against me, time and time again. And thinking about it, I do like talking with my fares. She really gave me a boost and a fresh perspective on my job situation. For all the hassles, the drunks, the rude fares, the mean people, I am still my own boss. I can choose how hard I want to or don't want to work, and I meet a cross section of society that not many people get to see. Sure, dealing with the general public has its downside, but I will give the church lady points for sharing her view on my situation. It gave me that warm fuzzy feeling.

I like driving in San Francisco because it is the biggest little city in the world. I definitely would not consider driving a taxi in any other city. No way. Different mindset here, laid back. I worked a full ten hours tonight and felt spent. And I will work through the weekend due to financial constraints. I know this can lead to burnout. If you don't take some time off you get a bit stressed out. Balance is the answer to many questions in life, and a lesson I learn each day in whatever I may do.

As I rolled down Market Street on my way into the boneyard, I took one last flag. He rode from Market Street to the Power Exchange (a sex club). I dropped him off, wished him well as I do all fares, and called it a night while still thinking about the boost the church lady and her simple words of wisdom gave me. You never know what to expect with your next ride. It could be inspiring or fatal. Like the earthquake thing, it's best not to dwell on the negative because it will just bring you down. It's past 6 A.M. and I made myself a promise to avoid seeing any sunrises because this reminds me of too many all-nighters in college. Association, you know. So cock-a-doodle-doo, this Bud's for you.

Chapter Thirteen

BATTER UP

Taxicab Regulations: Section VII, Part A, subset 6
All calls must be dispatched and an individual driver must be assigned
to the call.

    As with most nights, the first call almost always provides some
heavy foreshadowing for the rest of the evening. Why should last
night have been any different? Hell, cab driving is ninety percent
luck according to the Book o' Bud. After washing my ride I clocked
in my numbers on my waybill. While the engine warmed up I listened
to the radio calls that were on the board. One that caught my
attention was for a pickup at Candlestick Park at the Player's gate.
To check in for this order seemed like a long shot, a real roll of the
dice, but that's the way I like it. So many factors could go against
me, traffic was my biggest concern. Hell, I didn't even know there
was a ball game.
    The sun was shining and the traffic was unusually light; I figured
the Gods were smiling down on me as I checked in for the call. I got
the order along with a bit of sarcasm from the dispatcher. I didn't
let him get to me though and laid rubber as I left the yard. So far
things seemed to be going smoothly on an otherwise gutsy call as

far as cabbies are concerned. When I arrived at The Stick, I darted by some cops who gave me a dirty look so I slowed to a snail's pace. I figured out shortly after zipping by the fuzz that I had entered through the exit. I circled the attractive nuisance (now called 3Com Park) full circle until I arrived at the Player's Gate. Usually this ends up being the loser gate because a cabbie might get anyone from Leon the janitor to some sleeper left in the park that the security didn't have the heart to hand over to the cops. Security noted my timely arrival and I was told to wait. The wait is something cabbies hate, but I started to get that warm fuzzy feelin' this call was gonna be a big winner.

I was reminded of a Gatorade commercial as I saw two bodies emerge from the tunnel and instantly knew I had a couple of ball players. After my fifteen-minute wait you would think I would be feeling impatient and frustrated, but watching the two ball players come closer mellowed me out and the experience began to feel a bit trippy. They got in the back and I greeted them in English (to their amazement) and gave them a hearty hello and Cheshire cat grin. I knew they would be a good load even if it was just back to the city. To my surprise, I recognized one of them and couldn't believe I had just landed myself two bonafide Chicago Cubs! Funny thing is the last Cubs game I saw was back during the 1989 playoffs when they lost to the Giants. Now being a Cubs fan and the Bud man, I felt like I was sittin' on top of the world; even more so when they directed me to take them to the best strip club in town, which I did post haste.

For those of you who have not had the pleasure of visiting ess eff, I'll let you know that the best strip club, hands down, is the O'Farrell Theater. This place was born in the early days of porn in San Francisco by the infamous Mitchell brothers, one of whom shot and killed the other, but that's entirely another story. You can rent it on video: Charlie Sheen and Emilio Estevez star in the movie of the local porn king's life. Better yet, rent the brothers' breakaway classic, *Behind the Green Door*.

On the way north on US-101 both of the guys handed me a crisp $100.00 bill, securing them my services for the evening. I think they figured out straight away that they would be dialed in with ol' Bud at the helm. Money talks and bullshit walks, I've been told, and covering gates and gas and then some before my first ride was even over was a rare thing. Needless to say, I rolled out the red carpet along with the barrel.

I pulled up to the intersection of Polk Street and O'Farrell Street and BINGO! I spied a legal parking space. Zen parking, oh yeah. Time, money, and a legal space were on my side. As we entered the joint I greeted the manager, Chuck, and let him know I had just brought in business who were some real celebs. My valid hack license got me through this gate free of charge. This is one of several strange perks that comes with being a member of the A-card team. They checked the place out and I got two thumbs up from my new friends as they were ushered back to a private room. I, of course, tagged along like white on rice. As I ducked to the other side of the curtain into the private room, it seemed somewhat small. Too many cooks spoil the stew, this much I knew. That's when I saw two of the most beautiful women I'd ever seen start their private show for the ball players. I was advised to make like a tree and grow, or leave, or however you say it. I could feel the temperature rise as I exited the melee. One Cubby handed me $60.00 and said to get some fun. That was on top of the two Franklin's I had already been given for retainer. I was on my own and feelin' fine.

At first, I had all good intentions of not spending the $60.00, but the force was with me this fateful night, so fuck the sixty I said to myself. I deserved to explore the far reaches of the galaxy along with this place, which felt like another universe. My cabbie ID badge along with my overalls and baseball hat had me marked as either a cop or a real homely looking soul. So there I was, at the best strip club this side of the Mississippi ready to drop $60.00. No sooner had the thought of spending the surplus cash gone through my head than we met each other's eyes.

She had me marked, for better or worse, and since I had no intention of marrying this heavenly body, it was most definitely for the better. She had a bit of that lost puppy look in her eyes, which made me hot and a bit bothered. I doubted my sixty would do anything but increase the bothered part. Boy, was I wrong.

She approached me and inquired if I might need some special attention. I explained to her where the money was and that I was just a driver as I pointed to my badge. She persisted until I told her I only had $60.00 and that the big money was in the private room. I reached in my pocket and pulled out the three crisp twenties, and as I gazed at my paltry sixty bucks she snatched it up. She said she would take care of me, after she realized the big marks were taken. I was quickly escorted to a booth in the back and because a current show was not going on we actually had some privacy. I can only describe this part of the joint as something out of the Madonna peep show video, except the booth only had curtains. I stood in the booth and she moved to the other side and told me to drop my overalls to the ground. Hello Mr. Wood. I barely had time to blink or even to think, and it was batter up. Was I dreaming or what? I did the opposite of my norm, put any thought of baseball out of my head and concentrated on one thing only, the finish line. The transaction and the reaction were soon done, both with great success. Now I was really smiling like that old Cheshire Cat Alice knows so well. Some girls just know how to do it while some will never know. Again, I felt that cosmic string wrapped around me like a warm blanket.

After an hour and a half had past I rounded up the superstars and we hit the town. We ended up at the Toronado, which is a kickass watering hole in the Lower Haight. Every time I enter the Toronado, two words always come to mind. Cash and Cow. The place has a linoleum bar that looked like it could withstand a nuclear war. The only thing they serve is beer, sake and some wine. A room behind the bar houses the 50 plus kegs. Low overhead, cash cow.

I got high marks from the manager and a couple of rounds on the house for steering the Cubs to 547 Haight Street. The bartender who makes only $5.00 per hour had gone to the same school as one of the guys and it goes without saying that we made his night. The Cubbies tipped him well. As we knocked down a few brews, we swapped stories and one thing about my story bothered my famous fares. They had laid out some serious cash at the strip club only to see two chicks do each other with a double dildo. Luck or fate, I scored the home run. After a few beers, the boys ran out of gas. It was around midnight and that's 2 A.M. in Chicago. Bedtime I guess. I returned them safely to their hotel. I drove until 4 A.M. feelin' on top of the world. But who is gonna believe me?

Chapter Fourteen

DAY OFF

Taxicab Regulations: Section VI, Part C, subset 10c
Every taxicab driver must advise their dispatch service when they
will be out of service or radio contact for more than ten (10) minutes
and when they have either returned back to service or radio contact
has been restored.

It's Saturday and I'm off tonight, my fingernails are starting
to grow back, life is good. I had bitten them down to the quick last
week, a victim of too many close shorts at SFO. I guess there are
worse habits to exploit than fingernail biting, alas, one show at a
time.

I caught the movie, *Score*, at the Castro Theater; a classic
'70s porn flick. They tried really hard to have a story back then. It
was still cheesy and I think I was the only man there with a female
date. No, I am sure of this. In a Travis Bickle turnaround, the
romance director of the local rag took me to this movie on a date.
I whispered in her ear that I will try anything twice, a working
theory that has fared well for me. I must say I ended up feeling like
Travis, and wondered who was the spider and who was the fly.

Having a day or two off during the week allows one to deprogram one's self. Fifty plus hours a week of dealing with the random public deserves some time to unwind and so far, so good. I'm trying not to think about going back to work. I need to take the Church lady's words of wisdom to heart. If she only knew the whole story. I doubt she will ever see this, although anything's possible.

Since I have managed to put a day of no drinking in front of me, I may try to take an unscheduled cab out from midnight to 3 or 4 A.M. I do this from time to time; a late short shift I guess you would call it. With day and night shifts running ten hours maximum, that leaves four hours to play with. An interesting shift. Lots of drunks for sure, and as long as it's busy I don't care how fucked up you are. Just pay me and don't get sick in the car, we will drive. Usually by the time the serious drunks climb aboard, they have already blown all the chunks they have and are at the dry heave stage. My instructions are always the same with people who have the potential. They have to sit at a window seat with the window open and if they have to puke they have to tell me so I can pull over, or at best, they have to lean their head out the window. So far, this has worked well. I haven't had anybody vomit inside the vehicle recently. I always, upon parting with a drunk or someone who has been drinking, tell them to put a glass of water by their bed. This is good advice since they have to get up in the middle of the night to go to the bathroom anyway, however, I can't verify if any drunks ever remember my parting words of wisdom.

I would like to think that I have a life outside of driving a cab, but often times I don't. I have become disconnected with the morality and judgments of everyday life. Not much would shock me today as compared with a couple of years ago when I thought I knew it all. Again, I remind myself that I'm not in Kansas anymore. Not many people have my hours while the ones that do also lead a strange and twisted life. I get to know some of my regular riders and have, I think it's safe to say, some off beat relationships. I do love people and would never have had a chance to meet so many if I were not a licensed San Francisco night cabbie. For this I am grateful. For this is what keeps me comin' back. See you on the road maybe and remember, I never pass up a flag. When you flag me down, I am ready to take you anywhere you want to go. I don't know where you are headed when I pull over, and I usually wait to turn the meter on until you let me know your point of destination. From the old lady who I took around the block for free (she forgot where her house was), to the couple I took to Twin Peaks, you just never know. So far I have been fortunate, some might say lucky, to have not been hurt physically. In the past, I've found switch blades as well as a bloody paring knife in the back seat, but better there than at my throat. See you on the road. Maybe sooner than you think.

Chapter Fifteen

BC PHONE HOME

Taxicab Regulations Part XIII, Section A, Subset 2
Every Taxicab shall be equipped with a Teflon shield separating the driver and passenger so any bullshit from the rear won't stick to the driver, also beneficial for avoiding traffic citations.

Working the airport is always a crapshoot, but last night I rolled boxcars on the first toss. Imagine that. It all started when a gent flagged me down in the Financial District at the intersection of California Street and Montgomery Street. As soon as he got in the cab, he forcefully told me that he had to make a 10 P.M. flight. "Never fear, Bud Carson here," I told him. I made it down to the airport in about seventeen minutes, which is pretty damn good. He was thankful that he didn't miss his flight and for that he tipped me well. He told me I drive like a Jamaican in New York. Thanks, I think. If I do manage to get a load down to the airport before 10 P.M., I usually loop around to wait in the queue for another pick up. After 10 P.M., it's a wash, and I will deadhead back to the city.

I was almost out of the concrete jungle after the standard forty-five minute wait. I kept my fingers crossed that I would get a load back to town, because by that time, I had grown tired of waiting in my own United Nations, and besides, my supper, a Diet Coke and Snickers bar, was long gone. Then the line moved and I found myself at the United Airlines terminal. That's when a gentleman sauntered over to my cab for a ride. I tossed his bag in the back and as both our doors shut, I put the car in drive and turned the meter on. I looked back in the mirror and I could not believe it. I had Steven Spielberg, the great movie director, in the back seat of my cab.

He directed me to a Nob Hill Hotel. Right off the bat I asked him the same thing I ask every airport fare, "Was the flight uneventful?" See unless you have a hot stewardess, an uneventful flight is a good one. Funny thing was, I could tell he was surprised and a bit miffed that I didn't acknowledge his presence in my cab when he first got in. Noticing this, I then gave him my standard follow-up line after the uneventful flight pitch. "Where did ya fly in from?" I said purposefully with disinterest. He replied impatiently in a rude tone, "Sun Valley, Idaho." I knew I had to play it cool if I wanted to get a good tip so I replied, "Beautiful area up there." My failure, or rather decision, not to acknowledge his presence was by this time obviously upsetting him.

"Ever been there?" he asked me, even more rudely than before. I told him the truth and said I had not, but rather that I had heard it was a beautiful place to visit. He then asked me if I knew that Hollywood actors live in that area of Idaho. Damn, he didn't want his toes licked, he wanted them sucked. Too bad, so sad. So, I told him I wasn't aware that Idaho was a hot spot for actors. By this point, our relationship had clearly been established; me as driver, him as passenger, painfully so. Because of this he finally loosened up a bit and began to talk to me with a normal voice. He told me that he had played golf earlier in the week with Bruce Willis and Arnold Schwarzenegger, and how the naughty Bruce got kicked off the course for wearing improper attire. I wish I would have, but no, I didn't ask what he was wearing. Tank top, I imagine.

Instead, I offered up a few stories of my own to him. I told him about the part I had in a Discovery Channel documentary on *America's Haunted Houses*. In that I played a workman who tries to save a girl who was drowning in the swimming pool of the Brookdale Lodge, an event that originally occurred back in 1955. The victim was the owner's daughter and supposedly still haunts the place. All the shots were filmed with me underwater, the deep end of the pool is seen though a window to the bar area, which made the filming easier on the crew, not me. After six takes of jumping into the pool fully clothed, I was close to drowning myself. I would not have been a happy ghost.

Then, Spielberg uttered the best line of the ride: "Must have been hard to get a speaking line in that role." Thanks a lot, Einstein. I would have taken this personally had I not already been inducted into the Screen Actors Guild. When we arrived at the Nob Hill Hotel he handed me forty bucks for the $28.00 ride and wished me well in my career as an actor. "You're well on the way." He didn't say where, so I took it as a compliment, and bid him farewell.

I phoned my mother immediately to tell her of my brush with stardom. Still pinching myself to make sure I wasn't dreaming, I then called a few other friends. The general consensus was that I should have pursued an avenue for future contact with him. I let everyone know that I thought it was better to show some respect rather than beg for a free meal ticket to fame. Hell, the tip, both monetarily and verbally, was great. I was a cool cabbie, not a toe-sucking lackey. In a strange way, I think my restraint and respect paid off.

When I checked in with the window guy, I was mighty excited that I had picked up the Hollywood mogul and quickly shared my story with him. As he pushed my change under the bulletproof window he calmly said, "Nice going, Bud, now you can get on your bike an' fly home."

A few days later, as I was getting ready for work and was watching Entertainment Tonight (ET), a report came on that said Spielberg had been riding in a Town Car limo in Los Angeles on his way to his studio's new movie premiere when the lame limo driver got in a fender bender, breaking Spielberg's shoulder in the process. He was taken to Mount Cedar Sinai Hospital, treated, and released. He missed the big premiere.

When we meet again, and I have no doubt we will, I will remind him of his safe cab ride, with yours truly, just prior. If by chance he does not remember I will have to remind him of the broken shoulder and subsequently missed movie premiere. I am confident this would jog his memory. I have to apply to the school of it's better to be associated with a semi-tragic turn of events, than not at all.

Chapter Sixteen

I NEED A MIRACLE
MONDAY

Taxicab Regulations Section VII, Part A, subset 3
Every Taxicab Driver who experiences any indecision on his assigned or appointed route may toss a coin or engage in a game of chance to determine his/her next destination.

I left the garage before sundown. With the traffic being a complete mess in the city, the question of where to go first was a coin toss. Tails never fails? Heads up? I could take a left and drive through rush hour traffic in the city, or I could swing right and jump onto US-101 south to the airport. Unlike my life, I took a right turn out of the garage and hopped onto the highway southbound in hopes of a quick fifteen—to twenty-minute ride to the airport. Unfortunately, the ramp was backed up as well as the highway. I toughed it out on the on-ramp, knowing that traffic will often free up once on the highway. I was wrong again. Once you think you have a traffic pattern figured out it will turn against you. The airport can be a crapshoot as well, but I was committed to go south, even more so after braving the initial onslaught of traffic.

US-101 southbound was bumper to bumper and showed no signs of relief. I was not happy, to say the least, as I rested my head against the steering wheel in frustration, a mostly symbolic gesture. I figured this was the better alternative to laying on my horn. As I raised my head up from the steering wheel I realized I was looking full on at a multicolor, Technicolor rainbow, due south and a bit east of the highway. I felt that warm fuzzy feeling and I hadn't even picked up my first fare. It's nice to know that money isn't the only thing that moves me while on the clock. Nonetheless, I was still going nowhere fast with the beautiful view being my only salvation. So I figured the rainbow was either a sign to go get the pot o' gold at the airport or bail out of the horrific traffic jam in hopes of a good load in the city. I bailed the traffic jam and exited into the Mission District to get my first fare of the evening.

He was an Irish guy who reeked of hard liquor. He had left a bar and asked if I could wait while he ran across the street to get some hot and sour soup. I hate to wait, but told him OK and promptly started the meter. After what seemed like a very long seven minutes, he returned with his soup and started slurping away. It smelled pretty good, but more so, it just smelled strong and thick, a bit more than I had bargained for. I'm glad I wasn't hungry at the time, some well vodka I consumed last night snuffed out my appetite. His fare was $7.10, he slid me a ten, then bid me farewell.

So I was off to the Financial District to look for any flag or radio order because it was hauntingly slow. Stormy Monday, I thought to myself. I think to myself a lot while on the road. Not out loud, only crazy people do that, with the exception of hands free cellular users. I darted across town then screeched to a halt in front of city hall. It was the streamer guy, a good friend amongst the cast o' characters about town. See he's always wearing horn-rimmed glasses with streamers hanging off each of the bows. You know, like the ones you might find on a kid's bike. The dude marches to the beat of a different drummer, in his own parade. He walks all day, skirting every neighborhood during his self-appointed rounds. He is a very intelligent man and is always dressed in clean clothes, though his hair and facial hair are usually a bit unkempt. This only adds to his persona. He's at the upper end of what I would call street people, different than bums, not a panhandler. For all I know he could be a millionaire. He would get my vote for being My Fare City's next Emperor Norton.

"the streamer guy"

I see the streamer guy walking around the city all the time. He only walks on the road, never the sidewalk like the masses do. Not sure yet if he perceives this tactic as living dangerously or simply better exposure. I'm always curious about people who are living on or beyond the fringes of our society. The streamer guy easily qualifies. When I see him, we speak on the meaning of life, good and evil, and many other insightful topics in between. Last time we bumped heads I asked him what's new, what was on his mind. I was hoping for some pearl of wisdom. He advised me that the business to get into was custom bicycle handlebars. I wondered if his streamers had some connection to or significance in this, but decided to cross that bridge some other time. He professed that the biggest problem in San Francisco was the familiar battle between good and evil. Explaining that half the people are on the evil side of life while the other half occupies the good side. The trick, he said, was that we have to learn to live together even while the constant tug of war between the two sides continues. He went into detail and made a lot of sense at the time, although the idea has simplified considerably since his word-for-word definition left my mind, and ended up in the same place all of my socks, keys, and other Bermuda triangle tangibles have gone. I have a gut feeling he knows something everybody else does not know, a key to happiness if you will. I hope to find out more from him as we find our paths crossing again. Until then, questions like, "Are you creating a never-ending crop circle?" or "Does localized movement guarantee freedom to wander the same locality in the afterlife?" will have to wait. In this strange city, the streamer guy is one person I can depend on, a constant in an ever-changing landscape. I consider myself most lucky to have met such an insightful and uncommon acquaintance.

As some drunk laid on his horn driving around me, I thought too many people are in a rush, folks forget to stop and smell the roses, or anything else for that matter. With it being a slow night, I was taking any flag I saw. Eventually I picked up three guys in the Financial District who were not going far, but at this point any load is better than no load. I was in a good mood as we spoke of nothing in particular, until they asked how much an airport run costs. Time for a curve ball, answer a question with a question. "When do you need to go?" I secured the airport run, a bit o' sunshine on a dark and damp night. They had flown in from Idaho, and had to connect through ess eff, en route to Santa Barbara. As I dropped them at their party, I wondered if they had any dirt on Bruce Willis's improper attire of late.

They were ready to go when I came to the fiesta to fetch them. I think it's safe to say they had a good buzz on. They were also very pleased to discover I allow smoking in my cab. There aren't too many more places to smoke freely in California, so we enjoyed a kind smoke during the ride south, toasting to the gray area in life. Happy with the high level of service I provided, I got $40.00 on a $27.50 fare. I hope they come back and visit soon. After they disappeared into the terminal I plopped back down into the driver's seat, closed my eyes, drifted for a moment, and pictured the rainbow from earlier. A horn from a small car behind me was more like a tap on the shoulder than a knockout punch, but it still killed my rainbow. I opened my eyes, then my carburetor. All I needed was to get through bartertown, the concrete jungle, then hope to find another diamond in the rough, along with a little sanity.

Much later, this Monday was somewhat uneventful, but bartenders and the like provided a decent late night boost. Being in the know, most of them take cabs home. I turned in after ten hours on the street, burnt to a crisp. I was not looking forward to my bicycle ride home as it's mostly downhill to work, but it's all up hill on the way home. A virtual mirror to my rider's moods each evening, more so on the weekends. However, I need the daily exercise, and the lesson. I do not want to become a fat, stereotypical cabbie, or at least not fat. I wonder who I'll see on Tuesday? Whoever it is, I'll make sure they have a nice trip.

Chapter Seventeen

TALKING LUGGAGE

Taxicab Regulations: Section VI, Part E, subset 4
A Taxicab Driver shall not refuse to transport a passenger's luggage, wheelchair, crutches or other property that can be transported within the confines of the vehicles trunk and/or passenger areas.

I have had some strange shit go down driving nights but I never cease to be amazed. Just when I think I have seen it all, some situation happens that keeps my life in perspective. Still other things warp my perspective so far beyond comprehension that I figure it to have been changed permanently. I can understand the drunks, the drug addicts, the freaks, the geeks, and even the business people. But the sex and fetish folks I doubt I'll ever understand. I will always be happy to cart them around and hell, their money is as green as the next guy's, but some of the shit they do, I just don't get it. I was doing my strange loop around the city as business slowed. Until the 2 A.M. bar rush, I decided to continue to drive, rather than playing some hot spot in the financial. I had just finished reading *The Neon Wilderness* by Nelson Algren and with no new reading material, I was digging for gold, or rather that diamond in the rough, as I like to say. I'm not sure how to describe what I ended up with other than an easy fifty bucks and some serious soul searching as to what makes people tick. Life often seems like some grand master plan while other times it's like a big cosmic joke. Reflecting on the man who flagged me down last night and how he directly reflected on me, I would have to lean toward the cosmic joke theory.

The guy I plucked up was right out of the heart of the Castro district at 18th and Castro St. He played the part well, dressed entirely in black leather and with a big mustache. Though it sounds like a stereotype, he did remind me of one of The Village People. And let's just say he wasn't going to the YMCA. We hadn't traveled more than a block when I figured it was time to find out where he was headed. It was not where I expected. He was straight away with his request, and boy was it a first. He waved a fifty-dollar bill in between the front seats, and did it look as good as a carrot to Bugs Bunny. The guy asked me if he could ride around for an hour, in the trunk of my cab. I pulled over right away and put the vehicle into park. As I snatched the fifty out of the guys hand I told him that for fifty bucks I would give him a half an hour, as I was not sure of the air supply much less the carbon monoxide factor in the trunk of the vehicle. This guy was truly a week shy of a fortnight. He nodded his head and smiled, like he had tried this before but without a willing driver. I was additionally comforted by the fact my photo identification was in my visor, and out of view. I drove around to a side street in case some concerned citizen thought some murderous business, rather than monkey business, was going on.

As I wished the guy well and shut the trunk I laughed to myself and thought what a strange fuckin' city I live in. He wanted me to pick up any other paying fares I could though I told him that there was no guarantee, business had been slow, but that I would if the situation arose. Since I already had the fifty I will tell you I was lying when I told him I might pick up another fare, no way would I want to blow my cover on this one. I headed towards the Mission district all smiles, the fifty already warming up my billfold. As I headed down Valencia St. southbound, I turned down the tunes and yelled to make sure he was OK. Sounding like Charlie Brown's teacher, he managed to get out a muffled "Oh Yeah!" I turned back up my favorite radio station, KUSF, and drove around the Mission, regrettably passing a few nice-looking ladies trying to flag me down in front of Bruno's, a popular club. "Maybe next time, gals," I mumbled as I slowed, but continued on.

I almost picked up a drunken Latino man later in the ride but had already clocked 25 minutes, and I couldn't be sure of where he would want to go. Arriving back in the Castro, I pulled over on Collingwood St., up the hill a bit from ground zero where I initially picked up the fare. Thankfully the automatic switch that pops the trunk was working on the cab, which came in mighty handy, more so than ever before. This would be the first piece of luggage actually to get out of the trunk by itself, and most likely the last. But never say never.

After the guy climbed out of the trunk I yelled back for him to please close it, at which he did. As I pulled away we waved at each other and I even caught a thumbs up from him in the rear view before I hastily rounded the corner. I'm not sure what he did in the trunk, and as I was not in my regular cab I'll probably never know. To be perfectly frank, the fifty bucks carried me over 'til the bars closed and turned a fair to middling profit margin into a decent wage for the evening. I'll chalk this one up to personal business. I'm not sure what else to call it, other than mutually beneficial.

Chapter Eighteen

GOOD BYE RUBY TUESDAY

Taxicab Regulations Section V, Part C, subset 2d
The taximeter shall be mounted no lower than either the lowest portion of the front window frame or the top of the dashboard.

Tuesday evening went very slow. From the start, it was a take-what-you-can-get kind of night. After toughing it out in the city for a few hours, I deadheaded to the airport. My first ride from the airport went to Foster City. This is about fifteen minutes south from SFO, which means you can just make the short, by the hair on your chinny-chin-chin. If there are any traffic delays, you lose, no matter how close. Thirty-one minutes? Too bad, so sad. Time among other things can blow a short. Today it was textbook, twenty-seven minutes round trip, a nail biter nonetheless. My next fare was also a good short, to Army and Folsom, about a fifteen-minute ride each way, only north. Traffic being light, I made the second short in no time. My third mark out of SFO went to the Hyatt at Fisherman's Wharf. Add it up and you get a good start, a good shake at a promising evening. Instead, it just got strange.

At the intersection of 6th and Market Street, round midnight, I noticed a late model Honda engulfed in flames. Cops were on the scene, though they didn't appear to be doing anything at all. A DPT officer resembled a fire dancer on loan from Burning Man; he had some serious wrist action going on with his light saber. The car fire blazed and blew in the wind with a mighty force and a putrid smell to boot. I stopped for a few minutes and spaced out on the flames. I didn't have a passenger so it was OK to watch it burn. I felt better upon pulling away though I couldn't put my finger on why.

Back in the Financial District I picked up a voucher client, a bitch in a power suit. I shot over her block and proceeded round the next when she started. She was very snappy when she asked why I went around the block. I told her the truth. I told her that I missed her block 'cause I was speaking to her, validating the popular theory that men just aren't multi-task oriented. I hoped this cutting-edge honesty would be enough, but it was not. I simplified it for her. I told her if I miss the block and go around it, it may cost about $0.30 to $0.60 extra and no cabbie wants to jam you for a block or two. Still trying to cross the longest yard and dump her off, I gave up. I finally told her to shut up. She shut up, and was a good girl for what was left of the ride. After she paid me, I could hear her dog barking inside her place. I think too much, too much of the time, but was sure glad I wasn't that dog.

"the financial"

The rest of the night was good timing. I got several decent orders out of the Financial, hence salvaging my shift. I kept the cab out ten hours, but took the last hour as my hour of power, or better yet moment of Zen. I decided to drive to the best view of My Fare City, the top o' Twin Peaks, a real visual treat. I relaxed and gazed at the glimmering lights of downtown and pictured myself racing around the streets from fare to fare like a worker bee buzzing and buzzing, from flower to flower. Warm, fuzzy.

Chapter Nineteen

EXCESSIVE HORNING

Taxicab Regulations: Section V, Part C, subset 13
The taxicab shall have a horn in working order.

    I picked up my cab around 6 P.M. and gave a friend a ten-dollar ride to the airport. This way I could justify getting down there to see if it was moving. I have already accepted my friend as a cheapskate, as I would have ridden empty otherwise. A large convention was just about to start; this meant many visitors to My Fare City would be arriving from the friendly skies. I ended up playing the airport until around midnight, with great success. My luck held fast with three nail-biting shorts; I made the last two in twenty-nine minutes. I missed what would have been my fourth short, due to a backup of cabs before the entry gate, then took my invitation to the fourth waiting lot and started round and round. The fourth lot's hamster wheel of movement ranks up there with walking through the Broadway Tunnel. Each time you come up to that gate and get another ticket to try again, a helpless and Orwellian feeling comes about you.

"bartertown"

Reality was a bit cold and pointless in bartertown, and my head was still ringing from the cabbie concert. I can tolerate the pagan rituals, the incense, the card games, the headgear of every shape and size, and the odor-iffic cabbies; however, there is one thing that breaks the fuckin' camel's back, and makes me crazy. Two words. Excessive horning. Let me explain.

Some idiotic cabbie gets tied up laying some cable, or at the famous tastes-like-chicken food bus, when the lot starts to move along. Nobody can move their cab until he does, so every cab not moving will sound their horn, all the way out of the garage. This can result in a unique and unequaled sound of beauty or it can result in an out of tune fart, as it happened to sound like tonight. Nobody will move any faster, but this practice continues as one of the only and most stupid signs of solidarity among cab drivers in My Fare City. As always, when this happens (tonight it happened several times), I roll up my windows and wait it out.

Emerging for my last time of the evening out of the concrete jungle, I took a deep breath and wished I would get a ride back to the city. My mood had been stretched 'n chewed like a piece of saltwater taffy. I pulled up to the taxi island of the international terminal and noticed a strange sound. It was a distinct humming. It's a very strange noise if you stop to listen; however, it blends into everything else if you aren't paying attention. White noise. You can hear it very clearly on the lower concourse. It mesmerized me into a place I had not been before. I'm not sure, but I would guess it to be the air ventilation system, or spirits.

Chapter Twenty

WHAMMY

Taxicab Regulations Section XIV, Part D, subset 1
Every Taxicab Driver shall notify in person any radio call being answered in the City and County of San Francisco, at said residence or business address, on arrival at said order. After proper notification a cab driver may then depart at any time, to continue normal service.

North Beach is a lively area in My Fare City. Filled with fine dining and quite a few bars, there is almost always foot traffic about. If you can't manage to get yourself a flag in this area of town, then things all over are likely as slow as molasses. One of the area's best-kept secrets is a little restaurant named Julius Castle. It is located near the intersection of Union and Montgomery streets. This joint is tucked away just enough up Telegraph Hill to be considered off the beaten path.

Cab drivers hate to wait. After I accepted the radio call at this little gem of a restaurant the last item on my agenda was to wait for my fare to come out. I waited, and waited. The valet acknowledged me when I pulled up and scurried inside, no doubt informing the hostess of my oh-so-timely arrival. New cab drivers would have a hard time locating this place so I was reasonably sure I would get my fare, but things seemed to distinctly slow down. I was hoping I had not broken my rhythm, and was getting miffed after sitting around ten minutes with nothing to do but watch my car rust. Finally I turned off the motor and headed inside to speak with the hostess and find out where, if at all, my fare was. The valet who originally saw me was off on an endless search for a parking space, and nowhere to be found. Thankfully the hostess greeted me straight away and advised me to sit tight, noticing my official taxi driver badge and casual attire. She whispered in my ear that the fare was Mr. Franklin, and then gave a sweet smile and wink. Waiting would not be a bad idea, now that I understood. I smiled warmly at her, making sure to meet eyes, then I walked outside to my cab. The waiting now had turned itself from being mildly irritating to a good prospect, maybe even a diamond in the rough, or Franklin in this case.

I sat and listened to KUSF for an additional ten minutes until my fare appeared. It was a famous rock star and some beautiful babe close at his side. I immediately recognized him, and would be ready to let him know this, unlike Mr. Spielberg. Hell, I listened to his music for the better part of high school. He looked great, or should I say he played the part well. He was wearing black leather boots, black leather pants, and a black leather vest that was laced tightly enough to asphyxiate any normal human being. His hair was indeed as wild as his music, and I don't know about you, but in my book, Sammy Hagar is no mere mortal, but rather a rock 'n roll legend. Having him as a fare you would think would be enough for one person to handle, but he had a woman on his arm who was blonde, buxom, and as beautiful as a sunset on Mt. Tamalpais. What a pair!

Sammy directed me to head north over the Golden Gate Bridge to Mill Valley, CA. This little hamlet is about ten minutes north of the bridge, and would net me a tidy sum, a hundred bucks with tip if the hostess wasn't bullshitting me. At this point, I doubt she was.

I darted through the streets with the greatest of ease, driving a bit reckless on purpose. I was catching all of the green lights and my passengers were enjoying the ride, no doubt buzzed a bit from some fine wine with their supper. At one point I was even encouraged to hit the pedal to the metal. I made it so.

As we approached the Golden Gate Bridge I remembered the recent crackdown on speeding over the span. The speed limit is strictly enforced at 45 m.p.h., violating this nets you a double fine along with some close scrutiny compliments of the California Highway Patrol. Bottom line is you just don't break this law unless you are looking for three hots and a cot, and I was not.

I zipped through the toll plaza (there is no toll leaving, just on the return) and slowed my vehicle down to the posted speed limit, 45 m.p.h. Sammy asked me why I slowed down. I turned to my fare and told him something that he had no doubt heard before but for me it felt like the sum of my whole life had brought me to this point, this setup, this line for Christ's sake. "I'm sorry Sammy, but believe me when I tell ya, I can't drive 55." We all got a good belly laugh and I did get a Franklin ($100) upon arrival at his crib.

Chapter Twenty-One

EBB 'N FLOW

Taxicab Regulations Section VI, Part D, subset 7
Drivers shall only receive a tip/gratuity when expressly issued by
the payee. Drivers may not demand, imply, suggest, assume, or
otherwise receive any additional charges unless permitted under
City Charter Municipal Police Code or the Chief's rules and
regulations.

I was happy to be arriving back in San Francisco around midnight
because the music on the radio on Sunday nights can't be beat.
Whatever your pleasure, you got it goin' on Sunday nights. I jammed
tunes and played the Financial District for what it was worth. Not
much. I decided to stick it out for the full ten hours mainly because
I had already cracked the nut and the music was good. Even when
a fare got in my cab and wasn't going far, I maintained a friendly
and mellow glow. This paid off when a nice man tipped me with a
bottle of red wine. I'm drinking it now. He probably stole it or got
it for free. Best not let it go to waste.

There are several places you can situate yourself in the Financial
District to wait for an order to hit. As I surveyed the situation, I
stopped a moment to realize how quiet it was, especially when

compared to what it is like during rush hour. I was parked by myself and just the whisper of the wind could be heard as I stared at the darkened towering monuments to our productivity. Things seemed a bit trippy, but in a good way. I've never had an LSD flashback, but my pal Wavy Davy has, at least he got truth in advertising. After taking in the moment, I thought about wrapping it up for the night. On my way to get gas, I took a radio call simply because the customer's name was Mindy. I know a few Mindys, all of 'em knockout gorgeous. The Mindy I picked up was about the weight of three of me and it's safe to say she wasn't what I expected. I need to remember to expect the unexpected on this roller coaster ride of life.

I drove over 200 miles this evening and can always think of several easier ways to make money than driving a taxi. The people and the freedom, total freedom separates this vocation from any other. Many of us, myself included, mistake the letters a and o. Vacation or Vocation? The experience of just living through the night is like nothing else, it has a magic all it's own. I have always been a risk taker, and know big risks reap big rewards. Only thing is, those rewards change on a daily basis depending on my mindset.

Chapter Twenty-Two

TIJUANA TAXI

Taxicab Regulations: Section VI, Part F, subset 1 & 2
No driver shall drive, or permit to be driven, a taxicab vehicle whose interior is not kept clean, orderly, and free of offensive odors. Every color scheme holder placing in service any taxicab vehicle in the City and County of San Francisco shall provide facilities to ensure the thorough washing of the taxicab vehicle. Whenever required in writing by the Department of Public Health of the City and County of San Francisco, every color scheme holder shall be responsible for the full disinfecting of each taxicab vehicle so operated under their color scheme causing said taxicab to be sprayed with an efficient disinfectant.

Have you ever wondered how clean the cab you're riding in is? With an average of two to three hundred thousand miles each cab has traveled in My Fare City, it's safe to say most everything has been replaced on 'em at least once. If the cabs themselves could talk you probably wouldn't get in them, for so much life, good and evil, goes down on a day-to-day basis.

What I ended up with today was surely the thing bad dreams are made of, though I had no idea when I squealed out of the yard what was in store for me. I ended up getting issued the "Tijuana Taxi," or so some old timers call it. I had not found out why; I just figured the name was born of the many miles, the funky seat covers, and maybe because the suspension sat a bit low. It smelled kinda funky as I tore off to the Financial, but not any worse than some other cabs I had been issued. In the end, it was not the smell that got to me, nor my poor passenger.

A very large black lady flagged me down on the way to the heart of the financial district. I wasn't thrilled when she asked me to take her to the Cal Train station, just six blocks total. As I have said before, you gotta start somewhere, and they can't all be long hauls or long legs, though I would end up with some long legs later.

I hit the meter as we puttered off towards the station when, after maybe a block, the 300-pound lady was screaming bloody fuckin' murder! I swerved the vehicle and pulled over. At the same time, my fare was trying to jump into the passenger side of the front seat. I skidded to a stop, fearing for my safety, figuring she was having some sort of psychotic episode. My fare had gotten herself stuck between the top of the passenger side seat and the roof of the car, in part due to my hasty halt. In a sad sort of way, it was kinda funny. I could make out some words from her, though it still seemed like nonsense. She was screaming, "Get them off! Get them off!" I had no idea what she meant, but got myself out of the vehicle and opened up the back door to investigate at once. I have been thrown off guard before, but what I was witness to not only shocked but grossed the living hell out of me.

While still stuck in between the seat and the roof, her legs flailing in the air—I'm at a loss as to what to compare this sight to. Crawling on her legs were several large roaches, and I'm not talking about the kind you smoke. It was horrific. I ran around to the front passenger door, opened it and pulled the lady over the top of the seat and into the front of the car. She got out, jumped around like she was on fire, or maybe doing the macarena on acid, and brushed the roaches she could locate off her legs. In shock she ran off, in the direction of the Cal Train, now just a few blocks away. Man, I figured this to be the dirtiest lady I had ever had in my cab; I wondered if she worked at some funky fastfood chain. She was not dressed in a power business suit and had reeked a bit of cheap booze, but who knows?

As she was a block away and almost out of sight, I was still scratching my head. "Fuckin' strange people in this here city," I said aloud. When I walked around to shut the back door of the cab, I looked in the rear area to see if she had left any other bugs or vermin in the back of the cab. I couldn't see any right away but did notice in all her kickin' and screamin' she had managed to knock the back seat loose. As I was positioning it back on, I saw one small roach run under the seat. I lifted up the rear seat to kill the little bugger and to my surprise, I was looking at a whole fuckin' colony of 'em. Small ones, big ones, and some rotten food they were using as a deity. The memory itself still haunts me. I now would have to take the cab in, and get some real piece of shit for the duration of my shift. I promptly took the roach coach back to the yard and parked it. The window guy was not too impressed with my tale of woe 'til he saw the unwelcome residents of the Tijuana Taxi for himself, at which time he gave me a new cab for the duration of the night. Before I got the new cab, he did query me as to the whereabouts of the ill-fated passenger. I told him as far as I knew, the shock and mental trauma of the event had sent her off into the sunset, or at least to the train station. Before I left the bulletproof window, he told me to please avoid the train station. "A-OK," I said with a smile, and was off again. The only long legs I had in my cab the rest of the evening were those of sweet young ladies leaving the clubs. This I could deal with. As to the whereabouts of the ill-fated rider, nothing was ever heard of her again. After I uncovered, literally, the roach motel, all the old cabs were promptly bombed so no more unwanted little passengers would be riding along free of charge in My Fare City.

"tijuana taxi"

Chapter Twenty-Three

HEAVY METAL

Taxicab Regulations Section XVI, Part D, subset 8
"A psycho driver twisted in my head. Silence broken, but there's nothing said."—Ozzy Osbourne

As a San Francisco cab driver, you see plenty of accidents, most of 'em after the fact. I personally have seen countless intersections littered with the twisted wreckage of unlucky vehicles. Their drivers, who I do take a gander at, always seem to have that deer-in-the-headlights look. In many cases, I am on the scene prior to any emergency services, and if I ever decided to be an attorney I would be one hell of an ambulance chaser. I have never felt compelled to stop and assist until recently.

There is a real dead zone (slow time) between the hours of midnight and 2 A.M. With the bars legally closing at 2 A.M. it's kind of like the calm before the storm. After 2 A.M. drunks and skunks all prowl the streets, looking for a ride home, with foul breath and bogus-smelling drag queens being the norm. In fact, I have never had a drag queen in my cab that didn't totally gag me with his cheap perfume.

Before the melee started, sometime after midnight, I found

myself northbound on Franklin St. in the heart of Opera Plaza. This area is notorious for many a blind intersection. Franklin St. is a three-lane one way, so it can prove to be hazardous, as it was this evening. I pulled up in the left of the three lanes on Franklin to a red light at Grove St. The only thing that caught my attention was a couple of brothers in a Chevy Nova in the right hand lane playing some drum 'n bass on a stereo that obviously cost more than the ride itself. As we met eyes, I nodded at them in approval, which they returned. My radio was tuned to KUSF, which had just finished playing the Devo Corporate Anthem, one of my personal favorites. Life was good, for the moment.

A four-door Volkswagen Jetta was puttering eastbound on Grove, safely, and on a green light. Then it happened, heavy fuckin' metal. And no, not comin' from the brothers' Nova, but in front of my very eyes. In the empty lane between the brothers and myself came a Mercedes station wagon, speeding like a bat out of hell. Like a bullet, the Benz roared between us, hitting the unsuspecting Jetta squarely in the passenger side of the vehicle, blatantly running through a solid red light on Franklin. The impact made a sound I shall never forget; boy was it loud and violent. I had my windows rolled down to air out the smell of my previous fare, which made the whole event that much more intense. When both vehicles came to rest, the Mercedes didn't look that bad, even with some smoke rising from the cracked radiator. The Jetta, on the other hand, had been tossed like a rag doll twenty or so feet, and what was left of it was half on the sidewalk next to the Opera House. A clear indentation of the Benz was punched out in the side of its German counterpart. The Benz had literally made its way through half of the poor Jetta. The scene was horrific, and a little unreal. I think the noise of the impact had burst a fat cell in my brain, as I felt a bit stoned.

I got out of my cab and walked over to the Jetta, expecting to see the passenger spattered all over the driver, as no passenger, seat belt or not, could have survived this wreck. As I neared the driver side of the Jetta, I could now tell the driver was intact, though in shock. Thank the Lord, he was the only one in the car. I told him everything would be fine, not sure if he understood me or not, and not to move, though he wasn't trying to nor could he, I suspected. Looking over to the Benz, I was surprised to see a white skinhead (I know, redundant) fall out of the driver's seat and then get up, only to start limping away in pain. His leg was fucked up as he was dragging it along, reminiscent of a wounded animal. With the skinhead moving slowly but steadily away, I yelled at the two brothers in the Nova who had witnessed the wreck to grab the oh-so-obvious felon. He in no way fit the demographic of a Mercedes Benz Station Wagon owner and it was doubtful to me he had borrowed it from mom for the evening. The two brothers gazed over at me, then at each other, and then one yelled, "You grab him whitebread, he's one of yours!" They jumped back in their Chevy and made tracks the same way I avoided my last bench warrant. In a strange sort of way, I guess I understood where they were coming from.

The skinhead disappeared into the night long before the ambulance and cops were on the scene, even though I had the dispatcher radio 911 posthaste.

I am pretty sure the guy who was in the car that resembled a half-opened can of tomato soup lived. It doesn't take a rocket scientist to figure out the Benz was hot as high noon in Death Valley, and that the skinhead also lived to see another night in My Fare City.

Chapter Twenty-Four

GO DIRECTLY TO JAIL

Taxicab Regulations Section VI, Part A, subset 3
Every Taxicab driver shall obey any lawful request or order of any law enforcement officer or his or her designee. A law enforcement officer or their designee has the authority to settle any fare disputes. This may include but is not limited to adjusting the disputed amount, persuading the passenger to pay, citing, or taking a citizen arrest of the participants.

I don't know how I get so lucky sometimes, but having dodged another bullet on the streets of My Fare City makes me realize the danger inherent in the occupation of being a San Francisco Taxi Driver. Remember kids, I do not drive one of those cabs with a shield separating the front and rear of the vehicle, nor would I want to. Thirty percent of my nightly take is on tips, and for tips, you need communication. There is little or no communication in a cab with a shield, the result uprooting the normal modus operandi between driver and rider. Physically and psychologically, it's a completely different balsam, one I would rather not play. The fact I speak English fluently is an asset in my particular line of work, and something I would like to take advantage of, among other things, whenever the opportunity arises.

"cop shop"

Notwithstanding my sometimes happy-go-lucky attitude, I assure you, it isn't always fun and games when the rubber hits the road. Yet another guy threatened to kill me, and how shall I say, it did not thrill me. This guy I think would have preferred, or better said, would have been more used to, speaking through a bulletproof partition, like back at the barn for me, or the big barn (house) in his case (pun not intended, but will take it). Any wingnuts who actually make it into my cab are always flags, this is standard. I don't know where they come from, but always find out where they are going. Usually crazy, of course, and/or around 6th and Market. California is the land of fruits and nuts, this is a gimme. Still, nothing could have prepared me for this ride, barring a .357 magnum and Clint "Dirty Harry" Eastwood at my side. The gods were smiling on me once again, and luck was all I ended up needing, and got.

The hombre hailed me from the corner of 16th and Valencia Streets, in the Mission District. He was a thin Latino man dressed in a white T-shirt, blue jeans, and wearing a tan-colored Carhartt jacket. For all intents and purposes, he looked like a regular, hard working, middle class guy. If you plan on making any money driving a taxi you have to pick up flags off the street sooner or later. You can't always pick and choose your fares, though you do end up being somewhat prejudicial, for your own safety.

When this cat got in, I paused and looked back and asked him how he was doing, my first mistake. We had not moved as he started into a chilling monologue. "How am I doing you ask, how am . . . I doing? Well, I'm gonna kill someone, that's how I'm doing." I couldn't get him out without a fight, I figured, so trying to play nice and not have me be the person killed, I asked him what was up, my second mistake. Mind you, his door was closed but I had not moved yet. He then started crying and told me his mother was denied parole again today. He said as a child "they were always together." He said when he was a kid, his mom and dad were having a party when he heard loud yelling and screaming coming from the kitchen, where apparently they both were armed with knives. He wasn't sure what happened after that until the "pigs" arrived. Weeping, he said, "Blood was all over, man. I had his blood on my hands. The pigs kept asking me what happened; I didn't know." The cops took his mom away; his dad was severely wounded and died that night. The cops let him go with his grandmother, whose house he needed to go to now.

He told me to take him to East Palo Alto, not only a meter and a half trip, but also a dangerous destination, having the title of murder capitol of the world a few years running. I had a gut feeling he did not have the funds required. A timely interruption went down as a car laid on his horn behind me. I slowly moved southbound on Valencia St. He continued by saying, "I never see me madre outside the joint since then," apparently not having any money for bail, or good legal representation.

I told him how much it would cost, my third and final mistake. He went ballistic. "Why didn't you tell me this back there, before I bought the shit man! You better take me there or I'll waste you man!" I distinctly heard the sound of a switchblade opening. I know this cause I own one too, though mine is safely stowed in my night table next to my bed.

OK, fun's over. As we had traveled a block south on Valencia St. I looked to my right and saw the Mission Station of the San Francisco police. After he threatened to waste me, I made the assumption he was not gonna pull out a fattie. I said, "No problem my friend," then veered a hard right into the lot holding all the cop cars, got out quickly, and ran for the door. Not looking back, I could hear his door shut as I went into the station.

Some cops looked at me suspiciously as I turned back to my cab. He was nowhere in sight. A fat and smelly cop sipping a steaming hot cup o' joe asked me what my problem was. I looked around and he said, "Yeah, you!" I looked again at my cab and said quietly, "Nothing officer." He yammered at me, "Do you know you can't be in this lot with your cab? It's restricted." I quickly conjured up a lie, telling him I had a radio call here. He told me to park next door and come in the main doors. Having a pocket full of kryptonite myself, I didn't want to go into the whole time-consuming process of making a report and hanging around the cop shop any longer. "Sorry, sir" I said and was off, checking the back seat before I got back in the cab. Tearing out of the lot, I did not pick up anybody else in the Mission, though I did have a few drops there later that evening.

Thinking back to my own childhood, I distinctly remember my daddy telling me that California was the "land of fruits and nuts." I thought it to be a funny joke at the time. This wing nut was no joke. I consider myself very lucky to have been driving by the cop shop at the right moment, or I may have ended up as another grim statistic. On the assumption he was telling the truth about his mom, I do feel sorry for him.

The rest of the night I felt like a cat with nine lives, not sure which one I was on. With short shifts long gone, I played the financial for the most part, hoping the stock market hadn't crashed or I might end up with some more disturbed riders, and frankly, I wasn't in the mood.

Chapter Twenty-Five

MONDAY NIGHT

Taxicab Regulations Section VI, Part A, subset 4
A Taxicab driver shall not hinder, delay, or knowingly make false or misleading statements.

I rode my bike down Haight St. to the garage with high hopes, high hopes, high apple pie in the sky hopes. The sky was yellow and the sun was blue, or whichever way you see it through.

I usually don't go to work until the sun sets, but today it was still light. Just another sign of the changing season which means more business because more tourists will be visiting My Fare City. I personally don't like to start work while it is still daylight out. Starting and ending while it's dark is much easier for me. I don't like having to bring my sunglasses to work, one less thing to lose. To me, starting and finishing at night just feels right.

I managed to get an early ride south to the airport and on my first try there, I got a fare back to the city. That was all the time I would spend rollin' the dice at the airport. But with seventy dollars in hand from my outbound/inbound airport runs I would now make something, no doubt. I wore on as the evening did by driving from neighborhood to neighborhood without any specific plan. Then I decided to play the Financial District, which is always good if you are in the right place at the right time. I started to get in the groove but all my fares were short ones. I just couldn't break the five-dollar-per-ride mark even with the tip.

"corner of haight and ashbury"

I remember one businessman mentioning something about "tolerance management" to his co-worker. Hah! What a joke. I wish my last boss had more experience in the field of "tolerance management." Hell, I might still be working normal hours towards a specific goal. Fuck it! I would rather be tuning into college radio and getting to know My Fare City better than going back to the rat race. If anything, as a night driver, I've joined the bat race. (Ha, ha.)

After I got back to the city I decided to see what would happen if I didn't initiate any conversation with my fares with the exception of, "Where to?" This was very interesting because it made most people uncomfortable and ninety percent of the time they would eventually start to talk. Of everyone who initiated conversation, only one person did it by not talking about the weather. It's our common denominator because it affects us all in different ways.

Frankly, I'm sick of talking about the weather. I would rather talk about anything else and often will segue from the weather to whatever subject is on my mind. An example of this is when some stuffed shirt comments on how our sunny day is quickly turning into a stormy evening, I'll mention how this will be a real drag for the folks going to the needle exchange on the Lower Haight later that night. "A needle exchange on Lower Haight?" they will comment. Then my clever, or not so clever, segue (depending on if you think clever and blunt are one and the same) would allow me to speak about something other than the weather. In this case, the needle exchange. So, with what looked like a boring evening ahead, I decided to turn it into a cross section of viewpoints that I otherwise would never have heard. As far as the needle exchange topic went, I couldn't find any supporters until after 10 P.M. I don't think they were current needle users, but rather street-smart folks in the service industry who had mostly liberal and well-informed views of the good and bad points on this controversial subject. I did find people to debate the subject with before 11 P.M., just nobody who supported it. And, as for where this cabbie stands, I think it is better to use a clean needle if you inject drugs into your system. And for those who do use needles on a regular basis, the exchange is a necessity, not a luxury. I assure you, it's a way of life for more people than you can imagine. If something doesn't affect you just because you are not a participant, think twice before laying judgment on something about which you don't know the whole story.

Ever tried on someone else's shoes? From needle use to breast cancer, nobody can know exactly how it is unless you stand in their shoes. So until you do, listen and learn and let's all keep an open mind in the meantime. An open mind was supposed to be the prerequisite to living in My Fare City. Unfortunately, a lot of prejudice still exists. I do my best to try to expose my fares to a fresh idea or two. I like to leave them thinking. When such a time comes that I get burnt out with deep communication, I close my mind and talk about city politics, the weather, sports, or the new ballpark. But most times I would rather dig a little deeper. If I don't, you sure won't.

"Tolerance management," this still gives me a chuckle. Business people direct everything down to each layer on the piece of toilet paper you use on your ass, no, each fiber, no, each atom. I do not appreciate unnecessary detail. Describe a puffy cloud, a sunset, a baby's smile, but leave the productivity analysis for a dry, stuffy boardroom full of fellow partners-in-crime and don't forget the graph to explain yourself. The crime I speak of is forgetting what is truly beautiful and filling your mind up with your ego and your "oh-so-important" position at the company and its agenda. I guarantee this won't mean much if this is your last day to live. Life is short; it's not just a saying. So yeah, you have my blessing to play hard. Just don't forget the roses and their wonderful smell. Though roses, like life, can prick if you are not careful handling them.

I tried to stick out my full shift but turned in a bit early. I felt spent, like the money I used to purchase my fourth Diet Coke a bit earlier. This night will not go down as anything spectacular except for the fact that nothing spectacular happened. I did not have anybody ditch me for their fare, I was not robbed, and I managed to make my gates, gas, and kickbacks. On top of this, I made some take-home money which I promptly put toward several past due bills.

I hope to have a more profitable night Tuesday, but only timing and the luck of the draw will help with that. The nightly kickback to my outbound dispatcher doesn't seem to be helping much either, but I really don't want to find out if it could get worse by not giving him his due. The old saying comes to mind: "Don't bite the hand that feeds you."

Tomorrow could be my best day ever or my last day alive. Best to look on the bright side, keep that glass half-full and continue onward and upward. I've got high hopes . . . I've got high hopes . . . I've still got high in the sky apple pie hopes! I think I am, no, I think I've gone crazy.

Chapter Twenty-Six

STONE COLD

Taxicab Regulations Section VII, Part B, subset 9
No Taxicab Driver shall be treated to anything other than a friendly, happy-go-lucky attitude by passengers when the taximeter is running within the City and County of San Francisco or Marin County, if the trip originated in the Haight Ashbury District.

Remember the infamous movie scene where the icepick-obsessed woman wasn't wearing any underpants? I sure do. I used to think she was a real babe, fresher than fresh. Alas, all good things, or fantasies in my case, must come to an end. She lives appropriately enough on Bush St., a coincidence I guess.

After she planted herself in the back seat, I told her how much I admired her work, as I recognized her straight away. She was not as sultry as I might have expected, but with her reputation as one of the beauties of Hollywood preceding her, I can say I was initially impressed. This, like my write up, wouldn't last long.

She told me to drive her to Tosca, a bar in North Beach, and not that long of a ride. The bar is located near the heart of North Beach, the intersection of Broadway and Columbus streets. Scenes from the opera of the same name are painted on the walls of the joint, this being the draw of the place I guess. Not to knock the bar, the grandeur of the place is subtly impressive. Locally noted for our mayor "Slick" Willie Brown hanging out there, the bar does good business and mixes some bitchin' coffee drinks. So, depending on your style and taste, you might enjoy giving it a looky loo if you're ever in the hood.

As far as my famous fare, I did not have much time to establish any kind of conversation or relationship whatsoever. She was wearing black and less makeup than she needed. Meaningful conversation was out of the question as she did face exercises for the entire $4.10 ride. Yes, face exercises.

I got a five for the trip, and that's about as exciting as it got. The dame was about as interesting as my pet rock, or should I say stone, Sharon Stone that is.

Chapter Twenty-Seven

IT'S MAGIC

Taxicab Regulations: Section VI, Part B, subset 4
Every taxicab driver shall ensure that their cab is equipped with a supply of receipts, preprinted with the taxicab company's name. Each receipt shall have the following information, but not limited to: driver's full name, badge number, vehicle number and amount of fare (written legibly), prior to giving it to the passenger upon request.

Three 40-something ladies jumped into my cab in front of the Fairmont Hotel, atop beautiful Nob Hill. It's around 5:30 P.M., and the evening rush hour has most taxis elsewhere. They flagged me driving by the hotel on the other side of the street. It's unlikely they were out of the PU (Pacific Union) Club; more likely they were jumpin' the queue at the hotel. The doorman's whistle had a certain pitch reminiscent of my alarm clock. I had only been up for a few hours, and to bed not long before that, so I wasn't in the mood for anybody being rude. See if you defy the vernal equinox, you can't make up that sleep. International travelers are hip to this, for me it just means to get to bed before sunrise. It was a photo finish this morning.

We hadn't even gone a half block when, unprovoked, no less, one of them stepped on me like a doormat and said in a very rude tone of voice, "Gimme a receipt." I thought of a thousand things to say to her, but before I could reply, she said again, "Gimme a receipt, buddy." I don't get paid enough to take that treatment from anyone. I waited 'til the first stoplight, another half block, took a look in the rear view mirror, met eyes, and politely asked her, "What's the magic word?"

I love catching people off guard, especially rude people. She gasped, got choked up, then caught her breath, and said again very rudely, "WHAT?" Excellent, I could tell nobody at home talks to her honestly, including the cab drivers.

I turned around this time, looked into her eyes again, and calmly said, "You know . . . the magic word." She got the clue at this point and muttered out, "Please?" I ripped off a blank receipt and handed it back to her. Could a blank receipt be the thing, or is she just a natural? I'll never know for sure. I would guess she wanted a blank receipt so she could burn the IRS. What she didn't know was I always give out blank receipts, it usually means a better tip anyway. As we pulled up to the restaurant I explained to her that I had been working on customer sensitivity training this month. Catching her not wanting to look like a total bitch in front of her fellow females, this comment did end up getting me a few bucks tip to boot and most definitely left her thinking. I was not what she expected her cab driver to be. Thankfully no need to use profanity, at least this early in the evening. Maybe next time she will think twice about treating a total stranger like shit, or at least remember the magic word.

Chapter Twenty-Eight

RAINY DAY

Taxicab Regulations Section VII, Part B, subset 7
Drivers shall, if fatigued or tired, park the taxicab in a legal space or stand and practice transcendental meditation for no less than 10 minutes.

As I left the yard to begin my ten-hour shift, it was raining hard. Traffic was at a stand still. I punched it through and zipped onto US-101 South to the airport. I always play loud hard-core music if I ride to SFO empty. The local college radio station was jammin' some funky rock 'n roll so the trip to SFO seemed like minutes. As I meandered through bartertown, residents were playing cards, reading, checking out other cabs and such. A mixed bag I assure you. I dropped my first fare off at a hotel at Fisherman's Wharf. As was his flight, the ride was also uneventful. His money was green, and that's OK. I then tried to work the radio in the Financial District and got two "no goes." Feeling frustrated, I tried again and got a radio order in the Financial though he only went for a short trip. I found myself south of the city and deadheaded down to the airport again. I couldn't resist after all the bad luck in town.

"one cab enter, two shorts leave"

The airport was still moving and I managed to get a ride back to the city. I was thankful I didn't get caught with too many shorts. I took a few flags here to there. I had a hooker, then a teacher, and then some tourists with their families. Lots of diversity. After a while of wandering around, I started to hit the bus lines to ask people if they wanted a free ride. Mostly, people were shocked but a few smart ones took the offer. Random acts of kindness, it felt good, but not as good as money. I got a lukewarm, fuzzy feeling. I drove a comedian home who was happy I was in the mood to listen. He works at a desktop publishing firm and does comedy on occasion. It's amazing what history people have and how they want to tell you about it. This chap worked as a card dealer in Vegas for about a year. He said he has never seen so much greed in his life. It had changed him, and I was glad to have a fare with dual careers. A competitor's cab stole my next order and I was frustrated as hell. After another few hops around town, I asked dispatch for a short shift, wanting just to go to bed and sleep, sleep, sleep. No go.

I was spent as I slowly cruised down the main drag through town, but the cabbie eye will always see a "possible," fare even if they don't raise their hand. As I pulled up to this guy and rolled down my passenger window, I actually recognized him. He is a cab driver from another company going to work! Two times in one week I would pluck this driver off the streets in the predawn hours. Though it is unusual between rival cab companies, we did share a laugh and a few stories. It made me think for a moment that maybe all of us cabbies could just get along, just be one, make a positive and real change in our attitudes to each other and the public. After I dropped him off I said to myself, "Keep dreaming kid."

Chapter Twenty-Nine

CROP CIRCLES

Taxicab Regulations Section VI, Part E, subset 1
No taxicab driver shall refuse, or direct or permit the refusal, of prospective passengers in any area or district of the City and County of San Francisco for transportation to any place in said City and County, or to the San Francisco International Airport, or to the Oakland International Airport, at rates authorized by law, if said prospective passengers present themselves for transportation in a clean, sober, and orderly manner and for a lawful purpose.

High-low, it's Sunday again and a lazy one indeed. I tried to get off to my usual airport high jinx as I would on any Sunday. Not the case today, I kept having short after short after short. I couldn't leave the Goddamn airport. I was starting to make some dough around the third short, but was tired of the lame card games and excessive horning. I figured whatever long fare I got next, wherever that fare went, I would beeline it back to the city to try to work it for what it was worth. I got another short after this thought, and made that one in 27 minutes, so it felt pretty good to be back to the airport all of a sudden. Thankfully, my next fare needed to go to the Hyatt in Fisherman's Wharf (a good long trip). So, after dropping my fare at Fisherman's Wharf, I ended up, as planned, back in the city. That's when I received a radio call from dispatch that my next pickup needed to go from Market and Sutter to the Glen Park area on the outskirts of town. My fare, an older lady, was quite pleasant and things were going as I had visualized at the airport. This was a good thing, but it was also a fleeting moment.

After dropping out in the Glen Park area I saw a young man standing on the side of the street flagging me down. This was a very unusual thing to see in a residential area of the city so late. But, as always, I pulled over for a quick stop and rolled the passenger side window down a bit to find out what kind of a fare I had there. I already knew it was a strange area for a pick up, but I had to find out what the deal was. The young man was in his early twenties and looked as if he didn't have a problem or a care in the world. However, I figured out real fast that he was a few fries short of a Happy Meal. He first directed me to the bus depot downtown. "Fine," I thought as I jumped on the highway heading in that direction. With it being a long night already, I took a moment to relax and as I accelerated I also rolled my window down a little. After cracking the window, the young man in the back asked me if he smelled or something. I told him he smelled fine. At this point there was no problem. However, just before the 101 US South exit, he directed me to the airport. "OK," I said as I changed the route trying to act as calm as possible because by this time I was starting to think that I would be mugged or something. I had to try to control my destiny here.

Everybody has a story and everybody has a place they come from, and somewhere they are going to and I try not to question a person's reasons for a particular destination. I just drive them to it. However, I will admit that this change in destinations from the bus depot to the airport was gnawing at me because I knew that all the flights had gone for the night. Although I was worried about what his response would be, I asked the kid flat out, "What's up with the change in directions? Is everything all right?" Like most fares, he opened up with just a little pry and told me his tale of woe. It turns out the poor kid was strung out on crystal meth. He told me that his few close friends were still into it and it was impossible for him to hang with them and avoid the meth. He just couldn't get away from the drugs in that situation. So, he was running away; running back to Southern California to detox at his parent's house in San Luis Obispo. He was leaving in the middle of the night. He was leaving in desperation and fear for his life. And somehow, he managed to flag me down. Random? I say no. On that ride, I talked with him not about life or what has happened or where he is, but I talked with him about what to expect for the next few days during detox.

Detox. I've been there. So, I let the young lad know the business at hand and what to expect for the next four days. "Hang in there at all costs," I told him. "Once the first stages of detox are over you will feel better. No pain, no gain." But to believe this, he had to get there first. By the time we arrived at the airport, I was feeling more relaxed from the conversation we had had. However, as I dropped the kid off on the upper level I started to worry about getting paid. The fare was $24.00. But, much to my relief, the kid gave me $25.00. He said it was all of the money he had. As I wished him well, I gave him back the change and a tip to boot. I told him not to call his drug-addicted friends in the morning when the sun rises and to make sure he follows through with his plan of the night to escape. I was actually thinking about giving him a free ride as I do on occasion, but decided against it. As the kid walked toward the entrance of the terminal, I hoped he would make it this time. However, I know it sometimes takes more than one try to rid yourself of a chemical dependency. I'll probably never see him again, but I do wish him well.

It's now past 2 A.M. and there is no reason to fight my way back to a nonexistent fare on the lower level of the airport. So I start to head back to the city when I see him, a lone traveler exiting onto the upper level of the airport terminal walking to the curbside. His bag is draped over his shoulder. He sees my cab. We make eye contact and he asks if I'm available. "Yeah, hop in the back, but please hurry" I say to him. I want him to hurry because cabbies are not supposed to pick up anyone on the upper level terminal. You might get a $500.00 fine if you get caught. For the most part, this fine deters cabbies from breaking the rules. However, sometimes we make exceptions if we think we can get away with it. The $500.00 fine is going through my mind as the weary traveler hurriedly hops in the back seat. I take off post haste and leave the airport heading north back to SF with a fare from SFO after 2 A.M. thinking to myself how rare this occasion is. I doubt this will happen again soon. I am actually glad to tell my new fare of how I made it back to the airport this late and I also inquire about his travels and such. I gave him my standard line leaving SFO, "Was the flight uneventful?" Remember, unless you have a cute stewardess or something of the like, an uneventful plane ride is a good one. My next line if no conversation arises is, "Where did ya fly in from?" I will admit though that when the man responded yes to the "uneventful" question and then said he had flown in from Tampa, he stumped me. He left me searching for some common ground that was not there. However, it was fortunate he wanted to chat on the way back to My Fare City because he allowed me another slice of life.

"Chad" had just returned from taking the entrance exam to become a full-fledged neuro-pathologist. The test is only given once every two years. It was his first time taking the test and he felt confident about his performance even after speaking with other doctors who have taken the test two times. He said the test is a very tough nut to crack and that most doctors fail it their first time. With this description, parallels of the drug-addicted youth came to mind because the failure rate seems so high for both riders' missions even though they are so very different. I chuckled to myself when the doctor mentioned that the neuro-surgeon testing location is located in Tampa. I thought not a bad location if you had to pick a place for a bunch of doctors to get together and golf. Nonetheless, he was glad to be home and told me he would be getting the results of his test in about two weeks. I discovered that a neuro-pathologist is a head and neck doctor and I heard a lot of other technical mumbo jumbo about neuro-surgery that fell to the wayside. After dropping Chad out in the Avenues, I zipped back to the garage and turned in my gate and cab fees, thinking to myself that the last couple of fares made my airport day a worthwhile endeavor. I didn't let Chad know it was a no-no to pick up fares on the upper level at SFO. There is a good chance he will be back in the same place in two years and will provide some other cabbie with that late night lucky run home from the airport. I doubt I will ever see the kid heading to Southern California or the Doc again, but I will remember them both, and the darker as well as the lighter side of life.

Chapter Thirty

MONDAZE

Taxicab Regulations Section XIV, Part G, subset 3
Every driver is required to give a minimum of (1) one free ride per month to guarantee good karma, even if the color scheme conflicts with this practice (i.e. Big Dogma City).

The city of San Francisco, seven miles by seven miles, has become much smaller since I started driving a cab. This is a good thing because with San Francisco as a popular destination, I kinda feel like the mayor of My Fare City when my friends come to visit. However, after my first month of driving a cab, I had lost all interest in driving my own car to the airport. I used to find such great joy in picking up or dropping off friends at the airport. And now I loathe the thought because I do it everyday for people who will pay me. That's the downside of driving a cab. But, every once in a while I can't avoid it. I had a friend visiting me for the weekend who had an 8 A.M. flight this fine Monday morning. My only way to get out of giving him a ride would have been to pay for a taxi for him. The chances of this were slim to none. I got him to the airport at 7 A.M. and felt extremely strange having done it in my own vehicle. I then took what seemed to be a long ride back to the city and hit the hay.

I awoke mid-afternoon ready and rested for the new day, or in my case, night. The days are gettin' longer and the nights are gettin' stronger.

The final days of the winter season are at hand and even though our winter here in San Francisco may have been wet, at least it was not below freezing temperature. Now, that would have been a real mess. Think about freezing-cold temperatures and rain combined in the city built on a mountainside. The streets would have been reduced to a macabre game of bumper cars with all the hills providing the inertia and the valleys providing the kill zone. I think it has snowed once here, but check the Farmer's Almanac for specifics if you so desire. I figured this Monday to be the calm before the storm because Tuesday is another hallmark of hallmark holidays: St. Patrick's Day. The Irish are a major force in the San Francisco bar industry right now and there are a lot of Irish living within the city limits. But ask any of them about St. Patrick's Day and they will tell you that besides the obvious increase in business, for most of them it's just another day to drink a pint, or two, or ten.

Chapter Thirty-One

MUG SHOTS

Taxicab Regulations Section VI, Part D, subset 4
Taxicab drivers shall be clean in dress and person.

My shift started with me winning two bucks on a lottery ticket. I tossed the other losing ticket on the ground for some soul to get a second-hand thrill by finding it. That is, they will be thrilled until they see it's a loser. My luck continued as I got a flag to the airport an hour or so into my shift. I dropped a nice lady off at the United terminal and came around to get in the waiting line to pick up another fare. But, as luck would have it, all of the waiting lots (all three of them!) were full. It reminded me of the never-ending line you meander through and through at Disneyland to get to Space Mountain. I circled around the infamous fourth lot five times before I could even get in line to wait. When I finally got into a line, I saw something I had never seen before. I saw another cabbie eat, wash, shave, and finally drink with the aid of only a simple coffee mug. It was interesting to me because I try to keep an open mind to alternative ways of living. With each new task the old Asian cabbie used his mug for, I became more shocked and surprised. And just when I thought he would be done with the use of the mug after shaving from it, he emptied it out and got himself a hot cup o' joe! I couldn't believe it. I started to have a conversation with myself about the cabbie and his frugal use of a coffee mug but stopped myself because having a conversation with one's self is the first stage to going insane. I'm not crazy; you're the one who's crazy. In fact, you're driving me crazy.

Chapter Thirty-Two

ST. PADDY

Taxicab Regulations Section VII, Part C, subset 2
Drivers may, when needed, provide emotional support to passengers
while the taximeter is in use. This may not be considered a
professional service but rather an informal counseling session. The
passenger, when asked, may provide the same to said drivers within
the City and County of San Francisco.

This Tuesday would no doubt be a winner because St. Patrick's
Day is one of the few holidays left dedicated to drinking yourself
into a stupor. Most people in San Francisco are street smart enough
to take cabs when the heat is on, as it was last night. And let me
tell you that Irish or not, people were getting toasted real good. All
through North Beach out to the avenues, the Irish bars were stuffed
to the gills. Bar owners were loving life just as I was because if
their business rocks, mine will too.

A good time was being had by all. Well, that is most
everybody. My hooker pal Vanessa and her unemployed boyfriend
Jose have a heroin habit that has gone from bad to less than

zero in the short time I have known them. She has always talked to me about quitting when she rides in the cab. She says she is tired of working to support her and Jose's habit and is in a constant struggle with the blind truth that is facing her. She knows the ride has to end, but after so many years, that old familiar heroin high feels very safe. And how did I happen to gaze upon this picture as it was finally coming to a close? I don't know. Dumb luck maybe.

Vanessa had found a new guy with a job and a coke habit. She was seeing him and living with Jose for at least the time I've known her. I would take her from place to place, each on the opposite side of town, back and forth. She was a good steady ride. That night, my mobile phone rang early. It was Vanessa calling to see if I could give her a ride. I told her I would be by to pick her up. She said that I would be giving her and Jose a ride to detox at San Francisco General Hospital. This is the public hospital in SF and it's in pretty bad shape. I would rather convert to Christian Science than wait my turn at SF General. Still, this was their only option and hope left. The cosmic string of the evening was beginning to get strung. As I waited outside their building for them, I decided to walk down the block to get a Whizz Burger. I ordered my munch as they got in the car, but since I wasn't there to drive away immediately, Jose got out and walked around the block to a liquor store. With the meter running, Vanessa and I drove around the block and saw Jose buying a 40 oz. with his last $2.00. I guessed it to be for the wait at the hospital. He didn't say. But, the meter kept ticking as Vanessa and I waited impatiently across the street. He took his time. I couldn't blame him. I think they had been building up to this ride for several years and now that it was finally happening, they probably still wanted to delay it. They were both in sorry shape and needed help, but had to find it on their own in their own time.

Lots of births and deaths pass by you every shift and some you might not even notice. At SF General you have to pay $5.00 per day to have a TV. Definitely a no frills flight and a real drag if you have spent thousands of dollars or more on your heroin run and are left without five bucks to watch TV while you detox. I won't even tell you what their arms looked like because it would be hard to describe their flesh below the blood and bandages that covered it. It was just patchwork to plug the dike, but it was the best they could do. And there was no mistake in my mind that I was supposed to be the driver on this fateful trip. This was very possibly, the end of the two as a couple as well as the end of a long, hard run. They had to be relieved. At any rate, I certainly was. I dropped them off early in the evening and drove away knowing that it would probably be the last time I would see them. I did not charge them for the ride because I wanted them each to have at least couple of days worth of TV. That's not a lot of TV but it beats having none at all because the detox phase lasts up to and sometimes beyond a week. Before I zipped off to greener pastures, I bid them both fare well. I then stopped at a private club and listened to some live jazz. I took half an hour off to let the whole thing sink in.

Then, I was back at it because all of the business was at the bars. From the bars to the homes I went, covering all sections of the city. The common denominator of the night was alcohol as was the general theme. Time passed quickly and profitably. I even took a few radio calls from the SFPD who had detained folks who were forced to cab it. One group was at an intersection and one group was at a district station. I was making money so work was that much easier and I was extremely happy. I drove 'til very late and when I answered a radio call that took me back to the Financial District, I knew it was time to pack it in no matter how good I was feeling. The pickup was a businessman who was reading the morning paper and who reeked of pungent cologne. It was definitely time to turn in. After dropping him off, I heard the birds chirping. Most definitely time to go home. I walked to the bus stop, which is something I rarely do and was harassed by a crazy guy who then tried to get a cop involved in the situation and was finally given a warning himself. Having had an overdose of San Francisco for the night, I was relieved to see the bus approach. I got on and was carried home with yet another day being born over My Fare City.

Chapter Thirty-Three

FULL MOON

Taxicab Regulation Section VI, Part D, subset 3
No Taxicab Driver shall attempt to use any physical force against any person except in self-defense or in defense of another.

My phone rings. Brenda needs to go to a hotel near the airport, like so many other times. I quietly stared at the full moon waiting for her to finish her business, and then we headed back to the city, like so many other times. But something was different, I could feel it. She has not been riding as high as she used to because she has quit doing heroin for the most part and by doing so the job of being an escort is pretty fucking real for her now. In fact, I would say she now knows what it feels like to be a hooker. Unfortunately, Brenda is not getting paid as much as she used to because her agency is sending her, or letting her go, on less profitable calls. Many of these don't even require cab rides. I was concerned, and saddened to hear that the night before, she had taken a cab down to an airport call that turned out to be a no go for her. With seventy bucks on the meter when she got back to her place, she told the driver she would run in for the money. She never came out. I was off that night.

What happened next is partly my fault because I failed to negotiate the rate for the ride to and fro, assuming it was unchanged from every other time. After we got back to her place, she gave up $30.00, which was half of what I expected to make. I told her the usual $60.00 would be fine, pointing out I waited forty-five minutes for her. I ended up getting $40.00, and a lesson in finance, from the school of hard knocks. I do not envy her.

As I pulled away from her apartment building in the Tenderloin, I was overcome with sadness because I was witnessing Brenda's life being slowly swept away down the gutter. As I thought about her situation, I realized I was in dire need of some inspiration and wouldn't you know, it was just around the corner.

I drove by the Golden Gate Theater and Warfield, both shows were getting close to end. Riverdance was playing at the Golden Gate Theater. First let me say that I really dislike that stupid fucking bullshit. And to make matters worse, my wasted time with Brenda was not helping my attitude much. I was looking forward to seeing the hodgepodge of people intermingling on the street. People on both sides of the street were flagging me down as I drove through them, trying to decide whom to pick up. That's when I spotted a mangy-looking rock 'n roll dude on the side of the street waving his arm for a cab. There I was and a decision had to be made between rock 'n roll dude and young yuppie snob. As you can probably guess, I decided for the rock dude. For a moment I thought I had made a mistake because as I pulled up to the curb, the rock dude waved to his friend who was behind a trailer with a bunch of guitars and equipment and stuff. But, despite my initial apprehension, they pleasantly surprised me.

They were going to the airport! This alone would have been a winner but what made the situation even more interesting was they were two members from the rock band Wilco. I like their music. They were pleased that smoking is allowed in cabs in My Fare City if the cabbie allows it, as I do. After they lit up the cigs, I pulled out a fattie. Ken and Jay, the Wilco dudes, were safely dropped off in time for the red-eye to their next gig, no pun intended. I was going to try to get on the guest list for the next time they play in the Bay area, but forgot to ask, being a bit stoned from the ride.

With a full moon, you know you're in for a ride. People always walk a step out of beat each time the moon shines full. But so far, I had been having an uneventful night as full moons go. However, that all changed with a simple radio call after midnight for a pickup in the Tender-Nob. This is the border of the Tenderloin and Nob Hill area. A merging of the lower class and supposed upper class if you will. Anyway, I took the radio call on Sutter St., but needed to stop to get some change before I picked up the fare. My last fare gave me a twenty and cleaned me completely out of change, so I had to get some right away. I pulled over to a convenience store one block down from the pickup address to make change for the twenty. The Arab guy behind the counter, who had obviously been abused in ways I'll never know, refused to make change for the bill even when I told him I was a San Francisco taxi driver. I walked out of the store knowing I needed to get change for that damn twenty. So, I walked back in the store, grabbed a Mini-Reese's Pieces (a ten-cent piece of candy) and laid it on the counter. The jaded shopkeeper refused to sell me the candy because I guess he deemed it not worthy for sale. I suppose he would rather keep the change in his register than make a sale. I thought it was a joke. The motherfucker wouldn't make change for me and now he was refusing to sell me a piece of candy. I knew I had to get to the radio call so I tossed the candy at his fat brown belly and it bounced off onto the counter in front of him. At this he started to reach for something below the counter. A red flag went up in my mind and I backed off. He ran around the counter waving a nightstick and screaming bloody murder in a language I did not understand. I knew it was time to leave.

I zipped out of the store as he chased me. I ran around and around my cab, which was parked in front of the store. He couldn't catch me because I kept running around the car always staying on the opposite side of the cab from him. How long was this nut gonna go on? After going around the cab several times he stopped at the driver side door and grabbed the mike. "Oh shit! Not the mike" I screamed as I reached for my mace. He started shouting something into the mike and was beginning to open the driver door when I gave him a face full of mace. He dropped the mike, screamed, and moved away quickly. What a stupid move I thought to myself. He ended up with a face full of mace because he wouldn't make change for a twenty. I had unintentionally pushed an overworked, underpaid, and obviously abused worker over the edge. Having repelled the crazy man away from the cab I jumped in the driver seat, slammed it into drive, and drove away. In my rear view mirror I watched him shrink as he waved his fist, cursing at me and disappeared in the distance.

I went around the block and picked up my radio call without change, but also without the crazy man riding shotgun. I let dispatch know what had happened so they would be ready for the complaint, but I decided not to call the police for the attempted assault on me by the proprietor of the corner store. The look in his eyes was one I'll never forget. He would have killed me in a heartbeat with no regrets. Before this night, I had never had to deal with violence as in this situation and hope I never see its ugly head again.

The mood was one that wasn't always good this evening. The full moon can be ecstasy or agony for people. With all my marbles still intact, I came in early and patted myself on the back for making it through the evening unscathed. You never know where someone's head may be and you might get into trouble as I did if you try to find out. Believe me when I say this: Your life is worth more than someone else's problems. When I look back at the attempted assault in a few days, I will laugh because attempted means almost, and almost doesn't count.

Chapter Thirty-Four

DAZE OFF

Taxicab Regulations Section VII, Part A, subset 1
No driver shall be allowed to be cynical for more than one shift, at which time a more noble, philosophical attitude must be adopted. Failure to do so may result in clinical depression and or mania.

I worked during my days off this weekend. I would classify it as working a late-short because the maximum time the day or night cabbie can drive is ten hours and that leaves four hours to play with. If the window guy and the cabbie have a good relationship the cabbie can come in after 11 P.M. Friday or Saturday night and take a car out for three or four hours. If they do this, they pay for the cab on an hourly basis. On Friday I worked from 11:45 P.M. to 3:45 A.M. and on Saturday night I worked from 2:00 A.M. to 4:00 A.M. However, I made some good money, which I desperately needed. At this point in time my social life is almost completely surrounded by driving. Who would date someone with my schedule? I can guarantee you that it's slim pickins. When I drive at night, I usually feel like I'm looking from the outside in. This is true even more so after midnight. After several years of driving a cab I'm finding it almost impossible not to become more and more cynical as I view life from behind the wheel. I try to hang on to the good things: the church lady who still calls me, the streamer guy who I gave a lottery ticket to yesterday when I saw him walking down the middle of the street, and all the neat people I meet while driving around. What is one to do when the burn out curve for cabbies is so skewed? For me, the late-shorts (a.k.a.: "the clean-up crew") are as raw as it gets. However, one thing is for sure, it keeps me honest. Yesterday I saw an article in a local paper with the phone numbers of all the cab companies in My Fare City. At the bottom of the ad it said the advertiser does not endorse any one company and they hope that the cabbie is on fewer drugs than the riders. Ha!

Working a late-short is nice because the time goes by fast and you tend to stay more disconnected from your fares than if it is earlier in the evening. You never know what is going through someone's mind at that time of night and many times you don't even want to. Also, it gets hard to remember the exact day of the month. However, I'm still OK with the names of the days. It's just the number that is supposed to be associated with the particular day that I am struggling with.

As I prepare for the start of another workweek I am trying to stay positive, although I will admit it's tough. Life on the streets doesn't change much. There are a lot of cosmic strings holding the fabric of reality together here in San Francisco, but what it's holding is not always good. I got a call from Jose and Vanessa last night. They bailed the rehab unit and are back to their wicked ways. Some things never change. Hell, I suppose I will still be available to drive for them. Don't think I lack compassion for them because of this. I am just hoping to make some good bank this week. I can see what is going down for them while at the same time I am powerless to change the situation. It is not my place. Recovery is for people who want it, not for those who need it. I have learned through experience that despite how much you need to change your life you will never do it unless you want to.

The late-shorts tonight were profitable but stressful. I'm getting burnt out a bit. But it's nothing a stiff cocktail won't take care of in the short run. We cabbies are a strange lot. I know I will look back on this time in my life as being pretty crazy, although I'll admit that it's hard to fathom that while sitting in the driver's seat. Flag me down again and I promise I'll keep my hands on the wheel and my eyes on the road.

Chapter Thirty-Five

HI HO HI HO

Taxicab Regulations Section VI, Part E, subset 5
A taxicab driver shall not refuse to transport any orderly and/or
contained animal but not limited to guide or service dogs.

With Sunday being my Monday, it is always hard for me to get
going. But I pulled a few strings and managed to get out of work
around 11:00 P.M. I can't remember the last time I was in by
midnight. Also, tonight I was dedicated to making the airport run
work for me. I took rides to the city, across the Golden Gate, over
the Bay Bridge and South to Palo Alto.

On my way back from dropping my second fare off in Corte
Madera, I picked up two young hitchhikers and their dog. Their
names were Chris (girl) and Don, and Kimo was their dog. Funny, I
thought, I grew up with a cat named Kimo. They said they had been
waiting nearly two hours for a ride. I was a little surprised by this
because they looked so harmless: a twenty-year-old hippie chick,
her skinny hippie boyfriend, and a cute, well-behaved hippie dog.
They said they were going to her Mom's house for the night because
their tent had been stolen the night before. They were visiting
from Oregon and thought that camping would be crime free as it is

back there. Sorry kids. Because of this, Chris's Mom was going to let them stay for the night. She lives in the nearby town of Tiburon. So, I drove them all for free to her Mom's place. As we turned down the side street to the Mother's house we saw her leaving the driveway in her mini van. Chris and Don said they had called her earlier and had left a message on her machine for her to come pick them up when she got off work. They thought they could get home before she did, however, it looked like she was now going to get them. This is where I sprang into action. I spun the car around in what can only be described as a *Starsky and Hutch* move and ended up peeling out and burning rubber. I pushed the accelerator to the floor and we chased her Mom down and pulled her over. After explaining the situation to Chris's Mom, we said our good-byes. In the future, I hope someone would do the same for me if I were in a pinch. They said it was their first free cab ride. Hell, I think it may have been their first cab ride ever. Whatever the case, I was happy to be in the right place at the right time to bring about something positive in a person's life. Chris even hinted to Don that taxi driving should be his next job. Don didn't look too excited about that suggestion so I mentioned how the law says a cabbie has to be twenty-five years old to be a licensed driver in San Francisco. I could see the relief fall over his face as I mentioned this fact. I am sure that being a cabbie was the last thing he was thinking of, especially after the day's experience.

After Chris, Don and Kimo, I took Tim, a San Francisco resident, home from the airport. He had been visiting his parents in Southern California. They have a place less than a mile from my parents' house. Surprisingly, we had a lot in common, especially with regard to our family dynamics. Tim had just taken a road trip with his Dad from Southern California to New York City. He said they had a really good time and it was the best experience he and his Dad had ever shared. I thought to myself that was strange because for the past four weeks I have been planning a similar trip with my Dad.

Tim was a bit buzzed from drinking in the sky, however he was not rude or anything. It was like he was put there in the back seat to tell me that. Nothing like a long drive to fill a cab driver's vacation, but it always ends up this way. As he described the trip with his father it was clear to me now that the message he was laying on me, with or without his knowledge, was that sometime this summer I had to do the same thing. Family is important and life is short. I will take this one to heart. It's random insights like that which keeps me coming back to work everyday.

Chapter Thirty-Six

OSCAR

Taxicab Regulations: Section V, Part C, subset 15
The vehicle shall be structurally sound and operate with minimum vibration and noise.

    This Monday was busy with all the Academy Award parties. Plastic and fantastic, I can assure you of that. Within the first hour of my shift, I was getting bored with the usual gab and decided to change myself for the night. I decided that I would speak to each fare with a thick southern accent. This seemed to beef up the amount people were tipping. I have noticed that people like to hear a pleasant southern voice and I have this one down. I told people I was from Texas and was new to the city. My fares ate it up. They believed me even more as the night dragged on and they got more drunk and more stoned. My first line to everyone when they sat down was, "How ya'all doin'?" My southern drawl is good and I had everybody fooled. I even fooled a group of people from Texas. Thankfully though, they told me what town they were from first because that allowed me to be from the other side of the state. However, after a while of doing this, I realized how bored I was with my job. I thought of a friend of mine who rides in elevators facing the rear to make his life more exciting. It's funny because people don't know how to react when they see a grown man standing the wrong way in an elevator. Some have even asked him if there was a door there that they didn't know about. Anyways, I think I may have felt some need to act tonight especially with this being Hollywood's big night. I was going to wear a tuxedo, but decided against it because I'm a cab driver, not a limo driver. The Academy Awards and the booze made for some big tippers as the night wore on. It was nice because I got to talk about the movies a lot which is always a safe and easy subject to get into. No politics or religion this evening. My job was easy.

I kept the accent for most of the night, however, I did drop it when Vanessa phoned. Since Vanessa has been my customer, she has talked about getting out of the business. But I know she never will until her health fails her or she is dead. When she rides with me, I never give advice to her. I always tell her what she wants to hear and never what she needs. I assure you that it is all part of the job. Having seen far too many women and men come and go I don't bother getting involved anymore like I once wanted to. I have realized that you can't change things in my line of work, you can only observe. Depending on the day, Vanessa might want to leave her heroin habit and Jose for the cocaine guy, or she may want to quit drugs altogether. It pendulates with each trip, indecision is always in her voice. Part of what makes a cabbie so cynical is that we get to observe the big picture of life. I remind myself on a daily basis not to get personally involved with my fares because it's not worth it. As the night wore on, I figured it to be a textbook night of $5.00 rides and good tips. However, that all changed when I answered a radio call at 2:30 A.M. in the Financial District.

I was a bit far from the order but the dispatcher gave it to me because most of the fleet was in for the night. As I waited for my pickup to come out of the high rise, I realized that I was tired of talking and that I really wanted to turn in. But, I also really needed the money. So, when the young blonde female came out of the building with a box of papers, I popped the trunk and jumped out of the driver's seat to load the boxes for her. I got back in and asked her, "Where to?" just like I do a thousand times a week with a thousand other riders thinking that it was going to be a $3.00 ride. She said she needed to go to Palo Alto and then back to the Fairmont. Yee Haw! I couldn't charge her meter and a half because it was round trip, but I was still looking at $150.00 or so. Score! Man, it felt great to finally get a long trip and a cute passenger too. With Palo Alto being forty-five minutes to the south, I chatted it up a little with her, but on the way back I let her sleep, figuring she was not interested in any more conversation. When we got to the Fairmont, she paid on a voucher and tipped me $25.00. With that, my net on the ride was $170.00. I guess I'll pay my phone bill now. I'll be holding onto the memory of this late ride for a while. I did ask the gal if she told dispatch where she was going. Her answer was no. If she had told dispatch her destination, the ride would have gone to one of the dispatcher's buddies.

The good-old-boy network still exists in the taxi industry and I will be part of it someday if I continue to drive. It's not really a big goal of mine. This job, which was supposed to last a few months, has gone on long past that. With each year that passes, I fear it will become more difficult for me to get out of this business. When I started, old timers would say to drive for as little time as possible, to exploit any other skill you have. Most every driver has done some other job and has either been fired or become burnt out from it. I personally have experienced both and now I am starting to feel a bit crispy from cab driving. I will get out someday, but I have no release date, I have no specific timetable. Either I'll die or wise up, but in the meantime, I'm gonna keep doing what I'm doing and keep hoping to find some kind of meaning in an otherwise meaningless job.

Chapter Thirty-Seven

MOOD SCHWING

Taxicab Regulations Section VII, Part A, subset 1b
In accordance with Municipal Police Code Section 1147.1, Educational entities may offer a "Cab College" for new taxicab drivers after applying for and receiving approval from the Chief of Police. All approved entities must follow the below listed course requirement:
Taxi Rules and Laws—1 hour

I have broken more traffic laws since becoming a cab driver than I ever expected to. You name it, I have broken it. Hell, you may have been cheering me on or you may have been curling up in the back seat. Remember, the fastest route between two points is a straight line and a horse always runs quicker on the way back to the barn. However, none of the traffic laws I break put the public or myself in any danger because the streets are really empty after midnight. I will admit it's still a thrill to get away with it. Illegal left turns are probably the best. Kudos to SF for wising up and making some previous no left turns now legal for buses and taxis. Another law geared for us is that cabs can cruise in the bus-right-turn lanes on city streets if they have a passenger. But make no mistake, this is only on the city streets, not the highway. Also, there is actually a law on the books that says cabbies do not have to wear safety belts in the city, but will get busted if they don't wear their seat belt on the highway. For example, one day about ten months ago, I was on my way to the airport. I had been zipping around the city without my seat belt on and then had to make a quick drop-off at the airport. Now, how am I supposed to remember to put my seat belt back on? I actually got a ticket for this last year, but the cop didn't show up in court for the court date and the charge was dropped. I'm sure all he wanted to do was to make me jump through a few hoops, compliments of the CHiPs. Eric Estrada, where are you?

I've been dreaming a lot lately. In some dreams I am driving, while in others I am crashing in a plane. However, the sickness of the street has not seeped into my time of solitude thus far. If I cross that bridge, I may have to hang up my spurs for a few weeks of beer drinking and kicking back south of the border in Rosarita, Mexico, where your dollar stretches, so you don't have to.

The rain last night washed off the streets as well as my dirty cab. In the words of Travis Bickle's now infamous line, "Someday a real rain will come and wash the scum off the streets." Well, today it's not raining and I'm in a most pleasant mood, so swing batter, batter, swing!

Chapter Thirty-Eight

SERENDIPITY

Taxicab Regulations Section V, Part C, subset 15
The Taxicab shall be structurally sound and operate with minimum vibration and noise.

I'm starting to bite my fingernails again. Oh well. I suppose it's just another bad habit to reckon with. Today, I got out late, but managed to get a brand new car. I felt so lucky because it was such a pleasure to drive, especially when compared with that old, beat-up, piece-of-shit cab that died on me recently. The city was dead because the night before had been a big party night. So, I did as I often do, I deadheaded to the airport.

The wait to get through the line was about one hour, which is average. While waiting in line, I had a good laugh when I saw this chunky funky cabbie. The Asian driver looked like the kind of guy who would wok his dog, rather than walk. I worked a few good shorts and headed back to the city with a German couple going to the tourist hell known as Fisherman's Wharf. On the way there, it started to rain and I started to feel bad because after I picked them up I told them about all of the nice weather they could expect while on their vacation. However, when I dropped them off, I got that warm fuzzy feeling when he handed me a $50.00 bill and asked for only $10.00 back. In all of my years driving a cab, he is the first German who has ever tipped me. For some reason, Germans do not tip. So, this guy was a breath of fresh air on a rainy and muggy day. From there I headed back to the city, where things started to shape up nicely. I had a $35.00 trip to the East Bay, which included the tip, and then I had a long ride to the ocean for $25.00 plus a tip. At this time I had made my gates and gas so I started to take a more laid-back approach as I hustled the city. After that, I had a few "no goes." But, they worked out well because when you have a "no go" the dispatcher will give you the next call from the area you are in. Luckily, both of my "no goes" were followed by good loads who tipped well.

After dropping off the last of the good loads, I decided to stop by the Pinecrest 24-hour house o' slop for some needed fuel. I was hungry as all get out and my head was starting to hurt. As I pulled up to the front door, I saw that they had closed for the night; the fuckin' cook had shot the waitress. My 24-hour diner was actually closed, for the first time in who knows when. Though it was probably there before the felony, I still found it tasteless to have a Help Wanted sign in the window. I was not a happy camper because I had been craving some greasy spoon all day. So, with my head aching and my tummy grumbling, I headed west on Geary Blvd. for some more action.

"pinecrest diner"

I saw two cops questioning a young guy in front of a church on the side of the road. I decided to drive around the block to see if anyone needed a ride. I pulled up and asked the cops if the guy needed a ride home and they talked it over for a second. They went over to the young guy who obviously looked drunk and talked with him for a minute or two and then sent him over to my cab. His name was Chuck and he told me that he had been partying at the Sir Francis Drake, up in the Starlight Room. Though his consumption of gin had nothing to do with the famous doorman at the Sir Francis Drake, it was worth a laugh.

He explained he had to work the next day so he left the party early. He had started to drive home and got about halfway when he realized he was too fucked up to drive the rest of the way. So, doing the intelligent thing, he pulled over to a legal parking place to rest for a little bit. That's when he fell asleep. He said that he was proud of himself for pulling over when he did and not causing an accident because he knew he was in no condition to drive. Not a bad idea dude. I wish more drivers would pull over when they realize they are in no condition to drive. Next time though, Chuck, recline the seat back so you don't lean forward against the steering wheel like a corpse. No wonder he got hassled by the cops. They probably got a call from a passerby who reported seeing a dead person in a car parked on the side of the road. Chuck was extremely relieved when I finally dropped him off at his home because he said he was about to get busted for drunk driving before I pulled up. Man, I never thought I would fish for fares from the SFPD, but so far so good. I'll take them wherever I can get them. A cabbie really needs to think creatively after midnight to get a fare.

On my way back to the garage, I was looping around on 19th Avenue on my way to the Marina. I hit the Marina Blvd. / Lombard split going about twenty miles per hour over the speed limit. A cop was sitting there with his lights out and I didn't see him until it was too late. My heart dropped to the floor as I zipped by him. I thought for sure I was busted and that I was going to have to pay a huge fine because of the speed I was going. Thankfully though, he must have had bigger fish to fry or been on break because I never saw him after the drive by. Whew! That would not have been a good way to end the night. So, after stopping for a Grub Steak to ease my hunger and aching head, I counted my blessings and my money and then called it a night.

Chapter Thirty-Nine

FRIDAY NIGHT

Taxicab Regulations Section XIII, Part C, subset 11
Taxicab Drivers classification as an independent contractor voids
any benefits employee status would have, thus nullifies any income
tax, not sales, or property.

Well, it's my day off and I went back to work anyway. Why?
It's simple. I need the money. This is what drives and motivates
a cabbie for the full ten hours of his shift and makes him want
to come into work on his day off. This is why a cabbie works:
tips and net earnings. Money makes me work on my days off
and it provides a dim wavering light at the end of the road. But
I know that when it is all said and done, the journey will reap
more havoc on me, physically and spiritually and mentally, than
what the money will be worth. The trick is to survive; to live to
tell the story as it is. I showed up at the garage after midnight
and got out onto the streets within the hour. On a Friday night,
there are always a lot of people out so I knew the few hours
would go quickly.

For my first fare, I took some drunk party people from North
Beach to SOMA (South of Market). They tipped well. Usually

after midnight on Friday and Saturday nights, the tips are better because most of the drunks are thankful for the ride home. And so far, the night up to this point had been a lot of drunks who wanted to go home. There was really nothing out of the ordinary, which surprised me. Around 2:30 A.M. I stopped for a flag who needed to go over the Golden Gate Bridge to Mill Valley. Not bad for a flag. Things were shaping up quite nicely. On my return from Mill Valley, I crossed back over the Golden Gate Bridge and dropped down into the Marina District. It was almost 3:00 A.M. and I figured that things would be winding down for the bar crowd. However, the drug crowd would still be going strong.

As I hit Lombard Street I saw two people wildly flagging me. I don't know why they were so frantic because I was the only car in sight and they were the only people on the streets. I guess they didn't want me to miss them. I hesitantly pulled over and a young twenty-something guy and a beautiful young girl hopped in the back seat. They directed me to Russian Hill. They introduced themselves as Kim and Randy. Kim wanted to know if she could smoke in the cab during the ride, and if she could smoke could she bum one from me. Because I always carry a pack for just this contingency, I told her no problem to both her questions. I gave her a Camel filter and lit it for her. She took a huge drag and sank into the back seat to relax. She wanted to know why I wasn't smoking with her and I told her that I don't smoke cigarettes. She pondered this for a moment and then asked me if it was just cigarettes that I didn't smoke. Upon hearing my reply, she pulled out a peace pipe and packed it full of the herb. She passed the pipe a couple of times and everything became, as it should be: relaxed, laid back, and mellow. We continued our conversation and I learned that she was from Boulder, Colorado. I could relate to this because I have spent a lot of time in Boulder. After Randy joined in the rap session, I learned that he grew up right across the street from my best friend and previous partner in crime, in my hometown. That was really bizarre.

I was wearing a baseball hat that was a promotional item from the movie *Half Baked*. His hat was of the same style cap but his logo read, "After Shock." He thought my hat was the goods and wanted to know if we could trade hats. I thought this was a strange request even for My Fare City, but thought about it for a few seconds and decided to make the trade. He thought he got a pretty good deal. However, I believe I ended up on the long end of the stick because I didn't tell him I had more hats just like that one at home. It was a bit strange how many common past experiences we shared, growing up and all. After I got them to their destination, I gave her my cell phone number and told them to call if they ever needed my taxi services in the future. Hell, I was hoping Kim would call me for pleasure because she looked like the morning star that shines brightly in the dawn sky. But I know that is wishful thinking. She is in her mid-twenties and I'm now thirty-something. While I hope to see them both again in the future, there is no need to get wrapped up in a fantasy world because reality always hits me like a ton of bricks when I wake up. I had to keep reminding myself to keep my eyes on the road and my hands on the wheel as I drove away from the morning star.

Chapter Forty

SPUNDAE

Taxicab Regulations Section XII, Part F, subset 2
A valid California Drivers License is required to operate a taxicab in the City and County of San Francisco, in addition to a valid A-card.

I was not looking forward to working today. In fact, I was quite crisp from working all weekend. The old cosmic string was woven around me once again. Sunday night was like any other Sunday consisting of a few airport runs and the hustle and bustle of San Francisco nightlife. Usually it dies out around 2:00 A.M. here although some things go later. However, it's definitely not a New York kind of nightlife. Everything about this Sunday had been textbook until midnight. That's when I decided to take the opportunity to read the current California driver's handbook during my downtime at the airport. I found a humorous topic that I will share with you.

Page twelve in the handbook lists the reasons a driver's license may be refused. The list states that a driver may be refused a license if the driver: 1) has a history of alcohol or drug abuse; 2) has used the license illegally; 3) has lied on the application; 4) doesn't understand the traffic laws or the street signs; 5) doesn't have the skill to drive; 6) has a health problem that makes driving unsafe; 7) has a failure to appear (FTA) or failure to pay (FTP) for a traffic citation on their driving record; 8) impersonates or allows someone else to impersonate an applicant to fraudulently qualify for a license; 9) has not complied with a judgment or order for family support payments; 10) uses a crib sheet for any examination for a license; 11) refuses to give a thumb print (news to me!); 12) refuses to sign the certification on the application (DMV form DL44); 13) submits a fraudulent birth date, legal presence document, or social security document. For more criteria see "actions resulting in loss of license" on page 74. After reading this, I think I will be spending more time cruising down near the DMV offices. I know where to look for new business now. If you take this test at home and you answer "yes" to one or more of these questions, I figure I'll see you sooner or later on the streets of My Fare City, flagging me down for a ride.

Anyway, after reading the handbook and becoming bored with it, I hit the streets to drum up some business. I was in the Union Square area when I heard the cross streets Golden Gate and Jones come across the radio. Hmm. Those sounded like Brenda's cross streets so I checked in a few blocks away and stretched a few blocks to increase my chances of getting the order. I got there and God Damn it, it was her. I was pretty excited because I had not seen Brenda in some time. I figured that she had faded away or been sucked up by the streets of San Francisco. Because her building turns off the buzzers at 10:00 p.m., she was out front waiting for the cab. She was wearing a knit cap that made her look like a cat burglar. As I rolled up to the curb she hopped in the back and was not at all surprised to see me. I asked her how she had been because I hadn't seen her for a while. She was in the mood to talk and told me what had happened to her since I last saw her.

She said she had been arrested for buying drugs on Klonopin Korner in the Tenderloin. It's at the corner of Turk and Jones. That's a corner where drugs are sold and it gets pretty rough. She was buying twenty tablets of codeine and five tablets of valium when a bike cop busted her and handcuffed her to a park bench. She said she was proud that they didn't get all the valium. I wonder where it went? She said the cop gave her the third degree about her life and asked her what was the pain in her life and why she needed to be buying codeine and valium. She said she told the cop that it was none of his business and that even if it was he wouldn't understand. She had heard about this cop before because her friend had told her that he uses the dilaudid he takes from addicts. Anyway, she was thrown into jail on her birthday and had to detox from heroin while in the joint. She said half the people in jail are kicking drugs and all they want to do is talk about it. While she was in jail she was able to get so far into her head that no one could touch her, not even the aliens she dreams about operating on her. She said she shared the cell with a chick that cried the whole time. She called her cellmates "Nancy Nice" and "Polly Pure." Her cellmate promised that she would never touch the crack pipe again. Brenda said they made them watch TV all day to keep their minds occupied. One of the shows was about an Olympiad who was stranded on a lifeboat for eighty days in the middle of nowhere. Strange. Brenda thought this was a lame movie because she rationalized that if you are floating in the middle of nowhere you still have freedom of action and choice. She didn't think it related to her situation at all. She compared her situation to 1984 because she had no choices and could take no independent action. She also said the cops were evil to her and fucked with her mind hard-core because she was kicking the habit. Her biggest beef was with all the people who kept asking her if she was kicking because she didn't want to be reminded of her situation. When she got out at 10:00 P.M. the next day, she went home and was so freaked out that she went to her bathroom and put on her makeup. That was all she could think to do.

Brenda's fare was a round-trip drive to pick up some take-out at the Pinecrest Restaurant off Union Square. Regardless of the staffing problem I mentioned, the food is still good. I dropped Brenda off back at her place and told her not to worry about things and that I wasn't stalking her. Still, when I hear them cross streets Golden Gate and Jones, you can bet I will stretch a tad. I told her I just happened to be in the area when the call came over the radio.

I gave her another one of my business cards and told her to call me if she ever needed a taxi in the future. As Brenda started to get out of the cab, a man walked up to see if I was available. I was relieved because it gave me a reason not to stay and talk to her any longer. As the man got in the back seat, he apologized for interrupting our conversation. I told him it was no big deal and asked him where he needed to go. As Brenda opened her gate to go upstairs to her apartment, I eased off into the night, but not before I told her she looked beautiful. She smiled and was then out of sight and therefore out of mind, at least for now.

After dropping off my fare at an after hours club, I had about a half an hour left to play with. I drove around looking for fares, and as I did, I thought about Brenda and her situation. Even though she was out of sight I still couldn't keep her from my mind. After all, it's my job to drive you down part of your path and as long as I get paid, your destination is your business.

Chapter Forty-One

LARRY AND THE BIRD

Taxicab Regulations Section VI, Part A, subset 10
Every Taxicab Driver, on a bi-annual basis, must submit to and
pass a medical examination. An examining physician must complete
the Taxi Detail's Medical Examination Report and a copy of the
report shall be filed with the Color Scheme Holder. The driver shall
retain the original report.

My roommate is one hell of a guy. His name is Larry and he has
lots of toys for big boys, most of 'em hotter than my engine after
a full shift. I still own the same Sony television set and stereo that
I bought in college. Larry, on the other hand, has spared no expense
to be the boy with the most toys. From his Moto Guzzi motorcycle
to his Acura, he has the best of everything. And, like a nice boy, he
is always willing to share with his poor, humble roommate. However,
he will always let me know how outdated my stuff is whenever he
loans his. He likes to mention his cool stuff every chance he gets.
This is fine with me as long as he continues to share. All in all, I
think I lucked out when I found him for a housemate. Even when he
goes grocery shopping, he will offer to share with me. Every time
he goes to COSTCO he will ask me if I need anything. On each of

his last few runs, he has picked me up a case of Cup-o-Noodles at my request. For me they are easy to prepare and tasty as well. I'll eat Cup-o-Noodles almost everyday for a few months and then get burnt out on them and fixate on some other kind of food. I blame this on my addictive personality. It really transforms my diet into a very strange thing. I do eat a variety of different foods, however, I eat them consistently and exclusively for a few months at a time. I will eat something everyday until I am sick of it and then I will pick some other food that I like and move on. Addictive personality? Yes. Bad person? Not by a long shot. Anyway, back to Larry.

We have had some inspirational conversations in the morning after I get home from my shift. When I get home, he is always in the kitchen making coffee and breakfast to start his day. He reaches in the refrigerator for a milk carton and I reach in the refrigerator for a barley pop. The other morning after I got home, Larry was curious because he noticed that I have been living off Cup-o-Noodles for the past month. I'll admit to killing a few cases of them, but there is always a means to an end in My Fare City. It turns out that Larry had tired of seeing me eat Cup-o-Noodles and was inquiring as to why I didn't eat anything else. I explained my eating habits to him and left it at that. Imagine my surprise when I came home the next morning and found a freshly baked whole turkey in the refrigerator with a note from Larry saying to help myself. I immediately made a turkey sandwich to go with my morning beer. Now that's a pal. Also, he will often come home for lunch, which is my breakfast, and make salmon and mashed potatoes for us. Larry, I salute you for providing me with a balanced diet. After feasting on the bird, I decided that my favor back to Larry had to be something special and something that didn't cost much. I decided to make a huge pot of turkey and vegetable soup with the remaining turkey. I went to the store and bought some vegetables and spices and made the soup when my roommate was at work. When he got home he found a big pot of fresh, tasty turkey soup waiting for him. It was the least I could do especially since he is always kind to me and is always feeding me healthy meals. It's a bonus to be able to eat right because I do not intend to become a fat cabbie.

However, all didn't go so well earlier at the store when I went to buy the vegetables. The turkey soup almost wasn't because of an idiot store manager. When I got to the grocery store I realized that I had forgotten my bike lock so I brought my bike inside and leaned it against a do-it-yourself steam carpet machine. That's when Don, the scrooge manager or manager wannabe, told me I had to put my bike outside. "Someone might fall over it and sue us," he said. I got upset and called him an officious pinhead. He didn't care for that so he pulled rank on me and used his powers as acting "manager" to not sell me a bag of carrots, some celery, and two onions. Hell, it's not like I was a drunk trying to buy booze after 2:00 A.M. Anyway, this motherfucker decided to pull on me at the worst time during my turkey-soup mission. I think I'll write a letter to the home office with the hope that he will be reprimanded or suspended or fired. All I can figure is that because the store is located across from Hippie Hill, he was used to harassing hippies and runaways and now that their numbers have dropped, because that area of the park is fenced off, he is going after bike riders and vegetable eaters. Get a clue asshole. The grocery store at Haight Street and Golden Gate Park should be for the people and it should not have some overworked, underpaid, control freak harassing customers. Now that I've vented, I'll end this chapter by letting you know that I did get those carrots, celery, and onions. I gave a guy who was hanging out in front of the store a quart of beer to purchase these important recipe items for me. So, I got angry and it cost me a quart of beer, but in the end the soup got made.

Chapter Forty-Two

BETTER OR WORSE

Taxicab Regulations Section VI, Part B, subset 5
Every Taxicab Driver, while operating a taxicab vehicle, shall have in their possession a three (3) inch by five (5) inch laminated identification card with a photograph of the driver's face (without hat, scarf, sunglasses, etc.) a minimum of one and one half (1) inch in width by two (2) inch in length displayed conspicuously at all times in a manner that is easily readable by any passenger in the taxicab vehicle. The card must include the photograph of the driver, the driver's badge number, driver's last name, driver's first name and the color scheme of the taxicab vehicle. The taxicab driver must acquire this identification card, in a form approved by the Chief of Police. The colors on the picture identification card shall match the color scheme holder's color(s). The colors shall be aligned horizontally along the length of the identification card.

When I left the world of business and the nine-to-five rat race, I was extremely unhappy and unhealthy. I weighed in at a few pounds shy of 200. Since I started driving a cab, riding my bike to work, and eating less and better food, I'm now back to my fighting weight of 155 pounds. I look like a new person. Being employed as a San

Francisco taxi driver has changed my attitude about life and health for the better. The picture on my cabbie ID does not look like me at all. In the picture I look like an unhappy, overweight businessman. But, that was then and this is now, and today I am in great shape and feel excellent. I would even say I am happy most of the time now. However, being a night taxi driver hasn't completely changed my life for the better. Even though I am healthy, semi-wealthy, and more street wise because of driving the night shift doesn't mean that everything is good. Since becoming a night cabbie for My Fare City, I have found it more difficult to have a serious relationship with a woman and have lost a lot of my friends because the job is all consuming. I have found that it is all or nothing. Hell, even with my Friday and Saturday nights off, it is still pretty hard to find a cute gal to date. So far it has been slim pickin's. And what makes it worse for me is I found out the other day that my forty-year-old roommate is dating an eighteen-year-old girl. She is still in high school. He told me that he met her when she gave him a facial at the salon. Eighteen years old. If I could only be that lucky. Who knows? Maybe in the future I will be that lucky because he also told me that she has a twenty-one-year-old sister who is single and free to mingle. So, if all goes well we may double date someday. But until then I will continue to drive and try to deal with the fact that most of my relationship's last about as long as the cab ride. At least I am getting paid to be in those.

Also, I don't see my old friends like I used to. It seems I only see them if there is a concert or some other event and this happens less and less as the time goes by. Because I drive nights I can't party like I used to; my friend Hemi knows this well. As he put it, "Bud, you just aren't in the loop anymore." I have so many short-term relationships with my fares that I think it may have affected the other relationships in my life. My buds were pretty tight in the past, but now we are disconnected and drift through our lives aimlessly, never in the direction of repair or good times. My old friend Wavy Davy still lets his freak flag fly when the wind is right, Hemi is workin' it, just not always my angle. I have seen so many beautiful and horrific sights lately it isn't always easy to "take the good with the bad." Working as a night cabbie puts me in the front and center row of the classroom of life. And because I have chosen to take this class, I am getting an unforgettable education that no other school can teach. So far it has been a unique experience that I will always remember even though there are times I cherish and loathe it in the same breath.

Chapter Forty-Three

COMMUNITY

Taxicab Regulations Section V, Part C, subset 11
The Taxicab vehicle shall have a rear-view mirror and side-view
mirror on both sides of the vehicle.

I took the bus to work today and it was full of hot, sticky people
that seemed to stare at me curiously. I think it was because I was
wearing my official taxi driver's badge on my shirt. They probably
thought I was a cop. I was tired because I had only dozed off for a
few hours the previous night and I took the damn bus so I could get
to work early and get the cab out early. And, I was too tired to ride
my bike. I usually don't take the bus, but when I do I like to observe
people and how they interact with each other. I think it's funny how
people on the bus will make eye contact with each other but will not
speak to one another. Everyone is looking and staring at each other
while no one has the courage to say anything. Not even a comment
about the weather is uttered. I find this very rude and uncomfortable
and yet, I find myself doing it as well. Anyway, that is one thing
that bothers me when I take the bus. Everyone is so disconnected
and afraid of each other. Things shouldn't be like that. That's why
I try to make eye contact with my fares whenever possible. It sucks

trying to carry on a conversation through the rear view mirror. Alas, I still try. It is so impersonal and I don't want people to think of that way. Anyway, I got to work early and got the cab out an hour early and started the night taking radio call after radio call hoping that my meter would not crack the $5.00 mark. See, for any fare under $5.00 I usually will get the whole $5.00. This means more tip for the buck.

As I was driving, I noticed an increase in the drunk homeless people who were weaving and bobbing from street to curb crossing the street haphazardly. I saw one homeless man saunter into the busy rush hour traffic completely oblivious to the danger. He was wrapped in an old blanket and it looked like he had stuck his finger in a light socket. We are talking about one bad mother fucking hair day. He looked like a freaked-out Don King. Somehow, he made it across the street without getting hit. I think it was his hair that saved him. I mean, it was impossible not to notice him. I stopped my cab and watched him as he continued to stagger down the sidewalk, aimlessly bumping into light poles and parking meters. I don't think he had a care in the world.

After a few minutes, I took a call and drove to North Beach where a bartender loaded an old drunk man into my back seat. He looked like he was paralyzed because his legs were like dead weight. He was drunk as a skunk and it wasn't even 5:00 P.M. yet. However, he wasn't quite in the "sleeper" category yet so I had to listen to him mumble as I rocketed up Russian Hill to his place. He yammered at me the whole ride about nothing and made a short seem like a long. By the time I dropped him off I just wanted the old fart out of my cab so I could make some money in peace and quiet. When we pulled up to the front of his building, I waited for about thirty seconds and then realized what I had to do. So, I bit the bullet and got out and helped the drunk old man out of the cab. I left him sitting on the bottom step to his building staring at the ground still mumbling to himself about something. As I put the car in gear and rolled away, I made a mental note to myself that I would never let the same thing happen to me when I get that old.

My next fare took me to the airport. After dropping her off, I got into the wait line and played a few card games. One that we like to play is called "Tonk." I didn't do too well and ended losing $10.00 to a rival cabbie. Also, while in the concrete jungle, the radio reception fades because of all the concrete that blocks out the signal.

"concrete jungle"

However, as we were playing "Tonk" on the bottom level of the six-story parking structure, the radio started to play. I looked around to see what, if anything, could be causing this when I saw a fat Indian cabbie standing directly in front of my parked vehicle. I couldn't believe it. The fat cabbie was acting as an antenna for my radio. The music only lasted for about a minute though because he waddled back to his cab. As I headed out of the first waiting lot to the terminal, I noticed the fat cabbie again as he passed by me with a Danish hanging out of his mouth. It looked almost artistic. I think the exhaust fumes were affecting me because I have never thought a Danish could be so profound.

I took a fare from the airport into My Fare City and decided to hang around for a while. After a few shorts, I decided it was time to take a break and headed to a friend's place for some dinner. It did not surprise me when I got there and found a feast of vegetarian Chinese food. Go figure. Kung pow, hot greens, tempe, green peppers, chow mien noodles, and a mix of teriyaki, peas, broccoli, tofu, and garlic in a black-bean sauce. Nice job Wavy Davy. After dinner and some good tunes, I got back on the road with a ska beat in my head and the chant, "William Shattner . . . William Shattner . . . William Shattner." It was really starting to bother me. It was like some damn jingle to a commercial that you can't get out of your head. To erase the tune from my memory I searched the radio dial for a panacea and found it with Rush. I have a lot of drug-abusing memories associated with that band. In fact, the highest I have ever been was when I was at a Rush concert in high school. I had eaten a bunch of mushrooms and by the time they took the stage I was flying to the stars as I melted into my seat. I usually saved the LSD for Jerry and the most "Grateful Dead." It's a different trip to get to each scene and you know how I like to drive.

After having a nice break with Wavy Davy, my batteries were recharged and I was ready to get back at it. As I was driving around looking for a flag and waiting for a radio call, I saw an Ecstasy dealer I used to know back in the day. He was standing outside 1015 Folsom, taking a break from the rave that was going on. They call it "community" and they usually rock well into the night. I stopped and said hello to him even though I was not interested in buying any extracurricular for the evening. Maybe some other time I told him as I drove off to pick up a radio call. After thinking it over, I have come to the conclusion that one can succeed at failing or one can succeed at success. Both of these results are outward expressions of the attitudes you hold for yourself. You either think rich or poor, abundance or absence, plenty or poverty. Either way, the choice is yours. When you consistently maintain positive attitudes toward situations and circumstance, the outcome of that event will always reflect the attitude. Anyway, that is my mantra.

Chapter Forty-Four

CCCP

Taxicab Regulations Section V, Part C, subset 33
All taxicab vehicles shall have both a large print sign and a braille sign mounted on the right rear door indicating the cab number and the company name so the vision impaired can easily identify both the cab and the driver.

Wednesday night was its usual self. It was a sea of drunks, whores, businessmen, couples, extroverts, introverts, and a lady who smelled like rotten fish. A potpourri of fares as usual. However, tonight I got to wear my dumb cab driver hat for one of my fares. Around 8:00 P.M. I took a radio call for pick up at a hotel on Van Ness Ave., which was only a few blocks away from where I was. I picked up four people from a nice hotel on Lombard and as they piled in the cab, my first impression was that they smelled nice. There were four of them—a woman and three men. The woman reminded me of a James Bond girl. She was wearing a short power skirt and a loose-fitting designer top of some kind. She looked like a high-priced call girl. She was with three men who were all dressed in nice power suits, the businessman's special I presume. One of the guys jumped in the front and the other two sat on each side of the woman in the back seat. I asked where to and only one of them even came close to speaking English. I was surprised they had made it as far as my cab, to be perfectly frank. However, they were well dressed and they were white so the man wasn't keeping that third eye on them. As we rolled away, one of the guys in the back who spoke English at the pre-school level directed me to Pierce Street. I asked them if they wanted to go to the Pierce Street Annex, which is a popular bar with the wannabe Melrose crowd, and they all nodded in approval.

At this point I thought it was funny how I was having a hard time understanding them. The old role reversal for sure. I myself have had many cab drivers whose English consisted of "thank you" along with a smile and a nod. Anyway, I drove the Russians to the Pierce St. Annex and they didn't get out of the cab. They were talking to me in Russian and I couldn't understand one word they were saying. All I could do was nod and smile. As they continued to talk one of them wrote on a piece of paper an address that read 39 Pierce Street. So, I drove them to 39 Pierce. It was a ten-minute drive and strangely enough, it took us to the Lower Haight. We entered into the dead end where 39 Pierce St. should have been and found nothing. There was no building with any address near number 39. At this point I gave up because I couldn't understand Russian and I had no idea where they needed to go. However, I do know that they capped on me pretty good because some languages are universal. So, as I started to drive them back to their hotel, I had a brainstorm and I radioed in to dispatch and asked the dispatcher to put out a call to any driver who spoke Russian. I thought that is was worth a shot anyway. Well, sure enough, a Russian-speaking driver was available and the dispatcher instructed him to meet me back at the hotel on Van Ness. As we pulled up, the other driver was there and I greeted him, explained the problem to him, and told him he could take the fare because I had personally had it with them. I was just happy to hand this problem off to someone qualified to handle the situation. He was happy to get the fare and I was happy to get rid of them.

Oh well. It was just another trip of trips in the capitol of the universe. I was so glad to be rid of those folks, mainly because it got very tense toward the end of the ride. I wasn't sure but I think they were armed. And I wasn't even going to charge them for the ride. But as the woman and the two younger men sauntered over to the other cabbie, the older man pulled out a wad of bills the size of which I have not seen since the last time I bought pot. As he flipped through the wad of mainly fifties, he plucked one out and handed it to me. He nodded and then briskly walked to the waiting cab. There was a split second I thought about interrupting him but decided against it when I saw all of the cash he had. I figured they saw a side of town they would not have seen had it not been for me. I hope they remember me back across the pond. Well, I guess the cosmic string today would be the irony of a fare not speaking English where usually the joke is on the non-English-speaking cabbie. The cabbie who picked the Russians up said he took them on a tour of all the major landmarks in My Fare City. I told him I was happy to help him and that I was glad things turned out positive. To you I will admit that it was the $50.00 that I was most happy with.

Chapter Forty-Five

DAY OFF

Taxicab Regulations Section VI, Part A, subset 1
Every Taxicab Driver shall comply with the provisions of the Charter, Police Code, Planning Code and Traffic Code of the City and County of San Francisco, The California Vehicle Code, California Worker's compensation Laws and these Taxicab Regulations, The provisions of all ordinances and regulations applicable at the San Francisco International Airport, San Francisco City and County Department of Agriculture and Weights and Measures, and all other governmental jurisdictions through which the permit holders traverse.

Well, I have another day off and I'm gonna go into work later tonight. I slept for almost 24 hours yesterday. The body heals itself with sleep so I was happy to get some much-needed rest. I awoke around 11:00 A.M. today. I went to sleep around noon yesterday. I called my friend Charlie, a friend who sleeps a lot and asked him if this was OK. He assured me it was, so I figured to make the best of all the rest I had just gotten and decided to go into work later. This is because as I searched for what I might do on my day off, I kept coming up with work. Most of my interpersonal relationships have headed so far south that they now are out of sight, but not out of mind. I have dug myself a hole so deep that anyone who would stand next to me would be crazier than me. But, this is what happens when you become a night cab driver. I at least still have fun with it whenever possible. I will roll with the punches just as I have always done in my roller coaster life. Up or down, I am never right in the middle. I think I like it this way even though it is taxing at times.

After waking and showering, I ate an Eggo. No one was around to take it from me. I ate it plain and it was just the ticket. My cell phone rang around 1:00 P.M. and to my surprise it was Brenda. I was happy to hear from her because the best orgasm I have ever had in my life was with her. I knew she had some angle for calling me but I didn't care, I was just glad to catch up with her. She asked me if I could come over and of course I did. We chatted for a while. She, like me, has not done any heroin in some time. I am not surprised I am clean but I am surprised she is. She has been to a few Narcotics Anonymous (NA) meetings but refused to call herself an addict. Though she was clean and had been for a while, her apartment looked like it always had, a total and complete mess. Everything from peanut shells to books about the occult was strewn about the apartment. There was a hole in the ceiling and after looking at it for a minute, I had to ask what the hell happened. Apparently her building is going through earthquake retrofitting. She said she was in her apartment when she saw a drill bit come through the ceiling. This would have freaked me out if I had seen it happen. We chatted for an hour or so more and she told me about her recent bust and how the cops wanted to make her an informant. She was unable to help at the time so she did not become a narc. Still, I was careful to be completely legal because I smelled something wrong from the get go. But folks, Bud says paranoia self destroya.

I gave her a ride in my own vehicle to her new boyfriend's place and left her, feeling happy we were able to catch up and I could look into another person's world while off the clock. She looked good but had not changed a lot. Even though she claimed to be free from heroin, she was still a hooker who was one step above the street. I hope she finds her way in life no matter which way that might be. She is just one of a cast of characters in the bizarre play I call "My Life in My Fare City."

Saturday night. The freaks were definitely out last night. From drunk tourists to local babes, it was busy and I managed to work the radio until the bitter end of the night when even the freaks had gone home. Zipping down Pine Street at exactly 2:00 A.M. was a real treat. All of the lights turn to flashing yellow one at a time and, if your timing is perfect, each light will begin its graveyard shift one by one for you as you speed through them. Other streets in the city all turn to flashing yellow as well, which provides an unmatched freedom to drive. And at 2:00 A.M. there is no traffic to deal with except for the random drunk, which you think about as much as the next earthquake. Both will probably happen unexpectedly and soon, but all you can do is drive on. I drive as safe as any other working man on the clock, so I don't think about what could happen when I get down on the freedom time as I dart down city streets taking in the ultimate tour at seventy miles an hour. I can't even describe how cool it felt at 2:17 A.M. when the twenty-four-hour Jazz station 91.1 played the theme to "Mission Impossible" which is a great late-night driving tune. I was on a mission and I lived to tell you about another night.

Last night a mangy-looking punk wannabe got into a deep thought session with me. I had mentioned that Nietzsche has said, "that which does not kill us makes us stronger." I may have been reaching a bit but the guy seemed like he might have some inspirational commentary for me. When I asked him what he thought about that, he told me that you can't use what you can't abuse. Hmmm, both meanings were swirling around in my head like a toilet bowl flushing on the other side of the equator as I sped down the empty city streets. After that Zen experience, no one stood out until I picked up a hip-looking gal and her boyfriend on the Lower Haight about 3:00 A.M. As they hopped in the back, they directed me to "The Stud" which is a local gay bar that is great for dancing. When they got in the cab, KUSF was playing some strange country tune and I could tell they thought it sucked. But, as we pulled off the curb, the tune ended and "No Quarter" by Led Zeppelin came on. The mix was perfect. The tune lasted as long as the ride and both seemed epic indeed. After I dropped off the Led Zeppelin experience, some real bitchy, cute dykes loaded themselves in and completely ruined the epic mood. I gave them a ride but the energy was definitely not positive. That's OK because even though they may not like guys, at least they did have someone to keep them warm at night when the fog rolls in.

After 4:00 A.M. I picked up a flag at 16th and Valencia, which is a seedy corner in the Mission District that turns even seedier after 2:00 A.M. Normally I would not take a flag from an area like that late at night, but for some reason I did. The guy got in and muttered, "San Francisco General." After that the guy did not speak one word the rest of the trip. I felt completely uncomfortable to say the least. I dropped him at the emergency room entrance not knowing if he was ever going to be seen again. Then I thought that maybe a relative or someone close to him was very sick. But then reality hit me and I was just thankful that I didn't get mugged because I got some bad vibes off him for sure. I'll never know what the deal was and I took it as a sign to end the evening. So, after collecting the fare, I b-lined it back to the safety of the gas pump at the garage. I had KPOO tuned on and the Blues were playing loud. It is a great radio station to listen to after midnight in My Fare City. I kept busy all night and fared well, but I fear that with each mile I spend on the street, the better my chances of experiencing that earthquake become.

Chapter Forty-Six

LIGHTNING STRIKES TWICE

Taxicab Regulations Section VI, Part E, subset 9
Every Taxicab Driver shall inform passenger(s) whose announced destination is or may be more than fifteen (15) miles, as recorded on the taxicab vehicle odometer, from the city limits of San Francisco that the fare charged will be 150% of the amount registered on the taximeter.

I took the bus to work again today. I always find this interesting because I do not have to pay attention to the road so I can look upon the streets freely. As I was waiting for the bus, a homeless man sitting at the bus stop caught my interest. He was not waiting for the bus but rather he was sitting at the bus stop killing time. I noticed he had a pack of smokes in his hand and an unlit smoke in his mouth. It didn't look like he was going to light that smoke because he kept fondling it, content with the fact that he had it. It was his pack of smokes and he did not have to bum one from anyone. And even though he looked like shit he still had a sense of security about him. As the bus moved away from the stop, he continued to play with his cigarette. I figure that if nothing else in the world goes his way he will at least be content with the memory of that moment. I wondered about him as we pulled away and I prayed I would never end up at a bus stop with nowhere to go. The bus came to a stop near the garage so I headed to work and that's when it all began.

"bus ride to work"

It was another Sunday and there was no doubt I would deadhead to the airport to look for that "diamond in the rough." So, I headed South bound on US-101 and tuned into my favorite radio station KUSF. For some insane reason they were playing the theme to the *Teletubbies* TV program. I found this sick at first but slowly I got into the beat and the weirdness of the rhyme and meter. I was really getting into it by the time I approached Candlestick Park and that was the same time it faded away into a buzz of static. Sometimes the strangest things make me feel so good. The "Teletubbies" got me off on the right foot. I think "Teletubbies" are almost as sick as Barney, but I dig the baby in the sun that smiles at you during the show. Yes, I have watched it. Yes, I'll try anything twice. Upon arrival at the airport, I ran to take a whiz and then picked up a sensible dinner from the food dude. I got a Diet

Coke and a Snickers. You know the commercial, "Not going anywhere for a while? Grab a Snickers." Not super healthy but it did the trick and it's better than the other crap the guy sells. Don't leave your cat at the airport because even cat tastes like chicken. After my meal I lost ten bucks playing cards with some Russian dudes. Not a great beginning but you have to start somewhere.

My first trip from the airport was a good one to San Jose. This runs around $100.00. The Indian man I drove was interested in me and I gave him the standard story of "What Bud is doing with his life." It sounded pretty good. So good I almost had myself fooled. As I headed north, I felt happy because I had made my gate fee on the first run of the night and I got a ten percent tip on the 100.00 to boot. Not bad for a Sunday. And because it was Sunday, it only took me one hour to complete my journey into the South Bay. Since I had to drive past SFO to get back to My Fare City, it was a given that I would stop back for another fare, and wouldn't you know it, lightning struck twice after a short thirty-minute wait. I picked up a man from the south terminal again. He almost got in another cab but was directed to me by airport personnel. He had to pick up his car at the outer parking lot of the San Jose Airport! Now that was truly a milestone. Two airport fares in a row and both of them needed to go to San Jose. The San Jose Airport runs about $95.00. I couldn't believe my good fortune. As we pulled up to his car the meter read $63.30, but because it was outside the city limits, the fare was meter and a half. This meant $95.00 in my pocket. But the guy only had $65.00 in his pocket and because I didn't have time to fuck with the other $30.00, I took his business card and a wholesome promise that he would send me the $30.00. I have his work address and e-mail should further collection efforts need to be taken. He was surprised I trusted him and I was too, so before he left the cab I told him it was in his best interest to send me the $30.00. I think he will. If he doesn't he will get a personal call from Bud's Collection Agency and eventually he will settle up. But, as with everything in life, we shall see. I'll be sure and let you know what happens. Despite being shorted $30.00, it still proved to be a good run. So, I headed back North on US-101 around 7:40 P.M.

The sun, which usually you can't look at, was not a problem to look directly into last night. It sat like a huge harvest moon on fire, setting ever so slowly in the West. As I headed north, I watched it sink behind the hills. It was beautiful. It made all the shit I put up with worth it. My momma told me I would go blind if I looked directly into the sun, but she was obviously wrong. As I steamed past Mountain View, the sun faded over the hills, leaving only its rays shooting up from behind them. Everything was as it should have been. Too bad I forgot to roll that fatty on my last wait at the airport. But that's OK; there would be enough time later for monkey business. Back at SFO, I had dinner again. Yes, another Diet Coke and a Snickers. After making it to "the concrete jungle" I heard a strange noise. It was someone playing the saxophone. I looked to my left but could only see the blackened marker reading, G33=level 1. Trust me, you never want to see or be at this part of the airport garage. I managed to find and snap a picture of the mystery sax player and then it was back to My Fare City for a few more hours filled with drunks, tourists, and prostitutes.

Chapter Forty-Seven

KARMA POLICE

Taxicab Regulations Section VI, Part D, subset 6
Drivers shall ask for and receive permission from the passenger to
play any audio/video device (AM, FM, radio tape player, etc.)

"karma police"

It was raining last night and I had the radio tuned into "All Along the Watchtower" by Jimi Hendrix with the seat tilted back as I left the yard. The rain is always good for business, but during the rush hour it means the regular riders have to wait longer. It never matters though because as long as I can keep a fare in the back and the wheels turning, things will be just fine. The first of the month had come and gone when I realized that I still had to pay my rent. That motivated me early on last night to crack the nut. After that I had hoped to make enough money to cover my rent, but this idea fell to the wayside as soon as I started to pick up fares. Last night I was driving more for the experience than the dough. I don't make a lot of money when I drive with this in mind, but I never lose any either. I always make sure I crack the nut before I slack off.

The first mistake of the night came with the first fare. He was a flag I picked up at 4th and Folsom Streets and I really don't know what the hell I was thinking when he got in the car. He had to go across town to Polk St. near Jackson to pick up a pair of sandals. He wasn't sure if the store was still open, so instead of taking him there to find out in person, I phoned the store like an idiot and found that it was closed. This ended the ride right there. I wasn't even half way to the store when I dropped him at Union Square. Nice job Bud. I made a mental note to myself never to do that again, especially since I needed the money. As the night continued on, the rain provided a steady stream of fares and a steady stream of income. As I drove I tried to put the first run out of my head, but not so far that I would make the same mistake again.

I took some Brits down to their hotel in the Marina and pointed out that they were only a stone's throw away from the best pepper steak in the city. I told them they had to eat at the Brazenhead Restaurant. I also told them about the time I was having dinner there with my Dad. We almost ended up having to wash the dishes because the place used to only take cash and all my Dad had was a credit card and a little cash. Luckily, he had enough cash on him to cover the bill, but unfortunately that was the cash he was going to give me so when I asked to borrow $20.00 he was fresh out. After dropping the Brits off I tried to play the radio for a while. I had a "no go" south of Market and got another radio call to an address that took me to the East Bay. From there I rolled the bones and ended up picking up a flag for a ride to Berkeley. The traffic was so bad on the way back to the city that for the time spent en route I would have been better off running around town. The peak of rush hour is the only time a trip over the Bay Bridge will backfire and it was just my luck that it happened last night. And to make matters worse, I received a call on my cell phone while I was stuck in traffic from a friend who was actually gonna pay for a ride. Usually when my cell phone rings, I can count on it either being friends with no money who need a ride or an ex-girlfriend calling to see what I am doing.

Because I was stuck in traffic, I was unable to help my friend and upon arriving back in My Fare City I ended up in the Upper Haight neighborhood, where a lone ragamuffin flagged me down. She said she was going down to see Radiohead at the Bill Graham Civic Auditorium. I asked the girl if she was going to the show alone and she replied that she was but that she hoped to see some friends there. Good luck, I thought, because the place was buzzing with a hell of a lot of people; it was general admission. She said if she found her friends by the end of the show, she would be happy. I dropped her off and kept moving on. I then ended up having a series of fares that were all headed to the Radiohead show. One couple had been given some tickets as a wedding present. The only thing was that the person who gave the tickets to them also gave them to the rest of the wedding party as well. It sounded to me like someone got some free tickets. Now I call that cheap with a capital "C."

Personally, I really wasn't interested in seeing the concert because I have seen them before. It was several years ago at a free lunchtime concert at the Justin Herman Plaza in the Financial District. It was back when I worked in Finance behind a dummy terminal rather than a steering wheel. It seems like a long time ago. I remember the day well though because I was wearing a blue dress shirt and my favorite pink polka dot tie. I like anything that is bright and a tad irritating and that is what I go for with neckwear, as those who suffered through my days as a businessman will attest. Radiohead was on their way up back then and they didn't seem to mind playing for a bunch of stuffed shirts for free. Promotion and publicity was the name of the game back then for the band and it was sink or swim. I felt so lucky to catch the free show during my lunch hour.

Anyway, back to the night. I picked up a group of people going to the show. They introduced themselves as Martin, Melissa, and Michelle. When I picked them up, they were already late for the warm-up band but because I picked them up from a bar, they all had a nice buzz on. On the way to the concert, Michelle started to rub my shoulders and she made the comment that I was a cute cabbie. OK. Complement accepted, but please don't tease me. I have a vivid imagination and left to itself I could be in big trouble. Martin offered to sell me their extra ticket to the show but I refused because I was not really interested in the band. But it felt nice having a stranger run her fingers through my hair and I was hoping they would just ask me to go in with them for free. When I dropped them off, that is what they did. That's the nice part about this job. I can work as hard or as laid back as I want to. Last night I was in laid-back mode so I parked the cab and headed in to see the show free of charge. I ended up losing my kind friends after several tunes because it was time to move on. So, I hit the road after enjoying most of the show. I figured that the free ticket was a karmic bonus I couldn't pass up, even though I lost as much in wages as it would have cost to buy it. When I left the show I found my cab still safely and illegally parked. The parking Gods were smiling on me again. Hee hee. After the concert ended I drove by the auditorium several times to pick up fares. With each trip back to the auditorium I was hoping to run into Michelle because I wanted her to rub my shoulders some more. She was a cute brunette and as I thought about her, I pictured her rubbing more than my shoulders. But, as luck would have it, I never saw her again. She was just another stranger passing in the night; a chance meeting that is to never be again. Regardless, I think it was as much fun for them as for me and definitely a concert I will not forget.

Chapter Forty-Eight

CLEAN UP CREW

Taxicab Regulations Section VI, Part E, subset 2
A Taxicab Driver shall comply with all reasonable requests of any passenger.

Well, it was supposed to be another night off last night but I managed to stay sober so I could work and pick up all the drunks on "clean up crew." Clean up crew is the crew that drives an unscheduled shift Friday or Saturday night between the hours of midnight and 5:00 A.M. I got a car on the road around 1:00 A.M. and hit the streets. I could have worked the radio but it didn't matter because flags were everywhere and they were all buzzed pretty good. I picked up a stripper on her way home who seemed a bit drunk. I know I would have to be drunk to take my clothes off in front of a bunch of men. As I was driving her, I could tell she was hitting on me, but I wasn't sure of it until she asked me to show her my member. I have consented to stranger requests in the past and she was turning me on with her verbal foreplay so I decided to show it to her. My member was flaccid, not quite fully erect, but large enough at the moment that I felt proud enough to give her a look-see, family jewels and all. She said she was impressed. I was surprised I actually did it. When we arrived at her place in North Beach, I went in for a thirty-minute break, which is usually not a good idea when working clean up crew. But, she gave me the best head I have had in a long time. I can't even remember how long it has been. I kissed her good night on the cheek and remembered an old prom date. However, my prom date was never like this. The cosmic string was wrapped around me like a warm blanket as I bid her farewell. Yet another fringe benefit.

"north beach"

Broadway and Columbus intersect in the heart of North Beach. At that intersection there is almost always a flag around who is ripe for the picking late on a Friday night or early Saturday morning. Anyway, to cut to the chase, I picked up three very good-looking girls from there. After my last load, I thought I was the man. They directed me to the Upper Haight near the intersection of Haight and Ashbury. When someone is really fucked up and discolored from being ill, I always make them sit next to the window with the window rolled down all the way. All I ever say is that if you need to toss your cookies, you do it out the window or you tell me to pull over so you can do it on the curb. Well, the one that got the coveted window seat was beyond help. The first major bump we hit, I peered into my rear-view mirror to see my worst nightmare unfold behind me. I looked at the girl sitting next to the window and saw that her head was bobbing up and down and all around like a cork in a rough sea. There was no way she was going to make it out the window even if all she had to do was lean to her right. I could tell she was going to get ill and, unlike most drunks in my cab, she had not yet made it to the "dry heave" stage. I continued to stare at the girl in my mirror and prayed she would not get sick.

However, as her head bobbed up, her jaw went slack and her eyes filled with fear and without warning she violently projectile-vomited over the entire front passenger seat and dashboard. Thankfully, the seat was empty at the moment. However, her watery puke spattered all over. It dripped down the window and off the back of the seat onto her feet and off of her chin and into her lap. It was a complete fucking mess and it reeked like puke always does.

I had to use all of my self-control to keep myself cool, calm and collected. Soon after the incident, we arrived at their destination. They paid me $20.00 out of the drunk girl's pocket and each of them threw me $20.00 to boot. Usually fares are assholes and only pay the fare when they get sick, but this time I had made a handsome profit. I hauled ass back to the garage, cleaned up the cab and made a mental note which one it was to make sure I never use it again.

I went out to finish up the hour because I would pay for it anyway. My first fare immediately asked, "Who puked in your cab? Were they drunk on Gin?" I responded with a lie and blamed the smell on the age of the cab, saying it was an old cab and only used once in a while. Needless to say, I worked that angle for a few "mercy tips." It went really well and after the last few fares I had had enough. It was getting close to 5:00 A.M. I put on the 440 air conditioning and hauled ass back to the garage before the window guy would have an excuse to turn my head into a pumpkin. I cashed out with a pretty good profit. After four hours of work, I took home

$110.00. That is better than most ten-hour shifts minus the vomit on the dash. I thanked the window guy for tabulating my fees correctly and went back to give the dispatcher $5.00. All is well that ends well on "clean-up crew" in My Fare City.

Chapter Forty-Nine

SHORTY WED

Taxicab Regulations Section XIII, Part F, subset 4
Every Taxicab Driver has the right to refuse service to anyone, for
any reason, (no shirt, no shoes, etc.)

The city seemed really quiet today. I slept until 4:00 P.M., which
is much later than usual. I was feeling kind of crispy when I hopped
on my bike to ride to work. It was very nice out and the warm air
felt great as it dried my hair on the way. Because I had the time to
spare, I rode my bike slowly. I was wearing my sunglasses and truly
digging life. I saw a drummer named Leon on Haight Street. Leon
is a cornerstone at Haight and Fillmore streets. I gave him a buck
for the time. Everybody has an angle, with each one wanting more
and more of that pie. I stopped to chat with him for a moment,
snapped his picture, and moved on as I thought about the bizarre
city I live in. His lame harmonica-playing sidekick demanded that I
take his picture too. I love it . . .

I will admit that I was feeling unusually tired and lazy. I picked up
my cab, logged in the outbound numbers on my waybill, and hit the
road. I tuned the radio to the college station 90.3 KUSF. I usually
never know what I'm listening to on KUSF but I like what I hear. At

6:00 P.M. they switch over to Chinese radio for a few hours and then back to the ultimate mix. Fares are always taken off guard by the tunes I play and the image I project. People often tell me that it's the best cab ride they have ever had. Sometimes it feels good to be King of the Pagans rather than president of a frat house. I mean I have always walked in through the back door in my life and this cab thing has exploited so many of my talents. I can't believe I actually still enjoy it. I will say that after my first year in the business, it seemed the situations stayed the same while many of the characters changed. The bitchy boyfriend, the drunken businessman, and so many others. The cast of characters in the play called "My Life as a Cabbie" is a never-ending saga of ups and downs.

After taking a few flags, I found myself in the Castro neighborhood. A man flagged me down and as soon as he got in I knew I had made a mistake picking him up. He immediately gave me $17.00 which is a strange amount, but I'll take a prepay any day. As soon as he shut the door he said punch it, which I did. We wandered around for a bit as the guy kept ranting and raving about nothing. He was obviously on some hard drugs. He shouted at me and demanded that I pull into the gas station up ahead so he could get some smokes. He not only made me feel threatened but freaked me out as well, which ain't too easy to do. Inside the gas station I could see him arguing with the poor sap behind the bulletproof glass. After thinking about the situation for a quick second, I decided to turn off the meter at $4.10 and took off posthaste to get myself away from the immediate danger. Too bad so sad dude. I doubt he will even remember the ride though I know I will. It was just another bullet dodged and all in a good night's work. After the loony tune, I was not in the mood to meet anyone else. The guy I ditched was a threat to my personal safety as well as a few fries short of a Happy Meal. That was when the dispatcher called for anyone who wanted to short shift and I jumped on it and took the rest of the night off. I did not make much money, but occasionally I will cut my losses and bail out. Mental health can be just as, and sometimes more important than physical health. I guess it depends on the day of the week and time of day.

Lucky for me I had somewhere to go after work last night. I was going to free movie night at "The Cell" which is an art/performance space run by young, energetic, and moral folk. The emphasis at Cell (Collective Exploratory Learning Lab) is on art and not a quick buck. Wavy Dave is my preferred master of ceremonies at Cell, but it's the group of artists as a whole that keep things glued together. A free movie night is held at least once a week. You only pay for soda, popcorn, or whatever sweet your tooth desires. Occasionally Wavy Dave will bring out his private cookie jar, but better get ready for a blockbuster kinda night, and forget about operating any heavy machinery. Last night's film was *The Wizard of Oz* with "The Dark Side of the Moon" played along as the soundtrack. It was very cool and a nice relief from the streets. For the facts on this quirk of nature, take a look at their website (www.cellspace.org). After cleaning up the space after the show, I went home to bed and had some strange dreams. Yes, I did go over the rainbow too. I can say without reservation, "There's no place like home in My Fare City."

Chapter Fifty

HOME RUN

Taxicab Regulations Section XI, Part B, subset 1
Any person(s) or company who violates or causes to be violated
relevant statutes of law may also be cited or arrested.

    I did not feel like working again last night but if I don't pay the
bills, nobody else will. After I was on the road for several hours, I
felt better though because people seemed to be in a good mood.
Everybody heard my view on the taxi situation in San Francisco.
After a while I felt like a tape recorder because I kept saying the
same thing to each and every fare that got in the cab. But that is a
story for another time.

    My night got off to a strange start because earlier in the evening
an ex-girlfriend called me up and said that she wanted to see me.
We are mostly sex partners because we don't get along too well out
of the sack. So, I picked her up and took her on a ride to see the
new ballpark that is currently being constructed. Our new ballpark
was supposed to be built in 1989 but we had to wait until now.
Anyway, it was after dark and I parked the cab and we both snuck
onto the site of the new stadium. We found our way to the exact
spot where home plate will be and she laid down and we scored the

first "home run" of the park. I will never think of Pac Bell Park in the same way again. Every run scored there now will be one that came after yours truly. My friend Arch thinks I'm nuts and I'm starting to believe him. And no, we did not get caught. Other than the fantastic sex, my night was pretty lame financially. I came home with around $40.00. Granted, I did take several hours off. The entire time we were "scoring" I could have sworn we were going to get caught. But, it was yet another bullet dodged. If I had got caught, my lawyer would handle the incident painlessly. Actually, that wouldn't be bad for publicity. I can see the headline now: "Cab Driver and Fare Found Naked on Home Plate" or "Cabbie Scores Home Run for Home Team."

The only thing that kept me going after midnight was the radio and 90.3 FM KUSF. They kept the vibe alive and me awake too. Thanks guys! Once I even returned a car to the garage because the radio was busted. The window guy said, "We don't need no prima donnas here." So, I opted to take the night off.

The streets were empty and I meandered around looking for any action I could. I was even spying out bus stops, which, as you know, I occasionally will do if it's real slow. Finally, after a radio call, I dropped some ladies off at the Marriott. I noticed that across the street there were some middle-age-crisis guys lurking outside a bar. They hailed me down and wanted to cruise through the Tenderloin to go shopping for a whore. They were ready to walk there before I came along. This is a bad neighborhood centered on "Klonopin Korner" where a lot of drug activity goes on. Some guy even threw a rock at me as I snapped a picture in the middle of the day! Anyway, I told the guys to save their money and that I was not in the mood to take them on a risky cruise. I told them to go back to their room and chill. I pointed out Brenda's advertisement in the local rag and said to try that route if they were committed to that type of monkey business. I think things worked out fine for everyone this evening in My Fare City.

Chapter Fifty-One

BEN FRANKLIN

Taxicab Regulations Section VI, Part D, subset 7
Drivers shall only receive a tip/gratuity when expressly issued by
the payee. Drivers may not demand, imply, suggest, assume, or
otherwise receive any additional charges unless permitted under
City Charter Municipal Police Code or the Chief's rules and
regulations.

It was Sunday and even though the Financial goes seven days a
week, it proved to be a very lame last night. Nothing was hitting.
It's like I was a step off beat with the world and the natural ebb and
flow of things. I really needed a good day and was not sure how it
was going to happen. I had a feeling My Fare City would be the
answer so I headed out because up to that point every other goddamn
order went against me. I had to keep my chin up and my head held
high as I toughed it out. Frankly, I had had it with playing the
Financial and I headed to North Beach hoping for at least a flag on
the way.

As I passed the Holiday Inn that sits between the Financial and
North Beach, I saw out of the corner of my eye the doorman flagging
a cab. Normally, I would blow by to avoid carting some tourist off to

dinner. However, this time I swung over two lanes and screeched to a halt. The doorman professionally opened the door and two fares got in the back seat. They wanted to go to the Sheraton Hotel. The man identified himself and his wife as being from Louisiana and said that they would like to see Ghirardelli Square first. OK, no problem. So we went there and I parked on Larkin Street and waited for them. In the meantime several fares checked to see if I was available, but the meter was still running and I had to refuse. I figured what the fuck, I would take care of the business at hand even though thirty cents a minute wasn't going to make me rich. I was relieved when the couple finally came back to the cab because I was ready to dump them as a waste of my time. The man said he had two more pictures left on his camera and he wanted to get some meaningful shots. I suggested Coit Tower, but he said they had tried to get up there Friday and couldn't because of the crowds. So I really started to lay it on thick like Mr. Tour Guide would and we headed up to Coit Tower.

We walked all around and I gave them a great tour along with some nice pictures of themselves to take home. In New York your camera might get run off with, but not in My Fare City. They enjoyed the tour around the famous tower and when all was said and done we cruised down to the Sheraton Palace at New Montgomery and Market. The meter read around $20.00 and the guy handed me a one-hundred-dollar bill and told me to keep the change. He said I was the best cab driver he had ever had and that he could have used me all week long. I knew I deserved a good tip, but not that good. But I'll take it. As I bid them farewell, I thought about how one event can change the spectrum of a whole evening. The rest of the night did not matter because the pressure was off. I quietly cruised through many fares smiling to myself about my new friend from Louisiana. Thank you for making my day, sir. I now have a new record for the biggest tip received and I doubt that I'll exceed $80.00 anytime soon.

Chapter Fifty-Two

MONDAY SERENADE

Taxicab Regulations Section VI, Part C, subset 8
Every Taxicab Driver shall use the waybill format as prescribed by the Chief of Police or the Chief's designee. The waybills shall be completed in indelible ink, and shall include the driver's signature at the commencement of the shift as well as the badge number and total number of hours worked. This waybill is to be filed at the Color Scheme's principal place of business at the conclusion of each shift.

I picked up a flag right out of the garage that wanted to go to the Financial. It seemed strange to be going back at quitting time so my mind began formulating questions. Was he a night person like me and so many others I have met? Was he a businessman, a lawyer, or a bike messenger? When I dropped him at 101 California, he paid up and gave me a couple bucks for a tip. He scurried off as another fare jumped right in and I took her out to Bernal Heights. After dropping her off I took a call for a pickup at Candlestick Park. Usually this is not a good idea, but I took the call anyway and got it as an "en route" to that end of town.

Finding my way out of Bernal Heights was a nightmare, but I

made it in good time. I zipped in through the gates at the park and saw some men who wanted to go back to the city; however, they were not the ones who called. There were no other cabs around so I told them to sit tight and I would do what I could and drove on. I found the radio call at the designated gate and when he hopped in, he told me to take him to the airport. I was hoping to "double up" and make some extra cash, but with one fare going south and the other to the north, the idea of doubling up seemed to be too complicated. As we passed the guys trying to get to the city on the way out, they asked again for a ride. The airport fare told me to have them jump in and to take them from the airport. Wow, now that was a good idea. The radio call gave me $20.00 for a $14.00 ride and the northbound cats from Denver gave me $20.00 each because I provided them excellent service. They needed a place to eat and were excited when I made them reservations at Greens at Fort Mason. They had about two hours to kill so I dropped them at Bix for a cocktail. After dropping them off, I felt pretty good because they ended up going to both places based on my recommendations. Things were shaping up quite nicely.

After working the Financial and getting some good rides to the Sunset, I ended up doubling up at the Amtrak. Funny thing about the Amtrak is that it is not the actual train station. The train only goes as far as Oakland and then a bus completes the journey, dropping you at the base of Market Street. Fares coming from here are often overlooked by cabbies because the nearby Financial District usually attracts them. One very large lady said she had been waiting over an hour for a cab. I don't believe she called my company, but nonetheless, I squeezed her into the back seat after I loaded her bags in the trunk. Two ladies going to the Wharf wanted to double up because they were anxious to go as well. When I dropped the large lady off, I backed into the driveway of her building to make it easier for me to exit. Only problem is she lives on a hill and she had to exit the rear passenger side door uphill. She got stuck in the door for a bit until I got out of the cab and pulled her out. The tourists going to the Wharf did not bother to pinch themselves. They were in San Francisco and a bit overwhelmed to say the least.

It was interesting to me to see the tourist's reaction to the situation. I have helped plenty of folks out of the back seat, but this was the first person in a while to get physically stuck. I tell you it was an uphill battle.

The Financial provided a few more fares for me until I took a friend to Cafe du Nord to meet a gal. Then the bars started to call right on time around midnight and I made a distinct transition from working the Financial to focusing on the Haight and the Mission. At 2:27 A.M. I crossed over Market Street from 3rd Street. It was a late Monday night and the anthill was empty. As I rolled up to a stop at Market I looked to my left and saw a lone sax player, Raoul, playing the blues to the ghosts swirling around the Financial. Except for me, there was not a soul in sight or within earshot. The sax sounded great as it echoed off the sides of the enormous skyscrapers and down the deserted streets. It sounded crystal clear because there was no other noise to drown it out. It was pure, fresh, and most definitely worth the buck I left in his case before walking away. It was an acoustically perfect studio. I left the motor off for a while to experience the full effect of the concert and was amazed that it was just Raoul and me on a corner that later would be infested with progress and numbers. For those fleeting few minutes, it was the most beautiful corner in My Fare City.

Chapter Fifty-Three

STREET PERFORMANCE

Taxicab Regulations Section V, Part C, subset 23
The taxicab vehicle suspension, steering, brakes, emergency brake
and exhaust system must be in good condition.

I was having a lousy morning, as I kept missing radio call after
call. Why the hell did I agree to take this daytime shift? I was just
not in the flow of things and needed a breather to collect my
thoughts, as what was left of 'em was not so complimentary. With
Union Square within spittin' distance, I descended down Powell St.
into the cab line at the Westin St. Francis. I noticed people lined up
to get in Sears Fine Food restaurant up the street. This place has
no affiliation with Sears Roebuck and Co., by the way. Thing is, the
place sucks, in my humble opinion. I mean waiting in line at The
House of Nanking is a rite of passage, but not this place. The only
meal I ever enjoyed at Sears was when an old woman who
complained about her food was silenced by my chivalrous gesture
of picking up her tab. The lady then came over and thanked me,
and would not leave my table until I promised to take care of her
parrot after she died. I hoped she wasn't going to keel over right
then and there, but I gave her my cell phone number to put in her

will, or at least in her purse for the time being. Too bad I have had to change the number several times because of resentful former lovers and bill collectors haunting me, both of which I have had plenty. I would actually make good for the old hag if I ever got the call. Of course my sick mind thinks that after she croaks, she just might leave her fortune to the parrot, with me to take care of both, but with my luck it would probably be just a fortune cookie to feed the bird. Anyway, that was my most memorable meal at Sears Fine Food on Powell, across from the famous doorman in the Beefeater duds at the Sir Francis Drake. It was definitely not for the food.

While sitting in the cab line on Union Square, I was bothered by some guy doing solo Shakespeare across the street. He was so loud and obnoxious about it he would have given a woodpecker a headache. At first I thought he was one of the crazies left over from Ronald Reagan lettin' 'em out, and very well may have been, but for the fact he broke his persona for a moment when I walked over from my cab to take a picture. I guess he found it humorous that a cab driver wanted to take his picture. He wasn't laughing when I went back to my cab without giving up any money, or maybe because I told him that Halloween is in October (I was in a lousy mood, OK?). The man I picked up from the hotel wanted to go to hell, I mean tourist hell, a.k.a. Fisherman's Wharf. I put on a happy face and we were on our way up and over Nob Hill en route to the Wharf. Rocketing up the hill, he asked if he could ask me something. As he had already done this, I replied, "You can ask anything you want sir, but I can't promise you will get the answer you want." He was not the first to inquire about my cab driving technique, referring to my feet working the gas and brakes. He asked why I use one foot for the gas and the other for the brake, and my answer was the same to him as those wondering before him: "response time." I went on to let him know that often I would be giving the vehicle gas while applying the brake; this would be categorized as kind of brake torque waiting to happen. "Brake torque" for those of you who actually never drove as a teenager, is when you apply pressure to the brake while gunning the accelerator, and then letting off the brake while the engine is at a high r.p.m. and doing a burner, or "laying some rubber" if I may be so bold.

So depending on the mood I may be in on any given day, my driving style may change. For that special descent down some of My Fare City's hills, I will use both feet on the brakes, always a magic moment, and usually in a spare cab to boot. Other times I will drive like I was taught in Driver's Education, using the right foot for both gas and for braking. I took Driver's Ed the last year it was offered at my high school, and got a C for those of you who were wondering. Little did my instructor, who was on loan from the Phys Ed Dept., know his student in the back row would be a shining star on the famed cobblestone hills of San Francisco (I think there are two of 'em, cobblestone hills that is).

Chapter Fifty-Four

BO BO NO NO

Taxicab Regulations Section VI, Part D, subset 2
No Taxicab Driver shall threaten, harass, or abuse any other person
while in the course of their employment as a taxicab driver.

I was on the road this morning before sunrise, and were it not for
a jumbo cup o' joe to warm myself up before my engine warmed itself
up, it would have been one rude awakening, for sure. KUSF was kickin'
out some funky tune that had dubbed-in sound bites from the classic
movie, and a personal favorite of mine, *Willie Wonka and the Chocolate
Factory*. Specifically, the part when Mr. Wonka, played by Gene Wilder,
is singing that macabre tune of fright while going through the tunnel
on the rowboat powered by those funky little Oompa-Loompa's. For
those of you who may have forgotten the words, here's the skinny:

> "There's no earthly way of knowing
> Which direction we are going
> There's no knowing where we're rowing
> Or which way the river's flowing
> Is it raining? Is it snowing?
> Is a hurricane a-blowing?

There's not a speck of light a-showing,
So the danger must be growing
Are the fires of hell a-glowing?
Is the grizzly reaper mowing?
Yes, the danger must be growing
For the rowers keep on rowing and they're certainly not showing
Any signs that they are slowing."
Willie Wonka

This beginning to my day was a flashback to my childhood, as would be the main event in a bizarre turn of circumstances that ensued. First off, I don't really like being taken back to my childhood unless I'm paying my shrink to take me there. Second, you push the wrong buttons my friend, and you had better hope I have been taking my medication. Third, the happy-go-lucky carefree child that lives in me, twenty-four hours a day, is just the resentful little shit you better be careful of. (My dad is constantly telling me to quit looking for the inner child, and start looking for the inner adult.)

The dub mix playing was innocent enough; it was after the flag that followed when things started to go downhill. The simpleton wanted to go to hell, tourist hell that is, a.k.a. Fisherman's Wharf. I was not thrilled about the ride but as I have said before, you gotta start somewhere—in my case, oversleeping and taking whatever came my way was where I had to start. Many things are new to me as I get the ebb and flow of being a day-tripper down, waking up being one of them. Alas, the fat lady having already sung, my days of starring in the night cracker suite are history, and good riddance.

After an uneventful trip, I parked my ride at the cabstand and opted to purchase myself a large coffee with a depth charge (shot o' espresso in coffee). Briefly, things went my way as the coffee girl at her stand gave me a buck off, giving me "employee status" as a worker in hell. I tipped her the buck as we in the service industry take care of each other, kind of an unspoken thing. I did appreciate the gesture.

As I sauntered back to my trusty steed, a clown greeted me, trying unsuccessfully to hold my attention; not knowing my span was much shorter than the beautiful Golden Gate in the distance. A picture of Krusty the Klown flashed through my mind for an instant as I smelled cheap booze on the clown's breath, and it wasn't even 9:00 A.M. for Christ's sake. It then comforted me to know there are those sicker than I out there, a disturbing thought unto itself. As I looked back at the clown before getting in my cab, he yelled over to me, "Hi, my name's Bo Bo!"

"bo-bo"

As I sat empty at the cabstand, time ticked away ever so slowly. Time passed, and business being slow for Bo Bo too; I was shocked by the alcoholic clown's decision to start heckling me. Oh it started innocently enough: He acted like he was trying to get me some business, when all he was doing was getting under my skin. In fact, his bogus clown epithets were scaring away any prospects left and right. I snapped a picture of him so he could be identified when I got through kicking his sorry ass. If the sadistic motherfucker only knew what childhood memory he had just unearthed. When I was still a twinkle in my momma's eye, she mailed away for some tickets to a TV show, *Bozo's Circus*. The tickets were revered, with a waiting list a mile long. Actually, receiving the tickets was as much of a ritual as getting a taxi medallion in San Francisco, both items being highly sought after and taking years to finally receive. So in my unadulterated youth, the news of the once-forgotten tickets arriving was, how shall I say, magical?

A segment of the show was called "The Grand Prize Game," reminiscent of playing the airport. The game consisted of throwing a ping-pong ball in a series of buckets, with number six netting you a shiny new bicycle. I was lucky enough to be chosen as the boy; they picked a girl too, to play The Grand Prize Game. I rose to the occasion, making the first three buckets. Then to my amazement, I made number four on a lucky bounce, and a year's supply of Jiffy Pop popcorn with it. I was trained at the local carnival that these things were rigged, but this was TV, and things seemed different.

Then was the time that separated the boys from the toddlers, the meters from the meter-and-a-halfs. I lofted the lightweight plastic sphere in an arc, praying to whatever god I had back then (I pray to the parking god these days) to help me get that shiny new Schwinn. It was an air ball—I had choked, and in front of not only Hemi, who I took along, but also the whole fucking TV-viewing audience. Controlled only by instinct, I clenched my fists and blurted out, "Awww shit!" Bozo ran up to me, cameras rolling and all, grabbed my shoulders with both of his stupid white-gloved hands and said, obviously trying to save face, "That's a Bozo no-no!" Still on autopilot, I retorted, "Can it clowny!" About as pissed off as I remembered being before I hit double digits. Cut to commercial.

I never got the Jiffy Pop, and was humiliated when, before the end of the show, I had to apologize, on the air and with my mom beside me. It was not a high point in my storied childhood, as my old man tanned my hide that evening. It hurt for days, though I did achieve a somewhat cult status with my peers for the duration of the school year.

Back at Fisherman's Wharf, I suggested Bo Bo move his act out of earshot, to no response. This sicko had nothing better to do than to keep using me as his shadow, and upon urging him to move along, I again got no response. I could feel the years of resentment, and the weight of my financially deficient day start to take over. I reached into my glove box and pulled out my six-inch locking blade knife, kept there in case of emergency. (Such as cutting off someone's tire valves? Next time, kids.)

I stepped out of my vehicle and opened up my trusty blade, the motion of me standing up ending with the "click" of the knife blade locking in place. Bo Bo heard the click and it's safe to say I got his attention with my shiny urban hunting gear. I ever so slowly walked to the front of my vehicle, lightly moving the blade across my unshaven face, for effect of course. When I got to the front of my cab I stopped suddenly and gazed upon my blade. Bo Bo asked me, "What's that?" He was stuttering a bit. Looking him square in the eye I said, in my best Travis Bickle voice, the now infamous line, "You talkin' to me?" Bo Bo quickly scurried off, looking once back to see if I was following. Lucky for him I did not.

The coffee girl smiled but refrained from laughing, not knowing if I was serious, I guess. As soon as I put the blade away some Asian tourists approached, giving me some sign language to ask if I was free or not. Obviously I was, and I motioned for them to get in, which they did and I affected an oh-so-timely departure from hell, past and present.

"pier 39—fisherman's wharf"

Chapter Fifty-Five

MODUS OPERANDI

Taxicab Regulations Section VI, Part D, subset 8
Taxicab Drivers or person(s) on their behalf shall not offer any gift, gratuity, or any thing of value in order to receive any preferred vehicle, assignment, dispatch call, shift, fare, or any other employment enhancement.

As a day man, I am allowed to drift on into the garage on weekends around midnight to start my shift, with the A.M. being the green light to start the ten-hour haul. Starting as P.M. literally turns to A.M. means it's a roll of the dice as to what kind of wheels you will get. On the other hand, business will surely be better on Saturday between the hours of midnight and daylight, than daylight on, for obvious reasons. It is very important to remember that playing in the night often resembles dipping into the ol' box of chocolates, lest we not forget our mother's advice that eating too many will give us a belly ache, and that we never know what we're gonna get.

As I sat around the garage after a minimal night's sleep, I looked at the sad sacks that were around me. There were some new guys who were told to come in early to get a good cab (and were taking the concept way too far) along with a few burnouts and soon-to-be burnouts like myself. I guess the one thing we all had in common was the desire to get on the road and start the ten-hour clock ticking, as sitting in the garage was not doing our health or sense of well being any favors. I was second up on the list, some tenderfoot got pole position. We arrived at the same time, but he got to the window to sign in first, as I had to lay a little cable in the executive washroom.

Having some time and an over-inflated ego to kill, I got my ass kicked at billiards by a guy twice my age. I was glad not to have wagered any dough, as for once I was following the "No Gambling" rule posted on the wall. I decided the next posted rule on the sign was worth breaking and spit on the cold and soiled concrete floor. Still waiting for a night man to call it quits and pull up to the pump, I sat down at the Cruis'n USA arcade game. Whoever installed this thing in the garage is one sick fuck, as you can tear through the streets of the United States of America starting in none other than Golden Gate Park and then moving on to the streets of San Francisco. Wreck your vehicle? No problem. Drive over 200 m.p.h. on city streets past cops coming head on? No problem. Run out of quarters? Problem. Finally, two cabs pulled in after what seemed like an eternity, one after the other. Before I even saw them, I could tell they were miles apart, literally. Poking my head around the corner I saw a shiny '98, and none other than the infamous Tijuana Taxi, having now been turned into a spare. The window guy saw the two cars pull in and yelled out the next two names on his list, the first I would not have the slightest idea how to spell, even having difficulty saying it to myself, with the second of course, "Carrrson!!"

I scurried up to the window as the window guy was writing the respective cab numbers on two blank waybills. As I peered through the bulletproof glass, I could see the cherry I was trying to pick. The window guy said I was second up as the new kid on the block was walking up behind me, not sure of the drill quite yet. Before I was told to stand down, I ripped a ten spot out of my pocket and shoved it underneath the protective barrier, with the airflow blowing it through and into his lap. He then slid the waybill I was looking for back under, and as soon as it was in my grasp, I headed for that fine American-made automobile, like Speed Racer running to the Mach 5. As I got in the driver's seat I could hear the new driver starting to whine to the window guy, realizing he was going to head for the border.

Having nothing short of a flashback leaving the yard at night again, and feeling somewhat manic from Cruis'n USA, I tore off into the cold night like a hot knife cutting into a stick of butter, for my bread.

Chapter Fifty-Six

THE CABS ARE FAB

Taxicab Regulations Section VI, Part D, subset 5
No Taxicab Driver may smoke, drink, or eat while a passenger(s) is in the vehicle.

When I hit the road this morning it was still dark, hence, the early bird gets the worm, I'm told. This concept seemed a bit far-fetched as I had not got myself a fare yet, and the only person I took notice of was a drag queen pushing his shopping cart past the front of the newly remodeled City Hall. It was a Kodak moment that found me out of film, and running a bit low on inspiration. I made a mental note and pushed on, over to Pacific Heights, with hopes of finding some stockbrokers on their way to the Financial. I was sorely disappointed with what I got.

I took a radio call in Hayes Valley, near the drag queen sighting. As soon as the old hag emerged from her doorway, I knew I had crapped out. When she got into the vehicle, I was overwhelmed with the pungent odor of what can only be described as a week-old soggy Filet-O-Fish sandwich. A light rain had started to make things worse, so I had no choice but to crack my window a bit. The only thing positive about this ride was she was not going too far, over to Geary and Fillmore Streets. As she was arguing with herself, I got a bit nervous and then she started shouting. A few blocks from her destination I pulled over, in front of the police station at Turk and Fillmore Streets and got out of the cab. "Ride's over lady," I said to her, standing in the drizzle. I asked her if she needed some help, and said that I would be happy to go get some. Seeing the cop shop, she must have made up with herself, as she got out of the vehicle and handed me some Paratransit script (voucher money given to the less fortunate so they can take cabs). I told her to keep it, as my company does not accept it, and now I was finding out one reason why. I jumped into the driver's seat and spun my tires on the wet pavement. The rancid smell stuck in the cab like a bad *Seinfeld* episode. I kept the fan on high and the windows cracked, but the smell hung around like an old bologna sandwich. I took a break for some coffee and fresh air, and thought to myself how the first ride of the day is a lot like a ball of phlegm at the bottom of your throat. You have to get it out of the way sooner or later, no matter how unsavory it may be to do so.

The coffee jump-started my body, and with the rain turning into a thick fog I was finally able to turn on the four forty air conditioning and forget about the wingnut that I got out of the gate. I wondered if my next fare would comment on the smell but the businessman had so much Polo on, it canceled out any prior smells I might have had in the cockpit. I secretly wished I had a Pepsi One. I dropped him off at the BofA building and got a five spot for a $4.80 ride. The Dow must have been down, hence, I continued on with a frown.

For no reason in particular, I headed to the other side of Market Street. I am one of those drivers who like to cruise, looking for that good load, rather than sitting in a line waiting for it, for the most part. I am a floater, and it's moving around in a kind of systematic/random pattern that I find my good fortune, though I don't see any good fortune until I have cracked the nut. The wind blew me past the Greyhound bus depot, not one of my most-loved pickup spots, where I saw a white guy wearing a poncho who was desperately trying to flag a cab. A yellow belly in front of me saw him but refused to stop. I had not had the greatest of luck thus far, but counted on it changing. Putting my best foot forward, I deliberately accelerated the cab into the pickup area, coming to a very sudden halt in front of him. He got in and said he needed to get to some ship down on some pier out in no-man's land to go to work, and he was running late due to several cabs refusing to stop. He seemed normal enough, but I'm sure Ted Bundy did too. I checked my guidebook for the pier the ship was docked at; it was way over on the other side of the city as I had suspected. Not a great area but I had been dealt the hand, now it was time to play. I turned on the meter and hit the pedal to the metal. His head went back a bit and due to my unsafe stop to pick him up and my quick start, I hoped he thought me to be a bit loony. KUSF covered the tunes.

After going deep into the wrong side of town, and so far out of the way, I was questioning my decision to pick him up, the pier finally came into view. Past the recycling plant and through the misty rain, a huge tanker sat docked, with a single plank leading up to a door in the lower half of the side of the ship. A bright light shone from within the hull, the only light for miles, other than the overhead I turned on in my cab to collect the dough the guy owed me. The ride being longer than he had anticipated, he grumbled about his lunch money being gone. He was talking to himself, sort of, a pattern that had emerged in my cab today. This guy was not crazy or on a cell phone but was fishing for some sympathy. By the bay, coincidentally. He had a twenty-dollar bill on him, and the fare was $19.60. I took the greenback and said he could have a few bucks back for lunch if he needed it. To my surprise, he refused. Happy to have made it in the nick of time, though he still had some sour grapes about his cash flow I guess.

"thanks bud!"

He thanked me and started up the plank into the ship. I was parked a few feet from the ship, unusually close to it, noticing the mammoth starboard side of the tanker towering above me. Before he disappeared into the vessel for his day of welding (his vocation), I yelled for the penniless seaman to come back. I popped the trunk and walked around to the rear of my vessel. I reached into the trunk as he stood quietly next to me. I pulled out my mini cooler and handed him my lunch, a chicken parmesan sandwich (I made enough for leftovers) and a Diet Pepsi (bought on sale). He graciously accepted the lunch and walked back to the ship, stopping at the entrance, turning around, and yelling with a smile ear-to-ear, "Thanks Bud, you have made my day!" I yelled back to him, "Later, Tater!" Then he disappeared through the shining hole into his place of business. I wondered if inside was heavenly or more on the beat of Poltergeist. A few hundred feet from the ship, I stopped and looked back. It was a mystic view: the light rain, the huge tanker, and the small light shining in the side of the ship. The scene was reminiscent of a movie, or maybe a foreshadowing? After he had walked the plank, I let the rubber hit the road for some more fun 'n games. With an open lot to squeal out of, I put it to the wood, and my trusty Crown Vic not only squealed the tires but all the engine belts as it came outta first gear. Mmm Mmm Good. I made a mental note.

As I drove back to civilization, KUSF was playing something by Cabaret Voltaire. The DJ came on afterwards and talked briefly about the band's first release, a seven-inch put out by them personally, an attempt at their own label, so to speak. Inscribed around the center of the vinyl are the words, "The Cabs are Fab." The DJ thanked all the cabbies driving around in the pre-dawn hours, mentioning one got her to work on time. I smiled to myself. Life was good.

Chapter Fifty-Seven

SOUTHBOUND

Taxicab Regulations Section XIII, Part A, subset 13
Taxicab Drivers who excel in customer service will be granted a fare to San Francisco International Airport by the powers that be, but like St. Nick, the powers that be know who's been naughty and who's been nice.

My senses were dull when I got my waybill, it was still dark and I was suffering from some serious bed head. My driver's license photo was more complimentary than my dull reflection in the thick glass, a testament to my morning. Pondering the bulletproof glass separating the window guy and myself, I wondered who exactly it was supposed to deter, cabbies or crooks. My thoughts stopped meandering when a light bulb flashed above my head that told me the management probably considers us one and the same. Takes one to know one, ya know, either or. As my waybill was slipped under the protective barrier, I switched the autopilot in my mind to on and headed off into the foggy pre-dawn hours.

I didn't even bother turning on my radio as I did not feel like

Speed Racer quite yet, and my ride most definitely wasn't sounding like the Mach 5. My engine had barely warmed up as I descended on Union Square, looking for some inspiration, but even more for a little luck. When I thought wearing a tie and working on a dummy terminal was my life, and I guess it was for a spell, my former boss used to always tell me, "Bud, sometimes it's better to be lucky than good." Wise words from the boss whose life I once saved (great job security). Funny thing, he was working on the premise that you need, or will have, one or the other, luck or skill. I had neither 'til well after sunrise, and what seemed like an eternity. I have mentioned before that if you do choose to play the hotels, you gotta be a home run hitter. Anything less than southbound to the airport will usually end up not only being frustrating but a waste of your time. Hence, I had made up my mind, or at least the part of it that was awake, that I would play a little baseball at the hotels in and around Union Square. As much as I often frown on the cabbies waiting in hotel lines for fares, these were the ranks I would join to begin today's journey.

"Cab line at the Westin St. Francis"

As I stepped into the dugout (cab line) at the Grand Hyatt, I sipped a hot cup o' joe I secured en route and browsed through the morning paper. Before too long, I was on deck, and then finally in the batter's box.

STRIKE 1
Origin: Grand Hyatt (Sutter / Stockton)
Destination: Cal Train Station
Time Departed: 7:12 A.M.
Time Arrived: 7:17 A.M.
Who: Two German women, mother and daughter?
Meter: $5.80
Tip: $.20 (foul)
Pain: Had Luggage (big tease).
Pleasure: Not speaking their language, all I had to do was smile.

STRIKE 2
Origin: Grand Hyatt
Destination: Wells Fargo Bank (Montgomery and Sacramento streets)
Time Departed: 7:33 A.M.
Time Arrived: 7:40 A.M.
Who: Two Bankers, mid-'fifties (at least lookin' like it)
Meter: $4.80
Tip: $1.20
Pain: Had briefcases that looked like small luggage.
Pleasure: I scared 'em a bit with my unsafe driving, with one saying I drove like a "hooligan." They told me to step on it initially, so I took this with a grain of salt and as a compliment. Remember, two of the biggest prerequisites of cab driving are to have thick skin, and an even disposition.

STRIKE 3
Origin: Grand Hyatt
Destination: 50 California St.
Time Departed: 8:02 A.M.
Time Arrived: 8:09 A.M.
Who: Businessman, around my age
Meter: $5.10
Tip: $1.90
Pain: Not only had luggage, but said was going to the airport
    later . . . in his rental car.
Pleasure: Friendly guy, tips were getting better.

. . . And yer out!!! That's out #1 (Grand Hyatt). I did not return to
play the not-so-Grand Hyatt again, having struck out, with the
luggage representing some good looks that ended up as pop
flies. With two outs left in my sadistic Abner Doubleday tribute,
I pushed on, this time to the Westin St. Francis, a hard luck
line for me in the past but with the sun peeking out a wee bit,
I got in the queue with the premise that "The Sun Always Shines
on Me." Funny, I know.

STRIKE 1
Origin: Westin St. Francis (Powell & Geary streets)
Destination: Ritz Carlton
Time Departed: 8:24 A.M.
Time Arrived: 8:33 A.M.
Who: Employee of Ritz
Meter: $5.70
Tip: $.30
Pain: Workers or Guests, The Ritz notoriously has very lousy tippers.
Pleasure: None

"southbound"

HOME RUN
Origin: Westin St. Francis
Destination: San Francisco International Airport (SFO)
Time Departed: 8:45 A.M.
Time Arrived: 9:05 A.M.
Who: A black guy
Meter: $29.90
Tip: $5.10
Pain: Some uncomfortable silences en route.
Pleasure: Made it south, to my own little United Nations.

Thankfully, I made it to the airport, and without even getting a full count. There are so many strange nuances that make up a cab driver's morning. No matter what piece of the daily pie you sink your teeth into first, I still say cab driving is about 90% luck. Other than the airport run, the most important part of my morning was no doubt the coffee I drank early on. A much-needed eye opener, the steam seeping out of the Styrofoam container reminded me of the steam pouring out of the streets, all over.

Chapter Fifty-Eight

THE EARLY DAZE

Taxicab Regulations Section XII, Part A, subset 1
If any section, subsection, subdivision, paragraph, sentence, clause, or phrase of these Taxicab Regulations or any part thereof, is for any reason held to be invalid or ineffective, such decision shall not affect the validity or effectiveness of the remaining portions of these Taxicab Regulations or any part thereof. The Chief of Police hereby declares that he would have adopted and promulgated each section, subsection, subdivision, paragraph, sentence, clause, or phrase thereof irrespective of the fact that any one or more sections, subsections, subdivisions, paragraphs, sentences, clauses or phrases be declared invalid or ineffective.

The first job I secured in My Fare City was one I will always remember with great fondness. Like cab driving, I kind of fell into it by accident. Funny thing, my pattern of reverse affirmative action was established even back then, when cab driving was just a twinkle in my bloodshot eyes. I was the last of a dying breed, I was a convenience store clerk. This racket is for the most part a "family" affair now, as the stereotype of the Middle Eastern store clerk really is true up and down the famed cobblestone hills of San Francisco.

Looking back, I had some strange foreshadowing of things to come in my life, though I had no idea at the time. Case in point. The night was a Saturday, one of my favorite shifts. Lots of cute women would come in, tired of all the Polo-stinking men trying way too hard to get laid. They in turn would usually be flirtatious to yours truly, as I did not stink of bad cologne or expect to get any of 'em in the sack. I was living in the real world; I was a fucking clerk for Christ's sake. The fog was thick and though we stayed open 'til 2:00 A.M. to service all the drunks in the Marina district, business was slower than usual. Around 1:00 A.M. with way too much time on my hands, I decided to perform a little experiment with the industrial BUNN coffee maker. What I had in mind wasn't rocket science, but more like rocket fuel.

I filled the coffee maker with the strongest espresso grind we had, using enough to kill an elephant, even a pink one. I could not believe it when the liquid slowly poured into the pot. I never intended this sludge for human consumption; drinking this shit would surely be risking life and limb. Remember, the only reason I even tried the experiment was that I had too much time on my hands and was, to be perfectly frank, bored. I mean this sludge could give some poor soul a heart attack at best. At worst? Let's just say I never want to have the heartbeat of a squirrel and find out.

After the initial brew was successful, I smiled to myself mainly that I did not make some huge mess. Phase one was complete with the advent of the liquid lightning in the pot. With this I retired to the back to prepare the ammonia and hot water for the nightly ritual of mopping the floor. I smoked a fatty of some kind buds to counteract being overpowered by the stench of ammonia, something I enjoyed very much. Feeling eerie, I emerged from the back of the store and immediately suffered a massive buzzkill. The shit had hit the fan. Someone had purchased a large cup of the sludge, as I noticed my experimental pot o' joe to be short. The pot was no longer full to the brim. My coworker affirmed some sad sack had just left with an extra large helping of the shit. He had no idea of the grave physical danger he had just put someone in. He was not at all happy after I gave him the facts on why I appeared uneasy. I was not looking forward to facing the consequences of my actions in this particular matter. What did I do? I did what any young red-blooded American kid would do. I closed the store early. A sense of well being wrapped around me like a warm blanket as I locked the dead bolt.

I turned out the main lighting and tried to mop up quickly with only the neon of the beer signs to light my way through the aisles. Just my luck on the final aisle, I heard a pounding at the door. My coworker affirmed to me, it was the guy who left with the experimental java. I had baked this cake and now I was gonna have to eat it too. As I slowly emerged from the back to face the music, I could make out a badge on the guys waist that only added to my anxiety. Even closer still, I could now clearly see him shaking his styrofoam cup. Boy, was I gonna be in the doghouse for this one.

I tried to tell the guy we were closed, hoping for an easy way out, but no such luck. As fate twisted one more time this night, I could now hear the guy's voice. He was asking me for a refill, I couldn't believe it! How could this guy want a refill, much less still be alive?

In all the confusion, the now infamous pot o' joe had not been disposed of. I hustled over to it and poured the wingnut a refill, on the house. Locking the dead bolt for the second time, I paused to wipe the sweat that had accumulated on my brow. Looking up, I could not believe my eyes. The man ran across the street and into the driver's seat of his taxicab, yes, taxi cab. As he laid rubber and sped off down the road, disappearing into the fog, my jaw was still dropped all the way to the floor. That was one crazy motherfuckin' dude, I thought, not knowing that years later it would be me walkin' in his shoes.

"Life is a test; if this were a real life you would
be shown where to go, and what to do."

Letters to Bud

BUD@MYFARECITY.COM

Saturday, February 21, 1998
Bud,
I rarely find anyone else with the presence of mind to speak what he thinks without reservation. What else can I say except . . . way to go.

Mara

Thank you Mara,
When you are in the position that I currently am in, you tend to see the agony and the ecstasy magnified ten fold. A lot of light is shining on me, but I brought the sun block. When I was young, my father always asked me at breakfast if I wanted "a sip of hot coffee to burn my mouth." I always refused, until one fine day I mustered up the courage, or curiosity, to take him up on his offer. I took a sip . . . and burned my mouth! I never much liked coffee after that.

B.C. over

Sunday, March 1, 1998
Hey B.C.,
One time me and my two buddies got in the cab, and as always the cabbie was foreign. My buddies pretended we were all gay and we

started hitting on the cabbie. I felt bad inside. After 15 minutes of poor humor I gave that guy a nice tip. Oh here's another . . . I did a bunch of Nitrous in a cab and the whole way I just threw the empty canisters on the floor.

Mr. Needlemeyer

Mr. N.,
Sounds like you might have some issues.

B.C. over

Wednesday, March 4, 1998
Hey there Bud Carson,
I'm a fellow cabbie in Wisconsin and I just wanted to say your stories are right on the money. Keep up the true to life tales of a S.F. cabbie.

Jeff Garcia

Jeff,
Well, I imagine things are not quite as liberal out your way, and the bud ain't as good . . . but you know first hand about the mystery of not knowing who or what you will see next, and this is a unique experience. Keep on driving and let me know how you fare. Keep the faith . . .

B.C. over

Friday, March 27, 1998
Bud,
I don't have a story of my own, but I always ask my cab drivers what their craziest stories are. The weirdest one I've heard was by a driver in San Francisco. He had a passenger ask him if he would watch him jerk off in the back seat for $10.00! The cabbie said he really needed the money at the time so he did it. He tilted the mirror back and watched the guy do the deed. The cabbie told us that he felt terrible afterwards and that he would never do anything like that again no matter how badly he needed the money.

BJ

BJ,
Like the sands through the hourglass, so go the days of my life. It's pretty intense all the life I am exposed to in just one evening. Each time I think I have seen it all I get involved in or am witness to some new strange fucking situation. This is real life, in your face kinda shit. You just can't avoid it because it will catch up to you sooner or later. Case in point. I had taken an airport fare to the south end of the city with a few minutes to spare to make a short back to SFO. As I approached the highway, a young guy was flagging me down while standing in the entrance to the freeway. Hmmmmmm. Maybe he lived to the south and would be a decent fare. I figured I would give it a shot and fuck the short. Well, fuck me silly because the kid wanted off at the next exit because he was headed back to the Tenderloin. I figured I would try to make the best of it and started to talk to the kid. I thought he was in his early twenties. He told me his name was "Sky" and he said that he was sad because his girlfriend of three months had broke things off. I thought to myself, "three months and you're feeling like that? What a puss. Too bad, so sad my friend." I didn't have the heart to tell him three months doesn't mean shit. But, I sensed that there was something else eating at his soul. I asked the kid if there was anything else bothering him and surprisingly he spilled his guts. It turns out the kid has been turning tricks for a gay escort agency in My Fare City. He told me he did it for the money, of course, and said he never told his girlfriend about it. I felt bad for the kid because he was wrapped up deep in a gay prostitution ring and all, but there was nothing I could do except talk with him, not at him, and hope we both might gain some insight into this game we call life. After confronting him and finding out the prostitution angle, I at least wanted to talk it over with the kid. He was not too happy with himself or his life. He was more upset about losing the chick than turning the tricks sucking dick. I think he enjoyed speaking with me because I had an open mind and chose to be a participant rather than a combatant in most matters. All I could really tell the kid was to be true to himself and everything else would move along as it should. As I dropped him off I knew he

got a lot off his chest. I bid the young kid from Boston farewell as he smiled and shut the door and walked off into Polk gulch, which is where a lot of male hookers hang out. Hey, you gotta do what you gotta do. Nobody said life was gonna be easy. The children of My Fare City need to grow up or continue the spiral down. It's up to them. I feel sad when I think about how I have to witness people's quest for money while I am on mine. Everyone has an angle and that's OK with me. I doubt I'll see "Sky" again but I do hope he finds a means to an end. The kid was the only thing that stuck with me from last night. Real life knocking at my door. Come on in I say and hit the meter for some more.

B.C. over

Friday, March 27, 1998
Hi Bud,
It's really cool to read your stories. I used to be a cabbie in Seattle, WA. It's like the last frontier, isn't it, always interesting, sometimes a little scary. I just wanted to let you know that your work is being enjoyed. You have done an exceptional job on your website too, it looks great (myfarecity.com). I will be bookmarking it so I can keep up with your adventures.

Lex Jarrell

Hey now Lex,
Thank you for your interest in my stuff. You mention the last frontier in your e-mail, I agree but would go further to say I travel where no man has gone before, on my way to the final frontier, or the "Final Final" (a local bar) in my case. Thanks for riding along.

B.C. over

Saturday, March 28, 1998
Bud Man,
I have this friend who does crazy shit when his buddies from college are in town. This one night we were headed to an after hours party after a day of boozing, and my buddy starts to take his clothes off in the back seat. We have about 5 people in this cab so the driver doesn't even notice what is going on. When we are almost to the address the driver hears a voice from the backseat, "Is this enough

of a tip for ya!" The driver looks in the mirror and sees this guy's ass right next to him. He scared the driver so much that he swerved all over the road. As soon as this happened, one of the guys in the back seat threw this guy's underwear out the window. We finally get to the address and the cabbie is PISSED OFF! We all jump out of the cab, including the naked guy who is only half dressed by now and without any underwear. I don't even remember if anyone tipped the driver. Sorry dude.

Richard

Little Richard,
Sometimes the force is with you while on others it is not. Last week a cab driver was stabbed to death in his Tenderloin apartment. Apparently he had an argument over $45.00. He lost. I do not know who the deceased cabbie is, but I do know he worked for another company. Anyway, it seems like a real waste of a life to me. I suppose it doesn't matter much especially when you consider how many people are killed each day. However, for myself and the other cab drivers of My Fare City, his death matters a lot because he was one of us. Cab drivers stick together even through a rare occurrence like that. For the most part I am good friends with most of the guys even though three of them really dislike me and are not afraid to let me know it. But don't worry because I do not let them get to me because the real test of a good driver is on the road and not with some stupid intimidation gig. I attribute the bad attitude of most cabbies to their cynicism because they have had to take in more of life's experiences than anyone ever should have to. A cabbie never really knows how they will react in a certain situation until they are actually in that situation. Most things, no matter how much you try to describe them, just can't be truly felt until they are experienced firsthand. I'll do my best to keep you riding shotgun but my conclusions about the situations that occur inside of and outside of my cab may be very different than yours because I have lived them whereas you are reading about them. I have been and will continue to be open with you about anything and everything that comes my way. Am I taking a risk? You had better believe it. But remember; no pain, no gain. Last night a doorman at one of the hotels I scouted finally came through for me. I told him that if

he gave me an airport run that I would kick him back $5.00. That's not a bad deal when you consider if a cabbie takes a fare to the airport they will get one back to the city. Double your fun, you know? Anyway, he had a couple of guys that were taking the red-eye back to Taiwan. It bothered me that they spoke in their language almost the entire cab ride. It bothered me so much I finally had to ask them to shut up. They looked surprised after I said that, but they did shut up. They mentioned how crowded Taiwan is with twenty-one million people now. Wow! I was more impressed with them than their country now that they decided to speak in English, fluently I might add. Just wait until old Bud speaks a second language, or do I now and just play dumb? But alas, our journey came to an end and their money was as green as the next person's. As they exited my vehicle, a man jumped in, said go to Fisherman's Wharf. He was fighting with another guy for the cab. Even though it is not allowed, I could do nothing to prevent the two men from entering the taxi. So, I played the classic "man in the middle" and got the one to the Wharf and the second to Mill Valley, which is just north of the Golden Gate. With $35.00 from the first guy and $40.00 from the second guy I was feeling fat and happy for sure. I made some really good bank last night and I will need every penny of it to keep one step ahead of the man. Everybody wants a piece of my pie even though only a few actually get as far as dessert. A meal with more than one course means more than one fork. A good friend told me that if I take big bites out of life I won't leave the table with an empty belly. But, in that same breath let it be known that I rarely bite off more than I can chew. Confucius say, don't be a cheapskate!

B.C. over

Saturday, March 28, 1998
Hey Bud,
I found your site through Netsurfer Digest and I must say that it is the most interesting site I have come across in a long, long time. It is very well written. I have a question though. You were talking about the doctor that you picked up at the SFO airport on the upper level. Why do cabbies get fined for doing this? Is that where the limos are supposed to go or something? My last experience getting

a cab was when I was going from Meigs Field in Chicago to the United Center for a Bulls game. I don't know if you're familiar with Chicago at all, but this cab driver was spectacular. It's about a 25-minute drive, because it was right before the game so the streets were all packed. We also had to stop at our hotel to drop off our luggage. This guy said we had no chance to make it to the game on time, however, he managed to get us there in 10 minutes because he really knew how to cruise. This cab driver was also cool because there was a big gas guzzling jeep in front of us and the owners were throwing beer cans and pop cans out the window the whole time we were following them. However, when we came to a red light and the trash continued to keep flowing out of their vehicle, our cab driver opened his door and yelled "PICK IT UP!" and one of the jeepers jumped out of the jeep and picked up a few cans. I guess some cab drivers are also environmentalists. Anyway, I appreciate your site! Thanks for the stories!

Mikey Beckman

Hi Mike,

To answer your question, the airport rules are loading and unloading on the upper concourse only, baggage claim and ground transportation down below. All the cabs wait in three lots that slowly inch toward a toll booth where they stick us for $2.50 before we even see you. Keeping the taxis all on the lower concourse does avoid total confusion, not that there ain't plenty of that already on both levels. The airport has a taxi detail that directs and flows traffic through the waiting lots to the lower concourse, and eventually out of the airport. This detail was recently taken over by the San Francisco Police Department, lucky them. It's my personal opinion that it's best to avoid any or all conversations with the police, for whatever matter. I'll be showing you a picture of bartertown, and a few other hot spots, soon on the website. As for your Chicago cabbie, any back road, oh I like Mike, I do I do, and I think I like green eggs and ham too! I DO! I DO! Us cabbies are a mixed bag of nuts for sure . . . To put it into context; sometimes you feel like a nut, sometimes you don't, and sometimes you just don't feel at all.

B.C. over

Monday, March 30, 1998
Bud,
One time I had to get from North Beach (San Francisco) to Palomino's in a hurry to meet a friend at 8:00 P.M. on a Friday night. The cabbie was so sweet that I decided I would sing to him so I picked a fun song. "I Say A Little Prayer For You!" by Dionne Warwick of course. "The moment I wake up, Before I put on my make up, I say a little prayer for you . . . blahbitty blahbitty blahbitty . . ." He thought I sang so well (or so bad) that he gave me the ride for free!!! I tipped him a ten spot!

Kim

Monday, March 30, 1998
Hi Bud-O,
How do I get in touch with you when I need a ride. I am a good tipper and live in North Beach. Thursday, Friday and Saturday are my usual "need a cab" nights!! P.S. My father from Daytona Beach found your website!

Kim

Kim,
Good for dad, man have I had a few drunken spring breaks out in your neck of the woods. I always ended up staying in Ormond Beach, with the working class. Me and my partners in crime had to dig a septic ditch for our friend's father's place we were staying at. A magic moment I assure you. That same year several pounds of coke drifted up on the local beach at sunrise. We never got closer to it than the local paper. Hope to see you on the road. I'm all over North Beach.

B.C. over

Tuesday, March 31, 1998
Hello thar, Budman!
First of all I must comment that I am truly "captivated" by your website. What a perfect name for a wonderful read! Your method

of execution reminds me of one of my favorite authors, a woman by the name of Terry McMillan. Ever read her? Check out a few of her titles—she is instantly recognizable. I really want to say that I think what you are writing is essential. It gives me and the world a chance to see the other side of a job that I have absolutely no personal knowledge of. I live in Tampa, and we just have no need for a taxi unless we are totally trashed out in a bar with no one to take us home. (I never allow myself that situation because I'm 41 and know better at this ripe old age.) I am planning to visit your website on a regular basis because I really like the way you relate your life's happenings. It's as if we were talking on the phone. Keep up the good work, Budman. It seems your writing venture will be as beneficial to you as it is to your readers. Perfect therapy! (I envy you!)

Best wishes, Sunni in Tampa

Sunni,
Thanks for your kind words. I'm not very "well read" but will check out Terry McMillian as I do have the chance to catch up on my reading while waiting at the airport. Since becoming a cab driver, I have read quite a bit, more than before I started drivin', for sure. My favorite writer and greatest influence would have to be Hunter S. Thompson. "When the going gets weird, the weird turn pro."—H.S.T. Now that sums it up.

B.C. over

Friday, April 3, 1998
Nicely executed site and good stories. Tip o' the hat. Attached is a cabbie ditty I made up while driving for Veteran's in the eighties, when the flag dropped at $0.60.

The Light
Turn off of Union onto Van Ness
Hassling the brakelights, god what a mess
If I can just pass on this muscle van
I'll make three straight green lights, yes I can

But then this Wah Ching in a 280 Z
Slams into the hole where I hoped to get free
Sometimes you're just gonna lose the light
This suit in the back says my meter's fast
Spillin' paid-for whiskey from a stolen glass
He's gettin' cute about the route but I let that pass
I got eighty bucks over gates and gas
He thinks he's a lawyer, I think he's a load
One more one-liner and he's back on the road
I like to look'um in the eye when they get the light
Sometimes ya feel so isolated and small
Shadows of angel dust crawling the wall
There's so much ugliness to come
You're shakin' hard, your face is numb
You know you can't count on your own suicide
You're just gonna have to ride out the ride
You're just gonna have to keep gunnin' for the light

Yellow cab creeping in the left turn lane
He must be greenpea, doesn't know what he's sayin'
He thinks he's cutting me out for the light
Wants to put a rotten spot in the night
To make it in the city you gotta be slick
This dogfight attitude is makin' me sick
One eye on the rear view mirror and the other on the light

Burning brakes, imploding steel, bloody fingers on the wheel
Shattered plexiglass reflecting flares
Half-drunk drivers stop and stare
The last thing on her mind was fixing her hair
She probably died in clean underwear
Reminds you to remember to keep your eye on the light

I heard last night in the shit and the rain
I wasn't surprised, I didn't feel pain
They told me old friend you finally went sane

Over Fort Point off the southbound lane
It's red up ahead but I stand on the gas
No way muthuhfuckuh you're gonna pass
Everybody sometime blows the light

Chip Seward

Chip,
Hit the road last evening and headed to the Financial District because I figured it would be busy especially since last night was a real dog. I was driving eastbound on Bryant Street towards the Hall of Justice which is the local courthouse/jail (a.k.a.: the little shop of horrors) when I saw a lone man trying to flag a cab down. That is never an easy task especially during rush hour. I told myself that I had to start somewhere and I may as well pick him up because who knows where his destination is. So, I pulled up to the guy and as he lumbered into the back seat he directed me to the Cal Train Station. I was disappointed to hear him direct me there because it was only a few blocks away. However, this was the exact kind of situation I needed to exploit in order to have a good night and I was sure glad I didn't smoke my lunch or my wits would have been dulled. On the way to the station, I asked him what he was doing at the courthouse. So, he told me his story with a thick Slavic accent. Paul, it turns out, is a real well-to-do guy and the owner of a 1980 Rolls Royce. Well, kind of. His Rolls was ripped off from in front of his country's consulate building at 550 Battery earlier in the day. I immediately asked him where he was taking the train to. He told me that he was going down to Redwood City which is about ten minutes south of the airport. After I heard that, I immediately turned around at the next stop light and said to him, "Paul, if you really drive a Rolls you ain't gonna be takin' no train to Redwood City. I can take you there for about $75.00 and you don't have to worry about no train and shit." He scoffed at the $75.00 and told me it was too much money. We bounced the price around like a ball falling down in a game of pachinko. The ball stopped at $50.00 and we were off. We had a nice chat on the ride and Paul turned out to be a real nice man. Although I still wondered where his Rolls was and if I might

chance upon it later as I was driving around. To be honest I would not have been surprised to see a couple gang bangers out joyriding in it. I have to admit my mood did sink a wee bit when I could not change the $100.00 bill he handed me. I wish I would have gotten the C-note, but no such luck. Still, $50.00 was a good start and it is always nice to have a good start. Thankfully, traffic was good and I dropped him off and got back to the airport within an hour or so. After an average wait at the airport I picked up a family of Swiss folks and no, their name was not Robinson. I dumped the parents and their three kids at the Hotel Monaco which is not a bad place and felt good about building up the quick $80.00 gross. So, off to the Financial I went because I did not want anything more to do with the airport unless I chanced upon a ride back to it. No such luck. I did pick up a businessman in South Park near where the jet engine was fired up earlier. I told him the story about Paul and his Rolls Royce, because his office was next to the scene of the crime. His only retort was, "There goes the neighborhood!" How profound. Anyway, most of my fares heard that story last night. Soon after dropping him off, I was on my way to the Castro with a guy from the Financial I drove home the night before. I explained to him that our meeting like that was like plane crashes and that they come in threes. I would see him again in the next day or two and then it might be a while before the next three rides. I don't think he understood the logic even though he smiled at the observation. After I dropped him off, I drove around in no specific direction with both my radios turned down because an old friend had returned a call and confirmed some bad news for me. I talked with her for a while as my heart weighed heavy again and I realized the weight of the world and how short life could be. I am reminded of this periodically and it's usually about as subtle as a slap in the face with a baseball bat. I really consider myself lucky to even be here to tell you this at this point in time after having so many close calls with that big scrap yard in the sky. I figure there must be a reason I'm still here. I mean, if my number came up, if it was time for my ticket to be punched, it would have been by now. Anyway, I will wait to tell you the sad news because as of now I am still having a tough time believing it myself. In time it will be known. After some heavy moments, I ventured to a radio call from a local Sushi restaurant. A few drunken women needed a ride to another bar and oddly enough inquired about local strip clubs. I rolled with it and advised them that the O'Farrell Theater on Polk Street and O'Farrell is by far the best strip club in town. They said they wanted to know so they could go with their guy friends who were also in town on business. Funny thing is, this weekend is the big Gay Pride Parade, which is an institution in My Fare City and with good reason. I do hope my mom is not upset that I am still unmarried and living in the gay capital of the world. I used to think that because of so many same sex relationships that it would be easy to find a nice girl. No way. More often than not, I end up taking a girl out on a casual date only to find out that she likes girls and will someday only use a man to have a kid. Well, let me know because I don't foresee any love on the horizon. However, it's always darkest before the dawn.

B.C. over

Wednesday, April 15, 1998
Dear Bud,
A group of my girlfriends and I were in Cozumel, Mexico many years back. Being one of our first Mexico trips, we of course thought we were on top of the world. The island is beautiful, but we had to take a cab to the small town to eat or shop, etc. Well, we were not only drunk but probably doing a few other things to go with it when our cab driver, who spoke no English, drove 100 miles an hour to blow our minds and then just stopped and abruptly in Spanish said what we thought was "Get Out." So, one of us opened the door immediately and a motorcycle slammed into the door! We never knew what happened to any of them. Us not speaking the language, feeling no pain and being a group of girls alone, just walked off. I still wonder to this day what happened to the cab driver and the motorcycle driver. Poor guy! We never could remember if we paid him or not.

Sharon

Sharon,
Sounds like a tip to remember.

B.C. over

Wednesday, April 15, 1998
Hello Bud,
Just wanted to tell you a story and also tip off other gals out there
that SF cabbies are hot, eager, and willing. Recently I was stood
up. All dressed up and nowhere to go. I called a cab. Not sure
where I was going but didn't want my new stockings and panties
to go unseen. The cab driver who picked me up was a real
sparkler. Big brown eyes, voice that brought my blood slowly to
a boil. He spoke of his hometown, of his lost loves. I sat in the
back seat and wondered what his hands would feel like on my
breasts and whether or not he was the kind of guy that would
appreciate my stockings, my full-bodied look, my thighs
squeezing his torso . . . I directed him to take me to China
Basin, I was thinking of doing the salsa at Jelly's. When we got
to the parking lot, I realized many of the cars had people in
them, windows steamed up. Lover's Lane? You betcha. But why
feel left out? I asked the cabbie if he'd like to "park" with me.
Nothing like loving in the backseat of a Luxor. By the time the
cab stopped rocking, a small crowd of teenagers had gathered
at the windows. We gave them a laying "O" and they gave us a
standing "O." Heaven.

Awilda

Awilda,
Speaking of Luxor . . . come visit www.luxorcab.net, for a peek
inside my world Awilda . . .

B.C. over.

Friday, April 24, 1998
Bud,
Sounds like you're having a hard journey at times. But in the words
of John Burroughs: "The flowering of man's spiritual nature is as

natural and as strict a process of evolution as the opening of a rose or a morning glory." But there is this difference: while the plant must have a congenial environment, the human flowering often takes place amid the most adverse surroundings.

Stanford Pepper

Dr. Pepper,
Sometimes it's better to be lucky than good . . .

B.C. over

Wednesday, April 29, 1998
One time I called for a cab after an extended stay at the local pub. I asked the driver if he minded if I put a 12 pack of beer and a pizza in the front seat. He said no problem. It was then that I threw up in the seat . . .

Uncontrollable

Uncontrollable,
That would cost you twenty bucks in my cab, along with the beer and pizza.

B.C. over

Monday, May 4, 1998
Nice writing. Good, genuine ring to the stories, like a tire iron hitting the pavement.

Jim

Jim,
My trusty tire iron is multi facet, it's safe to say. So far it's just been used to fix a few flats though I have had it in my hand ready to fend off a violent fare. The guy turned out to be so wasted, and broke, I just dragged him out of the vehicle and onto the curb. (We were at his home.) So ya see, it's not just a figure of speech that someone might end up "in the gutter." What a rude awakening I thought, too bad, so sad, life in the city ain't always pretty.

B.C. over

Monday, May 4, 1998
Dear Bud Carson,
I got lucky! I sit in my cubicle answering dumb questions all day and trying to look busy. While I sit here, I surf around looking for something of interest to help erode the time. Normally I find triple X sites, strange act sites and magazines. Today I found "My Fare City." It was great reading! For a moment I remembered what it was like not to worry about how "successful" I was or what I should be doing to make more money. Sure, I like money just fine, but sometimes it gets to be too much of a hassle. Your stories remind me of the real world right outside my door, almost like another dimension. We all seem to live in our own little circles that occasionally touch at the edges. Keep writin', I'll keep readin'.

Dave Strapko

Dave,
Thank you for checkin' in and hoppin' a ride with me. I, like you, used to sit in that cubicle all day. I feel pretty fuckin' liberated now. I still have my ups and downs, but having a job whose description covers every letter in the alphabet is always an adventure. I truly am my own boss, sometimes for better, sometimes for worse. I'm a natural at sales and I work every angle to make sure I'm gonna get a happy rider and a good tip. On occasion, sensory overload occurs and my morals get confused with my mission. Whatever happens, I'm here to tell. I am the man on the other side of the mirror.

B.C. over

Wednesday, May 6, 1998
Hello Bud,
Remember, if you're not here to write the stories, we can't read them. If Nietzsche wrote, "That which does not kill us only makes us stronger," then it must have been Nietzsche who said, "That which does kill us makes us dead."

Wild Bill

Wild Bill (a.k.a. Sweet William), a legend and an institution, was shot in the back while playing poker in Deadwood. Sometimes life is a gamble, perceived or not. I think Wild Bill knew his number was gonna be up soon, but he still kept playin', cause that's what he did his whole life, always pushin' the envelope. Always being true to himself.

B.C. over.

Thursday, May 7, 1998
Mr. Carson—
Did you really jump off the Golden Gate Bridge?

Matty Foxley

Matty,
Sure did! Funny thing, after I got out of the bungee jumping business my dad mentioned that I went and found the only job more dangerous!

B.C. over.

"bud jumps off the golden gate bridge"

Monday, June15, 1998
Hi Bud,
I like your articles! Could you tell me how steep the streets are in your city? Good luck with your life and your city.

Palten

Palten,
Have a look at San Francisco's Steepest Streets!
1) Filbert Street between Leavenworth and Hyde 31.5% grade
2) 22nd Street between Church and Vicksburg 31.5% grade
3) Jones Street between Union and Filbert 29.0% grade
4) Duboce Avenue between Buena Vista and Alpine 27.9% grade
5) Jones Street between Green and Union 26.0% grade
6) Webster Street between Vallejo and Broadway 26.0% grade
7) Duboce Avenue between Alpine and Divisadero 25.0% grade
8) Jones Street between Pine and California 24.8% grade
9) Fillmore Street between Vallejo and Broadway 24.0% grade

B.C. over.

"steepest streets"

Thursday, June 18, 1998
Hello B.C.,
How ya doing, man? Thought you'd like a quick note from someone in good old England (Winchester and Guildford). I've got to say a big THANKS for producing such an entertaining and enlightening read with "My Fare City"—I am truly hooked. I've been tuning in since the beginning and believe you offer an insight into other cultures and experiences I have never got from anywhere else. Although the taxis in this country do work long hours, they seem to have it somewhat easier than you do. There are virtually no guns or weapons of any kind in day-to-day life, and serious drug heads are few and far between. As our cities are generally smaller, a higher proportion of the cab rides are for longer fares—my brother and I are well known to our local cab companies and we pay an average of £8 (about $15, I think) for a 5-mile journey. Well, I won't bore you with any more, just to say thanks again, and please keep it going. Loved the piece on your daylight adventure to the darker side of the street, by the way. Please feel free to write back if you're curious about anything on this side of the big pond.

Simon Goodwin

Hey now Simon,
Thank you for your interest in a very strange side of life indeed. I have had some shit go down since being employed as a San Francisco taxi driver for sure. As to you spending $15.00 on a taxi ride, you would surely be on my list of "regular riders." I always say that thick skin and an even disposition are the prerequisites for driving at night in My Fare City. I am making a point of hanging around with new drivers as to do everything to keep my outlook fresh or at least as honest as possible. It seems with each week passing, my days off provide more and more the deprogramming needed for the coming week. You keep checking in and I'll keep driving, alone but one with the streets and my ride.

B.C. over.

Friday, June 26, 1998
First let me say that this is a cool page and I have read all your stories. I just got back from Las Vegas. I have been there at least twenty times. The cab ride to the Stardust was $17.30 and with tip

$20. The cab ride back to the airport three days later was $8.30 and $10 with tip. Thank me, thank me very much. P.S.—Your Bannanaz comparison about "the problem was it was the brown acid" made me laugh out loud . . .

David

David,
LOL.

B.C. over.

Monday, June 29, 1998
Hey Bud,
Another fan from the other side of the Atlantic . . . As an American living in the UK, I love reading the dispatch, drawing me back to the life and memories of people left behind. So often, the chord of "been there, done that, seen that" is struck in your powerful imagery . . . I love it so much, I send your address to everyone I know who is an Americanophile—so they can see the alternative vision of what life is really like for those not privileged, as so many are not. Love ya, guy.

Michelle

Dear Michelle,
So glad you were able to flag me down. I am happy to know that you are able to hop in for a ride, and from so far away. I will be the first one to say, driving a cab is one strange fuckin' business. I am one of those folks who has had my finger in just about every pot, but this one is the most bizarre without a doubt. I have grown up more than I could ever have imagined driving my nights away, which is better than the Kenny Loggins song, "Driving My Life Away." I'll stick with the nights. Thanks for your support; it's great food for my soul.

B.C. over.

Saturday, July 4, 1998
I just wanted to drop you a line to say thanks for putting out all your great stories. I really enjoy them. I myself am a cab driver too in the great city of Cleveland. Not as busy as where you are

over there but busy enough to support my family and spend time with my little girl. Well, I'm running off now, just wanted to let you know that I really enjoy your stories and to keep them coming.

Tim Monde (cab 812)

812 over . . . 812 over . . . hmmmmm, must be off the air. Hey now Tim, so glad to hear from Cleveland, I am still upset about the whole Browns thing, but I guess they will play in your city again. I salute you for supporting a family and driving to do it. Life ain't easy, and some of the shit we have to put up with, well, let's just say we don't get paid enough. Barring personal safety, of course, and unlike say, a waiter, if someone is too rude or has broken through my "glass ceiling," I can at least kick their ass out on to the street, which does happen on occasion. It's almost always drunks, and this fact alone keeps me from hitting the sauce like some folks do. Day drivers tend to drink to excess, mainly because they all get off work between the hours of 2 P.M. and 6 P.M. I would drink too if I got off then. In fact, way back when I thought the nine to five was the answer, I drank way too much. When I get off work there are no bars open, leaving me to ride my bike home, fire up the PC and anything else I might have, and write while it's all still fresh. Without documentation, driving nights would end up like dreams, if you don't get it down, it's lost in a blur of people, places, and situations. Funny thing, like you, I am off to another fun-filled night on the streets of San Francisco, hope your night went well, and of course I hope to find that diamond in the rough myself.

B.C. over.

Sunday, July 5, 1998
Mr. Carson,
You tell our tales well . . . The stories I have in my head from 10 years of cab driving. I am now driving in northern Maine, I've driven in Reno, Carson City, Lake Tahoe, and next year I'm moving to Boston. Once again I'll be driving. It's the only job I have ever had that I like to do . . . even years later. I just crawled outta my cab three hours ago, and what am I doing? I'm reading about it (laughing). Keep the stories coming.

Andrew

Hey now Cabbie!

Bud says beware of Boston, I hear it's a tough cab town, but then again I'm getting my info from riders, not drivers. I often ask myself how the fuck I ended up driving a cab, and like many things in my life, a situation presents itself to me, and I will usually bite. Thank god I don't have a mortgage or a wife, or a girlfriend, or even a boyfriend, even though Bud don't play that. Could it be the hours? Probably. Still, the amount of short-term relationships I have is fuckin' amazing. From the hookers who call me direct on my cell, to even the people I pull up to at a four-way stop sign at the same time, they all fall in to the category of relationships. Most are short ones, though certain characters keep themselves in Bud's life either by chance or fate. I would have never thought that "the streamer guy" would give me joy and a smile on my face each time I run across him. Still, I wish I could meet a nice girl who works nights, there ain't too many. Case in point, a cute nurse I was driving to work commented how she got off at 7 A.M. OK, she was cute, worked nights, and was not wearing a ring (us guys always check this). Upon arriving at her work, I turned around and told her I had been looking for her since my first day as a cabbie, and that I thought she was beautiful. I did not want to lay it on too thick and scare her while I did want to get my point across that I would like to see her again, on or off the clock. I gave her my business card, which has my cell phone number on it. She never called. Onward we go, where to, we never know. I will always give life "the old college try," forgetting I never graduated. Good luck in Boston, be sure and check back with the goods and don't forget to keep the sunny side up and the greasy side down.

B.C. over.

Sunday, July 5, 1998

Hey Bud!

Probably your farthest fare ever . . . all the way in Belgium. Reading My Fare City puts me right back to when I lived in the Bay Area for 10 years. It's like being "home" again, and reminded of what's important in life. Hope to catch a ride with you next time over in SFO.

Karin

Hi Karin,

So glad to hear from another rider from way over yonder. Life is most definitely like a box of chocolates. I have a special connection with Belgium wouldn't ya know. My senior year of high school I lived with a fellow student and his parents who moved from Belgium. Mrs. B, as I called her, was an angel. She would make me and her son eggs every morning. This was especially nice after a little wake and bake. She would put different meat in the eggs, usually spam. One day she tried to give us eggs and tongue, that's when Ken, her son, and I had to put our foot down. I guess the moral would be we went to school hungry, though we never got slipped some tongue from her again. Happiness to ya and thanks for flagging me down, from so far away.

B.C. over.

Sunday, July 5, 1998

I got hooked on "Waybill" several months back, and check back at the beginning of every week for your latest post. I just wanted to share a few thoughts with you. Bud, I guess you don't spend a lot of time hanging around the garage and playing cards with all your cab driver buddies like the TV show. I remember Alex's first line was something like, "Oh, he's an actor, he's a boxer, she's an art dealer, me, I'm a cabbie." Another thing, I was in Baltimore a month or so ago and didn't at all care for the cab service. First, they charge you by the time, which bothers the hell out of me, because you're just sitting there watching the meter run at a fucking red light. Second, none of the cabbies talked, and third, every time I got in one, my knees would dig into the "cage", which, ironically, were not used by any of the drivers. I was thinking these guys need to go to the Bud Carson Cabbie School. Keep 'em coming, Bud, and I'll keep flaggin' you down every week for another ride.

Mark

Hey Mark,

I do hang around the garage, but not as much as the new guys who play the waiting game for a cab. I have to show up between 4 P.M. and 7 P.M., grab my waybill and hit the road for a fun-filled ten hours. Tonight should be a real interesting one as I got up this morning to travel back to the Bay Area at 5 A.M., and I won't get off work 'til 4 A.M. tonight. I do smell a short shift if one is available, if not, oh well. As to the lame cabbies in Baltimore, I cannot speak for them but will say it has got to be a tough job in any city, thank god I drive in the capitol of the universe. Also, I am interactive in the way I will talk to you if you wish, and in English. Only a handful of the cabs in My Fare City, including the one I drive, don't have a shield. I like to think of myself as the shield. I have already sized you up and given you the shoe test before you sit down in the back and shut the door. I am sure I have had some runners that ended up liking me enough that they decided not to rip me off, still, in these situations, I guess I'll never know. One possible runner situation was a few guys I picked up from "Dead Head night" at Nikki's, a bar on the Lower Haight. They first needed to go by the park to get one of their backpacks they had hid in a bush. The one guy returned and we were off to the corner of Market and Van Ness, a perfect corner to ditch a cab driver. But during the ride I spoke of all the shows I had hit, and how I missed Jerry. We connected, and they paid, and tipped me. I was surprised to say the least, I would have for sure pegged these guys as runners, goes to show, ya never know. On the subject of the *Grateful Dead,* check out this great photo essay my friend has at *igc.apc.org/deadheadsontour.* Hi ho, hi ho, it's off to work I go.

B.C. over.

Monday, July 6, 1998
Hey Bud,
I enjoy reading your tidbits about cabbie life. I love cab rides. They are never boring. I love it when I leave a bar or party across town and step into a cab, a bit drunk and eager, and just sit back and relax till I make it back home. What's really intense is the time from the moment I put my hand on the door handle to when my ass kisses the seat—that whole fluid motion overwhelms me with joy. For me, it compresses the electric experience of urban life all into a few seconds. I also love the speed. I love being in the back seat

alone and contemplating wherever or whatever I was doing that evening. People say they get their best ideas on the toilet. I get them alone, in the back of a cab. If I ever made a movie, I would include an abundant amount of cab scenes—in the most romantic scope as possible, without excluding the vulgarity that the driver experiences. I would capture the truth of the experience, as well as its undeniable sensuality. My most recent cab drive, about a week ago, was with a guy who, when he saw me flagging him down, ditched his coffee break to pick me up on Market St. and drive me up the hill to the Masonic auditorium. We bonded within minutes and he gave me a card with his private pager number so I could call him for a cab anytime. After keeping it in my pocket until the end of the evening, toying with the idea of using it, I threw it away. Not because I am a young woman and this isn't a world one can trust. No, what really made me dispose of the card was that if I did have my own cabbie, it would only steal away from the pleasure of the experience as I know it.

Kimberly

Hey Kimberly,
Thanks for your interest in My Fare City, I agree that flagging a cab is as much a singular experience for the rider as well as the driver. As I have stated before, long rides and cute gals get my private line, which after handing out the number over a period of time, folks usually called only when it's raining or when they are in a pinch. Unfortunately, this is when I am the least available. I had hoped to get a few regular riders, who in turn would enjoy my company and tip well. The experiment flopped. I no longer give out my number and use the phone for emergencies or when I'm going from the airport to a "Destination Unknown" (I used to love that song). I know, the '80s are over but on occasion I will burst a fat cell in my brain and it all comes back. You are right that we live in a different world today. When I grew up, I played kick the can with all the kids from my hood. Today, parents and people are much more careful. I recently saw a film presentation titled "Why You Are Afraid." It was a series of educational films shown to baby

boomers. If you had seen these as a child, you would be scared of the outside world in a big way. My personal favorite was "Death Zones" (school bus safety). They had a kid from elementary, middle, and then junior high all get run over by a bus. The setup for each death was even more bizarre. "This bus driver has a perfect safety record, but before the end of the trip, someone will die!" The first to go was little Nikki Quean who got run over after running back to fetch her homemade valentine that dropped in front of the driver side front tire. Anyway, you get the picture. So many personalities come and go from my cab that if I don't provide some sort of documentation it will end up in a dream we both dreamed, one time long ago. As I don't intend to get rich driving a cab, contact me should you need a "technical advisor" on the flick. For a real good visual on taxi driving, check out HBO's "Taxi Cab Confessions." It will provide a visual to what I write and live each day I get behind the wheel. As far as anything being vulgar to the driver, sex is not one of them. I always get a smile and chuckle to myself that someone might be so brazen as to map out those uncharted waters. It's only if someone pukes or ditches me on the fare that I would consider vulgar. And even then, time marches on.

B.C. over.

Tuesday, July 7, 1998
Bud,
Keeper comin' . . . I miss driving in the cities . . .

Andrew

Hey now Andrew,
Glad to have you along for the ride. Just remember, always fasten your seat belt. It's the law if you are in the front seat or in any seat on the highway. What a stupid rule, made even more stupid by the law in My Fare City that it is actually legal to not wear a seat belt if you're a cab driver. To make matters even more confusing, a San Francisco cab driver has to belt up on the highway, but is the only one allowed to drive without a seat belt in the city. And the best

thing I learned at cab college is that it's legal to drink in a cab, except for the driver, unless the driver is in the back seat. It's like they figure we will probably end up in the back seat or something. I'll have to admit I have. Been in my back seat that is.

B.C. over.

Wednesday, July 8, 1998
G'day Bud!
'Ows it goin? Just found your site last week. I too am a fellow cabbie (at the moment just trying to put myself through uni—could be for a lot longer) working nights in a small town/city in New South Wales, Australia. I gotta say, great site!! As you would probably guess, the working conditions around here are a bit different to what you'd probably experience. For starters, this is no big city. The closest "real" city is over 200 kilometers away with nothing much in between. Only about 30 cars operate in this area, all controlled by one company. Out-of-town fares (generally around 20-30 km distance) are fairly commonplace with tippers, however, being pretty hard to come by. In my first week working, I scored a return trip to the coast ($300 return) though haven't had one quite that good since. Anyway gotta go but will write again.
Keep it up, Cheers

Kev

Hey Kev!
Thanks for flagging me from down under. I always like to hear from another driver. I just worked on one of my days off this week. I got a beater of a car and worked the sympathy angle hard. The vehicle was an old police car. I could tell by the speedometer. It went up to 140 m.p.h. where as the car would shake violently at 60 m.p.h. It didn't break down so I shouldn't complain. It's interesting that most any cabbie you talk to has had one paramount ride, a diamond in the rough I like to say . . . My experience has found cab driving to be 90% luck, so good luck down under!

B.C. over.

Wednesday, July 8, 1998
Dear Bud,
Awesome bit of poetry (Blue Sky). Have you ever read Charles Bukowski? He is your LA counterpart. Please take that as a compliment. I have read just about everything he wrote. The movie "Barfly" is about him. I have read everything you have written but I don't want to pump you up as a writer because I want to keep reading about your scene. You are truly a great writer. Thank you.
P.S. If I am ever in town I will bring a "Seattle Fattie" with me and look you up.

David

David,
Thanks for the kind words. I am fortunate in life that I have been given many of God's gifts. I find when I am true to myself anything is possible, even if it's just living to tell.

B.C. over.

Thursday, July 9, 1998
Bud Boy,
No offence mate but you sound about as interesting as a barn door. I've had better nights in a Swansea Night club with a fisherman's parrot. TAXI Driver? It's not vocation of the year, is it.

Jason Cicero . . .

Jason,
I personally suggest some Prozac; just to balance things out a bit, mate. Still, I would like to hear more about the parrot, and you don't even have to say a thing about the Fisherman, I'll use my imagination stud boy. Don't forget about that ol' barn door, you know the one. It always leads up to the haystack, where you can be anyone you want to be. Any comments are welcome Jason, have a beautiful day. (Read the Celestine Prophecy) P.S. No offence Cicero! Stand tall, be cool.

B.C. over.

Thursday, July 9, 1998
Hello Bud,
What's up man? I found "Captivated" a couple days ago and I have
been checking it out ever since. Keep it going.

Dan

Dan the man!
So nice of you to flag me down, enjoy the ride around Never Never
Land.

B.C. over.

Friday, July 17, 1998
Hi Bud,
I generally tip 15 percent in smaller towns and 20 percent in larger
cities. Is this about right?

Jim

Dear Jim,
Any tip is good tips though usually folks will tip up to the next buck
plus one or two more. Thirty percent of my money I make in tips so I
feel that friendly service and good driving should make a difference.
The definition of tip is *to insure promptness*. Now I would agree with
this but only after you get in the cab, not the time you might wait to
get one. Don't try for a cab in ess eff this Thursday, JULY 23rd, the
new moon (all drivers will be on strike).

B.C. over.

Tuesday, July 14, 1998
We have a lot in common even though I'm not a cab driver, I admire
your profession, it can be a rough ride, with long hours, and you
have to deal with some real assholes, I'm sure. I live in Omaha,
Nebraska, and I'm training to become a chef. I've been learning
my trade for about four years now, and I have some stories as well.
I think you have great talent as a writer, and I really liked your
story on life on the street. From the above it may not seem like I

can relate to your profession but I've seen the same characters all over my town. I've given a few bucks to everyone who at least tries to entertain me, and to some who I thought really needed the money, and like you, I feel the guiltiness and sadness that hangs heavy in the heart at the sight of these poor lost souls with no hope. Anyhow, thanks for listening to me and maybe I'll get some reply from you, if not, oh well. Thanks for your time.

Gavin

Hello Omaha!
I do have a few pals in your neck of the woods. My only experience in Nebraska is driving through it. If my memory serves me correctly (it doesn't always), I stayed in Lincoln on my way out west. It's nice to see middle America flagging me down. I often pick up chefs in training at The California Culinary Academy in My Fare City. When you feel the need, the need for my My Fare City, transfer those credits and "Come on Down!" as Bob Barker might say. I will give their site to ya (baychef.com). I am glad you share my sentiments regarding panhandlers bordering on street performance, they may not even know they have made it up to the street-performance level, and the ones who don't realize this are not just fresh, they be funky fresh. I would have never found "The Brazenhead" restaurant except for the fact I have a crazy chef friend who cooked at many different places during his time here in God's country. The worst place would have had to be the Black Angus chain in Vallejo, and the best of course being the Brazenhead. There was one lesbo restaurant around 24th and Noe that he got fired from. They should have stuck with all lesbos on the staff, he was out (wo) manned and outgunned. Working the night shift, it ain't gonna be easy finding someone who can tolerate all of my bullshit. Someone out there has what I need, and at this point, working nights and living a bit free and easy isn't a mutually respectful relationship. For Christ's sake, I went from working 9 to 5 in a suit and tie to undressing and sleeping from 9 to 5. Just like when I rolled and totaled my uncle's Blazer, I ended up on my wheels facing the opposite direction. Keep the sunny side up and the greasy

side down, and this goes for on the road, or in your case in the kitchen.

B.C. over.

Friday, July 17, 1998
Bud,
Your diary of driving really struck a chord with me. I can't help but think you are leaving out the most important people and things in your life that you feel, think, and care about—somehow. You have the makings of an interesting writer and you'll just seem to be getting somewhere and then you sputter out. You aren't staying with the thought and I am left wondering what really happened, what you really felt. Stop holding back! Often people have an eye to current and future readers when they write. It seems you're making things lighter, cheaper, easier, less intense. Why? For your "readers"? For friends? Are you afraid of what's really real in your life? Dance as if nobody's watching, love like you've never been hurt—and write with your heart and mind and leave fear out of it. I look forward to watching you develop. Keep passing the open windows.

Victoria

Victoria,
Fuck You, you sound like my ex-girlfriend.

B.C. over.

Monday, July 20, 1998
Hello Bud,
My Fare City is my home, but with such a grand world I have to explore I don't find myself there very much anymore. In New York, and readin' the tales is like being there. Don't ever stop.

Tizoc

Hello Tizoc,
Thanks for the vote of confidence, "East is the least, West is the best!"

B.C. over.

Tuesday, July 21, 1998

Bud,

I was just reading your waybills. Man it must be a lot of craziness to be a cabbie in San Francisco. I work the cab life in Milwaukee, and can only imagine the cabbie reality in SF. Lots of thanks for putting your life "on line." P.S. Go CUBS . . . Take care and keep up the good work, BC!

Beer City

Hey now Beer City.

I'm thinking of a cold Lieny and how innocently it goes down and how the hangover comes several hours later, headache city. Tune in to 92.7 "The Bear" in the greater Chicagoland area. The afternoon DJ is one of a kind. Mary Beth, whoever you are, I gotta say you sound mighty sexy over the radio waves. Spin some Jerry for ol' Bud and who knows, we may someday find each other traveling on that road of life and turn to each other and smile.

B.C. over.

Tuesday, July 21, 1998

Hey Bud,

You are truly a wild child! I have enjoyed your writing since the site has been up. Thanks for staying alive through it all so I can hear all your stories.

Charlie

Chaz,

I seem to remember some 500 mics we both ate on a sunny afternoon, in the land of plenty. I won't go on, but will say thank you for getting me to God's country. I won't forget sitting in the doorway of Saks 5th Avenue at Union Square waiting for you to come rescue me from the jowls of the big city. I remember taking some cash out of a machine at Opera Plaza and distinctly remember you telling me what a dangerous location that was. What a joke that seems like now.

B.C. over.

Tuesday, July 21, 1998
Just finished looking at your page and found it really interesting. I
have been a cab driver here in Christchurch, NZ. and some of your
stories bring back memories, others really amaze me. Good page,
keep it going.

Sheldon

Thanks Sheldon! Do you all really eat that adorable Kiwi bird? And
does it taste like chicken? Inquiring minds wanna know. Glad to
have you along for the ride, hold on tight, cause things just get
more and more bizarre, and the scary part is I feed off this like a
plug snug in a socket. P.S. My only memory of anything about New
Zealand is that little Kiwi bird. Strange are the memories we hold
on to, while burying others so deep they are snuffed out, at least in
this lifetime. Any major unresolved issues in life end up being
"bumped" into the next cause you never resolved it on this go
round. Oh yeah, and you guys Bungee jump, eh?

B.C. over.

Wednesday, July 29, 1998
Hey Bud, we talked briefly into your tape recorder at the "Further
Festival" on 7/24. I didn't see it on your web page yet, when is it
going up? Your page is great!!!

Ian

The Further Festival was epic indeed and I am currently working on
the chronicle of the event. Since that show, I have seen "Phil and
Friends" at the Fillmore, Bauhaus at the Warfield, and most recently
a friend got comp tickets to Emerson, Lake, and Palmer with Deep
Purple headlining. I think I covered the '60s, '70s, and '80s. Of
course this does leave a void for the '90s, but they're not over yet.

B.C. over.

Monday, August 10, 1998
Dear Bud,
I read of your site in the *Yahoo* magazine. It took a bit of hunting

to find it. *Yahoo* wasn't much help there. But I enjoyed reading your stories once I did. Must admit, I was kind of hoping for the type of rides from HBO's taxi confessions. But I guess every night can't be quite so exciting. Thanks again for a good read.

Jo

Yo Jo!
Yahoo! You found me! I am so glad to have someone find me out of that article. For those of you who haven't seen the story please pick up a copy of *Yahoo! Internet Life* magazine (Special Anniversary Issue, September 1998, page 84). I am in the article on "How America Uses The Internet." You know I do knock the Bud Carson who was a famous football coach out of the #1 spot on all the search engines I have tried when putting in my name for the search. I am assuming this is how you found me. Nice work!

B.C. over.

Friday, August 14, 1998
Sitting here in Seattle on an early Friday morning (can't sleep) and stumbled across the Captivated Site and your story . . . very cool . . . and I must tell you that every cab experience that I've had in San Francisco has been better than the one's here in Seattle. Although I do keep riding them . . . probably for the same reason that you keep driving . . . it's always interesting. I am a DJ (radio) here and thrive on personal experiences like this . . . keep it up. By the way, what do you think of KFOG? And is there a style of music that becomes the "soundtrack" for your adventures? Cheers!

Dean

KFOG puts on a great fireworks show every year for their "KFOG Sky Concert." They try to put a soundtrack to the fireworks show. Great idea, bad execution. KFOG's ads say it has "true variety." Also pictured on the ads are Tom Petty, Eric Clapton, and some other dinosaurs. I most definitely have a soundtrack to my night. 90.3 KUSF and 90.7 KALX are my top two for "Bud's evening soundtrack." You might hear some techno, house, blues, really anything goes. Also mighty fine are 89.5 KPOO for reggae and 91.1 KCSM for jazz. What do all these stations have in common? No commercials. I drive many a DJ around every evening. I can see them comin' with those cases of heavy vinyl and immediately pop the trunk. DJ's, as with most folks in the service industry, will give you a good tip for a good ride. For a real treat, check out The Skinny.

Wednesday, August 26, 1998
It seems like your nights run like ours (6 P.M.-6 A.M.). We are cabbies in Lima, Ohio, husband and wife. Drive safe and catch you later.

John & Ronda

John & Ronda,
Unfortunately, or fortunately, depending on your point of view and state of mind, they only allow us to have the cab for ten hours a shift. I think the few hours the cab gets to rest after the night shift helps extend the life of cab and the driver. Staying up past sunrise gives me the blues to boot. Thanks for checkin' in, I love hearing from other cab drivers. Funny thing, after I watched the tape I had of HBO's "Taxicab Confessions 5" before work the other day I ended up feelin' like I worked an extra hour. Go figure.

B.C. over.

Saturday, August 29, 1998
Bud,
4x40, I love the phrase! As an office worker I don't deal with people who provide the need for 4x40 air conditioning (thank God!). Keep the fares coming . . .

Dave Beedon

Dave,
Thanks for letting me vent!
B.C. over.

Sunday, August 30, 1998
Hey, Bud!
Awesome site. Very nice graphics and layout and your stories are raw and pretty cool. I've only gone through a couple so far but will be back, for sure. Believe it or not I play in a band with someone

you know way up in the north woods of Wisconsin. Yep, ol' Wild Bill Rodencal himself . . . A way cool dude and lots of fun. He clued me in on your site. I'm a forty-something high school art teacher myself, but at least I survived the seventies with most of my brain cells intact. They may be a little brightly colored by now, but most are thankfully still working. I understand my friend Larry is flying out to Frisco this week, and your escorting him around (?). Good luck, and keep him safe! Good seeing the site, and I'm drooling over Bill's "Mountain Grown Donkey Dick" stories. Onward and upward.

Mark

Dear Mark,
Isn't it great when ya burst one of those fat cells and everything bothering you gets washed away in a sea of good cheer? I sure think so. Oh yeah, make sure to never call My Fare City "Frisco." True story, two escaped convicts were questioned in Berkeley, CA. by a police officer as to where they lived. He knew they were not locals and ended up making the arrest after they referred to San Francisco as "Frisco." Don't get caught using uncouth grammar, being a teacher and all. Stand tall, be cool.

B.C. over.

Saturday, September 5, 1998
Budman,
Just read your story of the hearing. The photographs made me feel as though I had been there. Funny what one notices in a photo: In your first one, the bright yellow newspaper dispensers jumped out at me. Question: When you say that the wheelchair people were "crab cakes," do you mean that they were whiners? Janet Reno was there to see if there was reason to appoint an independent investigator to look into the possibility of a connection between the number of cab drivers in San Francisco and the death of Vincent Foster.

Dave Beedon

Dave,
Whatever you say guy. I'm just glad to have another chapter closed
and an uncertain future ahead. Two out of three voters in My Fare
City are anti-Willie Brown now. I'm surprised it's taken this long.
As far as the handicapped folks in attendance were concerned,
they just did not have anything positive to say, but I'm glad they
had a chance to speak. I hope the 50 new wheelchair cabs will shut
them up for the near future at least.

B.C. over.

Tuesday, September 8, 1998
Hey Bud!
Hope things are going well. Have a good, end-of-the-summer
vacation. I think I may do the same.

S.

S,
I hope this email finds you healthy, wealthy, and wise. As the summer
comes to a close I look forward to at least the healthy and wise
part staying up to snuff for myself. No cab driver is wealthy or
he would not be cab driving.

B.C. over.

Sunday, September 13, 1998
Dear Bud,
You dropped my wife and me off at a little Chinese eatery, in San
Francisco a few weeks ago . . . It was late on either a Tuesday evening
or Wednesday. You then gave me a piece of paper with your URL.
Thought I'd drop you a line and say g'day from Australia. Hopefully will
get back to SF in the next couple of months or so. Didn't mind the last
trip. Saw heaps of the city. Not a bad place—very similar to Sydney,
Australia, except we didn't build the city on a fault line! Anyway, you
can't help bad luck! Catch up with you later . . .

Gavin Brown

Dear Gavin,
Yeah, I remember. I hope the nutty husband and wife at The House of Nanking treated you with a good meal even if the place is somewhat crazed. Thanks for checkin' in. See ya down under someday.

B.C. over.

Thursday, September 17, 1998
Bud,
Just read your waybill on the 400 new cabs hittin' the streets of The City . . . Once again you guys get screwed without any gel to ease the pain. I like that there was such a large turnout of the local cabbies and fat cat politicos . . . Shit, they even had to invite Janet, the woMAN, Reno to see this fight. Nothin' like Slick Willie politics in SF. I myself just got the boot from my job. Oh well, life goes on. Shit, now I can finally see my kid, Jack, and play some golf instead of getting it in the butt from my boss. On an up note, how about the CUBS and Sammy "The Man" Sosa. He's da MAN, said SAM. Later from Milwaukee . . .

Sanswen

Hey Sanswen,
No doubt the new cabs will have an impact on the industry as a whole, but as long as my vehicle does not have any impact, I will roll with the punches.

B.C. over.

Friday, September 18, 1998
Your writing style is really great, kind of like a detective who crashed and burned, cynical yet humorous. I enjoy reading fiction about SF, as I am sure many people who live there do, but it would be a good book with great stories.

Anonymous

Anon,
Who said anything about fiction?

B.C. over.

Monday, September 21, 1998
Bud Man,
Ran across your site by accident, but what a GREAT surprise!!! I couldn't stop reading it . . . I was CAPTIVATED from the very first paragraph :-) I will be coming back often! Keep writing . . . and STAY COOL BUD!

S. Simpson

Thanks for stumbling across the site, it's usually me who gets to stumble from order to order, night after night. I have been through quite a bit since I began relaying my "tales of the city." I have not only lived to tell but have learned a lot about humanity along the way. Keep checking in and I'll keep it up. Captivated as a whole is an avenue that I drive along, and let you take it all in. As it should be. Trust me when I say it ain't easy being me, but who better to guide you through the madness and adventure My Fare City offers, for those who wish to take the good, and the bad . . . Oh yeah, the ugly too.

B.C. over.

Wednesday, September 23, 1998
Hey! What has become of Bud Carson? This is the second week of no-show for him. I'm having withdrawals! I will be forced to sue for mental anguish if this keeps up. Sing like you don't need the money. Love like you won't get hurt. Dance like nobody's lookin'.

Tonya

Hey Now,
Check out BUDCARSON.COM and find out!

B.C. over.

Wednesday, October 7, 1998
Hi ya Bud.
I've been reading your stories for some time now. Love your site. Great stuff! I'd been driving a cab for three years myself, in Brisbane, Australia, until The Man took away my drivers license. So many of your stories applies equally over here too. Now I'm on the unemployment heap, trying to find another job sans a drivers license. It ain't easy, gotta tell ya. At least the dole here is fairly easy to get, and keep. I'll be off the road until March next year. But at this point I fully intend to start cabbying again. I think it gets in your blood. But apart from that, it suits my preferred (single, unattached, and circulating) lifestyle. I used to pick the cab up at 3 P.M. Friday afternoon, and keep it for the weekend, then return it Sunday night/Monday morning. The rest of the week, I had to myself, to do whatever I wanted. I generally put in approx 42 hours driving out of the 60 hours I had the cab for, so I figured, that's enough hours per week for me. I work to live, not live to work. I get the same cab every week. Was a nice brand-new one too . . . well at least it was when I first got it. Had 302k's on the clock, but that was 9 months ago. All the cabs in Brisbane run on Gas (not Petrol). We have three types of pay-ins here. 1) Driver takes 45% of shift's take and the Company/Owner pays for fuel, 2) Driver takes 50% of shift's take and half of the fuel bill, or 3) Driver pays a set amount for the cab for the shift, and pays for the fuel. Personally, I do #1. It makes me enough. I generally take home $560 for the weekend (before income tax). My personal arbitrary target is $500, so any I make over that I see as a bonus. I really should be doing #3, seeing as I'm considered to be a "top gun" driver. Gas is cheap. From memory, the set pay-in for the days I drove is $509. If you do the math, you'll see that I'm ripping myself off severely. $560 is 45% of what I take. At that is approx $1250 gross for the weekend. Subtract my $560 and the $509 pay-in, that leaves me with $181 and the fuel bill for the weekend would approx be $70-$75. Tops. So, I'm stiffing myself over $100 a week. I should be doing #3, and mind you, this is during the medium part of the year. This time of year, NOW . . . geez . . . I'd be starting to ROLL

in the money. When I get my license back, I'll be doing some re-
negotiating with the company, I think. I drive/drove for the Yellow
Cab Company. They have been voted best cab company in Australia,
with the cleanest cabs, and the friendliest drivers . . . etc. etc.
(rolling eyes). They've never screwed me, so I don't screw them.
All our phoned-in jobs are given out via computer screen in the
cab. The fare rings the Co., and the operators put the job in the
computer. Our ranks system works thusly: All suburbs/areas have a
plot number. For instance, Coorparoo, a suburb of Brisbane, is
designated 124. OK. A car in the AREA plots area 124 in the computer
and joins the Queue. If he is the only cab in the area and is #1 in
the computer, he gets the next job available. Meanwhile, he is
hotfooting it to the rank, because, if another cab gets to the rank
before him, and plots in rank 124, the ranked cab becomes #1 in
the queue. We have the old radio setup too, built into the computer,
but only ever use that if the computer crashes, or if we need to
make an inquiry to the Query Operator about the job, or anything
else (like calling in radar traps, or mobile patrols :o)) We don't
have the graft here, to get a good cab. Don't have to pay the
dispatcher to get the good jobs. Basically, the new guys get the
clunkers. The drivers that show themselves to be competent, and
don't bend metal, get the good cars. That's the theory, anyway.
The Query Ops have been known to give some "good" jobs to their
mates, but we don't live in a perfect world, do we? Good ol' mobile
phones. Funny enough, the area I live in, 191, is also the cab number
I used to drive, pure coincidence. I've driven various numbers
before I became a known quantity to the Car Manager, the last
ones I drove on an every-week basis before getting #191, were #26
and #308. I shared the cab with one other driver, who drove it
during the week, Andrew. He was in the original #191 when it got t-
boned by a Ford F-100. I turned up for the start of my weekend,
expecting the old one, and here's this shiny brand-new car. Woo
Hoo!! So this NEW cab had more chance of staying in good condition,
longer, than most other cabs with only two drivers. Most drivers do
a 12 hour shift. Not many drivers get to keep the cab to take
home, like I do/did. Just the reliable ones, and those unlikely to

take the car and bolt interstate. :o Oh yeah . . . we have a population of approx 800,000, and we have over 1000 cabs in Brisbane. I'm not sure of the exact number, probably around 1300-1500. With 3 companies competing. Yellows (the BEST), Black and White (2nd best), and BC's "Brisbane Cabs", with the fewest on the road, but I digress. I have a gripe. What's happening??? I'm missing my weekly fix of reading your stories. I hope I haven't bored you with my tale. I really hadn't intended to say so much. It just all came out! First pic is yours truly with my ride, and the other, a view of cockpit, showing my CD player velcroed to the dash. Pics were taken with my Ricoh DC-3 digital camera, and modified in Photoshop to ease transfer via email. I have some more pics of around Brisbane, if you are interested, for your site? Cheers, and stay safe.

Chris Linek

Chris,

Nice ride my man! The pictures are great, truly inspiring. It is wonderful to hear from cabbies abroad, though it seems like you guys down under don't miss a beat. Remember ol' Bud needs a little R&R now and again. My cab number should have been 5150, that's an American term for getting locked up in a mental hospital for 72 hours against your will. For drivers who really need a break there is being 5250'd. This one keeps you medicated and in a smock and socks for 2 weeks. How would I know this, you ask? Good question. As for paying taxes . . . in the States you don't have to file if you make less than $7800 per year. Cash is king. I would love to get some more mail/photos from you anytime friend. My readers have been a bit hungry as of late with me taking a holiday and all. Cheers, I'll tell ya about being 5350'd and conservatorship some other day. P.S. Your steering wheel is on the wrong side of the cab! This would surely make for an eventful night in My Fare City . . .

B.C. over.

Thursday, October 15, 1998
Hi there Bud. This is Bob here, I've just recently started on an internet course which is how I came across your web page. I have downloaded

all your past stories and have still to read them all. I have also printed them out and passed them on to fellow taxi drivers who are not on the net. I will let you know the feedback I get from them. I can see from just reading some of your stories how much the similarities are from taxi driving in your Fare City and my own. I will finish off just now but if there is anything you wish to ask me about taxi driving in Glasgow I will be happy to oblige.

Bob

Thank you for spreading the word according to Bud. I really like the fact I am reaching other cabbies "off line." On that note I wanted to mention I taped the HBO special "Taxicab Confessions" recently. It came on at 11 P.M. so I just popped home to start recording it so I could watch it the next day. The program, for those of you who have not seen it, is actual video of passengers in the cab. They don't tell the folks they are being taped until after the ride. Then, those who choose to, let them use the video on the program. I would venture to say a tidy sum of cash exchanges hands. Anyway, I put it on and watched the one-hour show before work the next day. It was awesome, as true to life as I have seen other than my personal accounts. Only thing, after the hour program, and an hour or two into my shift, the only feeling I was left with was that I had worked an extra hour. Go figure.

B.C. over.

Friday, October 23, 1998
Hey Bud,
Welcome back. I hope you're OK. That one about the Cubbies certainly tops any of my own experiences with carting celebs around town . . . you da MAN!

Chris

Hey Chris,
Thanks for checking in, mate! I have learned in my recent travels the wonder of Vegimite! On toast of course. Not bad for a hangover, that's for sure. I don't get how Vegimite works though. I had only previously heard it mentioned by the band "Big Country." A very

nice gal from down under (Sydney) introduced it to me. Vegimite: Yeast Extract, Salt, Mineral Salt (508,509), Malt Extract . . . mmmmmm, Natural Colour (150), Vegetable Extract, Thiamine, Riboflavin, and Niacin. I especially liked the fact you get 91 servings per package! If anyone would like further information on the wonders of Vegimite you can contact Kraft Foods at: Kraft, 850 Corimer Street, Port Melbourne, Victoria, Australia. G'day friend. Remember, for all you do, this Bud's for you.

B.C. over and under.

Sunday, October 25, 1998
Dear Bud Carson,
Just read about your encounter with Steven Spielberg. Sounds like fun, but I wish you had asked about what Bruce Willis was wearing.

Anonymous

Anon,
Didn't want to "ruffle any feathers" ya know.

B.C. over.

Monday, November 9, 1998
Hey Bud!!!
It's me again . . . S. Simpson (S standing for Sandy). *smiles*. You gotta be doing something right cause I just keep coming back for more! *Grins*.

Sandy Simpson

Hey There Sandy!
I do so love my regular riders. Funny thing, most cabbies you really don't get to know, especially on any kind of personal level. In my case, it's an open book, or website to be specific. As I am back on the road after a brief but well-deserved hiatus, I am finding many things different, while still other things remain the same. I feel a lot like David Byrne at the end of the movie, "True Stories." If you haven't had the chance to catch the flick I'll try to briefly summarize the end. As he (David Byrne) is driving through a barren and desolate

part of Texas he mentions to us about how when you first come to a place it seems so beautiful. You notice how blue the sky is, how green the grass is, the birds, and how everything seems so new, so vivid. But after you have been there awhile, you lose that perspective. Deep thoughts for sure, but oh so true. I am glad to report that things in my world look beautiful and new, once again. Lightning doesn't often strike twice in one's life, but if and when it does, don't take it for granted. Take it as a blessing, and take it to heart.

B.C. over.

Saturday, November 14, 1998
Bud man,
I'm hip to a "fatty," but who is Mr. Brownstone?

David (I read 'em all) Hofford

David,
I used to do a little but a little wouldn't do it so the little got more and more. I just kept tryin' to get a little better, a little better than before. I was dancing with Mr. Brownstone, he kept knockin', he wouldn't leave me alone. I thank my lucky stars that ol' Mr. Brownstone didn't end up leaving me with a tombstone.

B.C. over.

Saturday, November 21, 1998
Bud!
We have nothing in common. Still I follow you. You have made it.

Ann Renneus

Thanks for your kind words Ann,
I wish to live ever as to derive my satisfactions and inspirations from the commonest events, everyday phenomena, so that what my senses hourly perceive, my daily rides, the conversations of my passengers, may inspire me, and I may dream of no heaven but that which lies around me.

B.C. over.

Sunday, November 22, 1998
Hello Bud,
Yep, that's the cabbie profile, all right. Had to get to East St. Louis one night. Cabbie says, "Yer lucky you got me. I'm the only cabbie that'll go there." He got a pint of rye and a .45 auto out of the fare box on the floor, took a big slug out of the bottle, tucked the pistola under his leg, and away we went. Looking forward to your stories.

Jerry

Hello Jerry,
Jung said it best, and I quote, "The meeting of two personalities is like the contact of two chemical substances: If there is any reaction, both are transformed." Words of wisdom indeed . . . I have never packed a weapon of any sort other than my mind, which, on several occasions has gotten me in trouble. As I have told ya all before, the most dangerous neighborhood I ever had to drive in was my own mind, and I have lived to tell. So roll with the punches and do what ya gotta do. Trust in yourself, your perceptions are far more accurate than you are willing to believe, as I'm sure your drivers were. Food for thought.

B.C. over.

Friday, November 27, 1998
Dear Bud,
It's been a while since I checked out the latest waybill . . . brings back fond memories of my life in your Fare City! Well written, as usual, Bud. Peace

Mimi Hall

Mimster,
Benjamin Franklin said, "Time is the stuff of which life is made." So, like the sands through the hourglass, so are the days of our lives.

B.C. over.

Thursday, December 3, 1998
Hey Bud,
I used to do a little, but a little became too little and a little turned
into moa and moa.

David Hofford

David,
The moa and moa was like deciding to fuck a gorilla. More
importantly, when I was done, that didn't necessarily mean he was.
Deep thoughts. It is not what one does that is wrong, but what one
becomes as a consequence of it.

B.C. over.

Thursday, December 3, 1998
Bud,
Respect means first knowing who has their shit together, then
learning what ya can from them . . . and thanking them for taking
the time to impart their knowledge into our meager little brains . . .
Comin' to Frisco in 10 days, new job offer. Maybe I'll catch a ride
someday? Any advice on a great section to live (I know about those
vacancy rates; less then 1%!) or where to look appreciated. Enjoy the
ride; you write 'em, I'll read 'em . . . later.

Gene Porfido

Hey there Gene,
First and foremost, never, ever call San Francisco "Frisco." There is
no Frisco in the great state of California whatsoever. A few years
back, some felons on the lamb got busted when the cops asked
them where they were from, they replied, "Frisco." It also labels
you as not only an outsider but one with little or no class. So best to
avoid using this term on your visit if you want any respect in my My
Fare City. For information on neighborhoods, check out next week's
waybill section. As far as getting noticed, well, my advice is to just
be yourself and blend in. Jumping off the Golden Gate Bridge might

get you noticed, but you would have to be crazy to do that. As far as your take on respect, let me say this. I have learned plenty from folks who have not had their shit together, but did have something to say that was of meaning to me, and that I was able to use. No thanks were needed or wanted to boot. Q: What's the difference between me and God? A: God doesn't want to be me. Have a great time in My Fare City, see ya on the road.

B.C. over.

Thursday, December 3, 1998
Hey Bud,
Great website! I am interested in becoming a cab driver in San Francisco. Any suggestions?

Henry

Henry,
First and foremost my friend, remember My Fare City's Taxi Driver oath.
A San Francisco Taxi Driver is TRUSTWORTHY
A San Francisco Taxi Driver's honor is to be trusted. If he were to violate his honor by telling a lie, cheating, stretching, or stealing another driver's order, when trusted on his honor, he may be asked to turn in his official Taxi Driver ID badge, if he can manage to locate the thing.
A San Francisco Taxi Driver is LOYAL
He is loyal to all whom loyalty is due, the window guy, the dispatcher, his fellow drivers, the owner of the cab company, his country and last but not least, his mother.
A San Francisco Taxi Driver is HELPFUL
He must be prepared at any time to save a life, commonly his own, and to share the wealth with whoever has a kickback coming their way. He must do at least one illegal U-turn daily.
A San Francisco Taxi Driver is FRIENDLY
He is a friend to all and a team player with drivers on his team. He has a twinkle in his eye, and a spring in his step, and is not only open minded but will try anything twice.
A San Francisco Taxi Driver is COURTEOUS

He is polite to all, especially to women, children, old people, and the weak and helpless, though he is not obliged in any way to dole out greenbacks or even spare change to the lazy fuckin' panhandlers. He will accept tips for being extra helpful or courteous.
A San Francisco Taxi Driver is KIND
He is a friend to animals, even if her name spells trouble. He will not kill or hurt any living creature needlessly, but will strive to save and protect all harmless life, with the exception of his brake pads.
A San Francisco Taxi Driver is OBEDIENT
He obeys the window guy, the dispatcher, and the police if there is no other choice in the matter.

B.C. over.

Friday, December 4, 1998
Bud,
Don't let go of those starry eyes. Please?

Ann Renneus

Ann!
Well hello again my friend, thanks for flagging me down. I promise not to let go, and I trust you will not either. The real voyage of discovery consists not in seeking new landscapes, but in having new eyes.

B.C. over.

Friday, December 4, 1998
Bud,
I just saw the sights of your wild trip! Hope all is well in Budland and you can get more images over the holidays. I just got a new Gateway 350 so I guess this is the start of something wild for me if all websites are as cool as yours.

One of Jerry's Kids

Hey now my Dead Head Rider!
We are the flow, we are the ebb, we are the weavers, we are the web.

B.C. over.

Saturday, December 5, 1998
Dear Bud,
I gotta say . . . great work, man. Really enjoy your writing . . .
brings back memories of the city by the bay (the finest city in the
world, no doubt; and I've seen a bit of the world by now!). But to
be honest, I have a bone to pick. I saw your bit about the Taiwanese
business people in your cab. Come on dude. If you were in Taipei,
Hong Kong or Beijing with your bud, wouldn't you speak English
with them . . . even if you had the ability to speak Chinese? Be
honest man. Love your stuff dude, keep it up (I read it ALL!).
Thanks, and hope to grab your cab (even if it is at the airport)
later this month when I'm in SF.

Greg from Sacramento (currently in Hong Kong)

Greg,
Honestly, yes I would. But having some mental problems, many
times it's "paranoia self destroya" for me. Even when people are
laughing in the back of the cab and I'm not paying attention, I
often think they are laughing at me. The medication helps most of
the time, but not all of the time. See ya on the road, my reader
from Sacto abroad.

B.C. over.

Thursday, December 10, 1998
Budman,
I just wanted to write and tell you MERRY CHRISTMAS! and HAPPY
HOLIDAYS! I run a Men's Clothing store and Christmas is my busiest
season, but I still have time to read "MY BUD."

S Simpson

Hello There Sandy!
So good to receive some well wishes for this here holiday season.
Men's clothing, what can I say? The last Christmas party I
attended I went stag and when a cute young woman approached
me and asked who I was with, I was temporarily caught off guard.
Always trying to fit in, but never quite being able to, I quickly

answered her "I'm with the brothers." "Which brothers?" she asked. I looked her square in the eye and answered, "Why the Brooks Brothers of course." She eyed me head to toe, taking a extra few seconds to give me the shoe test, and replied that she was here with Laura, Laura Ashley. We shared a good laugh as the natural ebb and flow of life, and the evening was working in my favor for a change.

B.C. over

Saturday, December 12, 1998
Bud,
Thanks a great deal for the photographic tour of your Fare City. It is interesting to note that much is the same the world over, every city has its poor. It leads me to think though that there are opportunities for these people if they want to work at a goal, though not condemning them for their choice of lifestyle. The only thing preventing them from doing so would be their beliefs, and possibly that they are happy in their state of life. Also . . . these people are surviving on so little, how many extras does the average person lug around them in life. How many possessions do we really need?

Eric Camilleri

Eric,
All separation is fear. All fear is an illusion. We forget that we are one. I find comfort and support from many sources. I am cradled and embraced by loving forces which guide me to good. I am able, on more and more deep levels, to feel safe and protected as I move about the streets of My Fare City. I am grateful to have lived to tell.

B.C. over.

Friday, December 18, 1998
Bud,
Thanks for your great stories of San Francisco! It's really good to see The City from the front seat of a taxi once in a while. Keep up the good work.

Thomas

Tom,

The cabbie battle hymn comes to mind Thomas. From "Rebel with a Cause?": "Mine eyes have seen the glory of the clearing of the board; He moves up and down the side streets, the right direction he moves toward. He hath loosed the faithful lightning of his terrible swift Ford: His night keeps keeping on."

B.C. over.

Monday, December 21, 1998

Dear B.C.,

Wow, your writing style kicks ass! I was just meandering around on the grid and I just happened to pass by your site. Normally a site gets about three seconds of my time but when I read one of your life stories, I was glued. Your philosophy rocks! Don't stop cranking it out!

Scott

Hey there Scott,

It's rule #1, living right isn't fun. Be true to yourself. I have never done anything I have regretted while smoking the ganja, though I have had countless regrets under the influence of the last "legal drug." Word to your sister.

B.C. over.

Thursday, December 24, 1998

Bud,

Have I found you? Despite all the computer geeking I have done through the years, I still have a lot to learn. If I have found you, the merriest of Christmas, and the happiest of holidays. Gotta run, but it's not because I haven't more to say.

Davidism

Dear D,

In a desperate mind, little gardens grow. Oh I had a horse and his name was Bill. And when he ran he couldn't stand still, He ran away one day, and one day I ran with him.

B.C. over.

Sunday, January 3, 1999
Bud Bro,
Billy Bro here . . . Lake Tahoe Jan 22 w/ Baby Buzz and Big Buzz.
Like your column.

Billy Bro

Billy Bro!
There ain't nothing like a good Buzz, especially with Bill Bro in the
mix. I hope the tables treated you well, and lady luck was a lady
that night. If all else fails, those boots were made for walkin', and
that's just what they gonna do. Taking a trip, not taking a trip.

B.C. over.

Thursday, January 7, 1999
Dear Bud,
Great site! I got it in exchange for a site called "Great Mobile
Homes of Mississippi" from another ex-Bay Area refugee up here
in the Great Gray Northwest. Cab Driver Report: Cabbies here are
generally Ethiopians or wear turbans. Like the owners of convenience
stores, their ethnic ranks change as new Third World residents
discover the promised joys of this, the Promised Land. I did some
personal research on owners of acrylic nail shops, and they all seem
to be Vietnamese women. My nail tech, Mary (they all carry unlikely
monikers like "Kelly" or "Mary") at my favorite shop, Top Nails
(consequently, they are all named Top, or Dream or Star . . .)
gave me a pair of bobbing-head Dalmatians. "You have good
luck in New Year when you get gift of dog," Mary firmly asserted.
One of my cynical friends laughed when I told her
that . . ."Yeah," she snorted, "you get to eat!" So, good luck
to you and Seymour . . . tell him to mind his manners!

Powderfox

My cousin spent some time serving in the Peace Corps in the
Philippines. When he returned, he showed us all pictures of the dog
he got for his birthday. When he said they walked the dog I really
did think they just took it for a stroll. I was wrong. They, in keeping
with tradition, "wok'd" the dog, as in cooked it in a Wok. Though

this may seem like some joke, I assure you it is not. I more enjoyed his tales of duck hunting with M-16's. Now that sounds like some fun. I never did ask if the dog had a name or not. Penny for my thoughts. My sister last thanksgiving had two turkeys her family raised that were named Mack and Zack. We ate Mack, and Zack got leftover duty. It was an interesting lesson for the kids I suppose. Where I come from, the dog may go for a walk, but does not end up as the main course. It's all perspective. The demographic of cab driver in My Fare City is diverse, to say the least. I notice it most when I'm at my own private United Nations (the airport). The separate factions pretty much keep to themselves, though on occasion I will get in on some gambling if all my planets are in line. I am proud to represent the disillusioned white kids "living on the fringe", living their life on our own terms. I could not ever imagine having to slave over some meaningless business that fed my pockets but emptied my soul. I have already had a lifetime of that bullshit. Never again. For all of those out there frustrated that certain ethnic groups have cornered several markets, I assure you that I not only stand tall, but kick ass on all the funky cats that have overrun my industry, and will continue to do so. Should I have a bed head, I will go with my Cubs hat, but the day you see Bud Carson with a towel wrapped around his head would be the day I ended up with a lobotomy. Anything's possible I guess. Remember, it's all perspective. What really is the trash in the trailer? Only you really know, but I suspect there is someone's sister in the area that fits the bill. I'll do my best to keep my side of the street clean, which ain't easy, and you just keep on keepin' on, like a citizen of these United States of America. Do what you want, when you want, and how you want to. It's the American way. Keep the faith and thanks for checkin' in . . . I really do appreciate it. P.S. As far as the note on nails, I can't relate as I have chewed mine down to nothing again . . . Seymour sends his best too.

　　　　　　　　　　　　　　　　　　　　　　　　B.C. over.

Tuesday, January 12, 1999
Wassup, Bud?
I dig your site and read it all the time when I'm supposed to be

slavin' for the Man. Hope I ride in your cab someday. So tell me, was that store you worked in "The Early Daze" United Liquors? Cause I was a clerk there for a while, too. Not when you worked there, I would've remembered ya. Anyway, same deal: We stayed open late on weekends to serve the Marina drunks, which was OK since we also got to see the Marina drunkettes, and, whatever you may think of the Marina, you have to admit there's some honeys running around there. My partner used to think nobody'd notice if he smoked herb in the beer cooler, but as you probably know, the smell of herb seems to just get stronger when refrigerated. So everyone who bought beer from us would be like, "Whoa!" when they opened said cooler, and then look at me all knowingly like I was going to get them baked. Sheeyah. As if, funny shit. I always gave cabbies and cops free coffee, cause you never knew when you'd need one or the other. Sometimes I'd hook up the bums, too. But not usually. Our particular crop of bums tended to overstep their bounds a lot (one used to, somehow, manage to hunker down and piss through the mail slot . . .) and so they had to be harshed. Cool thing was, we sold kegs, and I'd always tell the rich Marina types who were buying them, "And sir, if you'd like, we can send a United Liquors Quality Control Team to your place of residence later in the evening." Sometimes they'd bite. We hung out with the Jell-O pudding heir one night. He was an inbred prick like most rich guys, but he had a nice place. I remember they called a cab for some chick 'cause she wanted to sleep in her own bed . . . in Palo Alto. Hope you got the fare. Drop me a line if you ever get time.

Your pal, Hugh

Yo Hugh,
Glad to hear from someone who toted the bottom of the pole in the old hood. To answer your question, no I did not work at United Liquors, though I was at several jobs in the Marina back in the early daze. And yes, the babes were always keeping my wood afloat. Most of 'em were stone cold beautiful, but then again, our relationship was short, and thus sweet. The only relationship I experience today that is about as short is pulling up to a four-way stop at the same time cars going in all separate

directions do. Though this relationship is short, it is still a relationship with decisions to be made, winners and losers, depending on your perspective. I never bothered getting stoned in the cooler, but after the doors were locked, like many bars today, it was "anything goes."

B.C. over.

Saturday, January 23, 1999
Wassup B.C.,
How's My Fare City been treating ya' lately? First off thanks for puttin' that other Gene in his place about callin' ess eff (as the late great Herb Caen called her) Frisco, man I hate when people call San Fran that. Anyway I was and still am captivated by your writings, I know where ya' comin' from, me myself being an ex-cabbie on the island, I had my share of adventures to remember. I like the gig a lot, but the money wasn't all that hot because this island is only so big. A little 'bout myself, I was born and raised in the city by the bay (man, do I miss it big time) so I know about every street ya write of. Of course being a bike messenger downtown for five-plus years helped a little (it was the most fun I've ever had working so far!). By the way, have you had any conflicts with any messengers or any stories to share about them? Most likely not since you're a night man, right? Back in '89 when I was a messenger, cab drivers and MUNI drivers didn't get along too well. Does that hold true today? I hate that movie *Quicksilver* with Kevin Bacon—but it didn't serve the messenger world justice at all, that's Hollywood for ya. "Taxi driver." Now that's a classic. Sure it was violent but the bottom line is that it had moral value. If I had my choice, I would love to drive a cab in the city. The only drawback is I have a wife and daughter over here. That's why I moved over here in the first place, so I could raise my little one in a crime-free place. As much as I love S.F. and drivin' a taxi, taking a chance on being shot down or something isn't worth my baby losin' her pops. So I give you much credit on doin' your thing night in and night out. I look forward on reading your fares and our Fare City. I get homesick every time I do. Your shit is better

than the *Chronicle* and *Examiner* put together! Keep it comin'
B.C.

Gene Verzosa, Jr.

Gene,
I wish to see the day I am chillin' in Hawaii, a proud father and
happily married. Until then, thanks for throwing me a bone from
the islands. I used to date a gal whose Mom was, still is(?), a well-
known psychic catering to the rich and fameless in Hawaii Kai, on
Oahu. On a visit to Oahu, I got her Mom to tell my fortune. She
basically said that me and her daughter were not gonna work out.
She was right; we were history after I returned to the mainland. My
roommate who made the trip with me did enjoy the perks, as the
old girlfriend was bartending during the day, which meant free
booze and kept our costs down. Much more meaningful was my
trip to the "Big Island" where I was best man at a dear friend's
wedding. I got to stay with some truly crazy locals south of
Hilo, known to you as "the punatics." For those not familiar
with the lingo, this defines you as someone who lives on the
Puna side of the Big Island where the weather is much more
intense and the beaches are full of naturally occurring black,
rather than white sand beaches like the Kona side has. I
remember drinking this homemade flower wine and dancing like
nobody was watching. A truly spiritual experience of the second
kind (since it was my second trip to the islands). The third time
promises to be a charm, but when, I do not know. As I am now
a daytime taxi driver (survival instinct ya know), I do the dance
with the buses and bike messengers all day long. The past few
days have looked more like a Driver's Ed training film than
reality, but all the baby strollers and little old ladies made it
across the street fine. Funny you found another skeleton in my
closet of life. I was also a bike messenger for a spell in My Fare
City. I worked for Black Dog bike messenger service where our
motto was, "We will get it there, with booze on our breath."
This job, like bartending, ended up being not so good for my
health. The cat who ran it, Tony, reminded me of Mad Max (had the
accent) on barbiturates and Bourbon. Anyway, the war does continue

between the bike messengers and MUNI, which is still fucked up. Some things are timeless. My favorite "fuck the MUNI bus" trick was to pull the two cables off the wires and cross 'em. Not only do sparks fly, and big time, but the bus then has to be towed. You need to be pretty pissed, drunk, or both to risk this one, but let's just say it works. Happiness to your family, I envy you big guy. "It is clear the future holds opportunities and also holds pitfalls. The trick will be to seize the opportunities, avoid the pitfalls, and get back home by 6:00"—Woody Allen via.

B.C. over.

Monday, February 1, 1999
Bud,
My husband and I were in your cab last week. You gave us your web page info so I tried it today. From the photo I thought you were going to talk about the robot in Union Square. Have you seen him? He's painted bronze all over: hair, face, hands, clothes, etc. He sat on the southeast corner of the square the day I saw him. He had a cup in one outstretched hand. When anyone put a coin in the cup, he extracted a card from his pocket and handed it to the person. All this was done robot-style, i.e., very mechanically without variation. I watched him for a long time. I moved away and watched from a distance. The only gesture he made was the retrieval of the card which he gave out, and then only in response to a coin in his cup. As far as I could tell, he never blinked. Was he real? Is he a robot?

Barbara Green, Washington, DC

Barb,
Q. Are we not men? A. We are Cabby. Remember the Prell Shampoo commercial, Barbara. And so on

B.C. over.

Tuesday, February 2, 1999
Bud,
I am a regular reader of yours, and being a second-generation San Franciscan (20th and Collingwood, 22nd and Noe, 17th and Stanyan) now living in Seattle, you keep me in touch with the city I love.

Thanks, Barry Ewing

Barry,

You have had some nice digs in My Fare City, with all of your cross streets telling stories of their own, as well as being a statement to your good taste. For instance, at 20th and Collingwood, you must have had an epic view of downtown, also to the East and North. My old pal Natasha (not the one with Boris) has lived up there for years and simply refuses to move, and I can't blame her. Your theme continues with equally spectacular views close by at 22nd and Noe. 17th and Stanyan rounds it out quite nicely there at the edge of Cole Valley, one of the best-kept-secret neighborhoods, at least until my review in NEIGHBORHOOD TOUR several weeks back. I hope you were additionally pleased with the four-star (five for many) rating your other two places got. You got great taste my man! As far as Seattle, I hear quite a few folk make their way up North for a spell, always, of course, leaving their heart in San Francisco.

B.C. over.

Friday, February 5, 1999

Hello B.C.,

Just wanted to thank you for the ride down to Ella's a couple Saturdays ago (there were four of us, two couples from San Diego). The ride started off a great day that had us hoofing from breakfast to the Haight and down to lower and our favorite bar in the city, the Toranado. We spent a good deal of the afternoon drinking great beers and just enjoying being. Your writing here at Captivated is very interesting and I hope to drop in other times to check in how things are going. Hopefully we can hop in your cab on our next trip to SF!!

Vincent Outlaw

Vincent,

Ella's sure does continue to be the hot breakfast spot. I hope you all walked over to the Haight by choice, and not for lack of coverage out that way. It's so nice to hear that you made it to the Toranado, the same place I took the two Chicago Cubs I drove around on an "all points tour" of My Fare City. As beautiful as San Diego is, (I love to surf PB, and grab a munch at the Daily Planet), to truly enjoy "being" as you described is meant for the capitol of the universe, San Frantastic, CA.

B.C. over.

Wednesday, February 3, 1999
To whom it may concern,
I was on vacation, visiting my daughter in S.F. (her new home). With great luck I hooked up with one of the nicest cabbies in that fine city. Showed us around, let us drink beer in the cab (we're from WI after all) and generally made our stay a very memorable experience. Yeah, hell yeah, we tipped him, bought him meals, beers, and we still probably owe him.

Thanks again, Lars

Lars,
You don't owe me a thing. It was a pleasure to take you down a road less traveled, and also to Cala Foods to buy sausage and beer. Give Wild Bill and the other Lizards in the band a big wet one from me. See ya before Y2K, when I'm counting on an unlimited supply of sausage and Point beer. Your daughter would be nice too, just kidding. Actually, I'm not.

B.C. over.

Sunday, February 7, 1999
Hey dude,
As a night driver you were interesting . . . i know, i drove cab for 10 years . . . this day driver stuff leaves a lot to be desired. are you making the money you used to make? are you having the fun you used to? i doubt it. but i'll just bet you're doing a lot of repitions, grocery runs, the same ole people day after day after day . . . good luck.

Aflan

Aflan,
Well hello to you also fellow. First off, let me say a lot of things crossed my mind when first reading your email. Your bogus grammar and resentful flare would have to top the list, to be perfectly frank.

Ten years is a long time to be driving a cab, my hat goes off to you for surviving. Don't be so angry at the world, it is bad for your soul. Life is short, and even after 10 years of cab driving, miracles still do exist. "By the light of the moon, by the light of a star, they walked all night from near to far. I would never walk. I would take a car."—Dr Seuss.

B.C. over.

Tuesday, February 9, 1999
Hey Now Bud Carson . . .
Man you are a renaissance man of the '90s . . . How else could anyone else but you, Bud, pull off being a cabbie by day and a literary giant by night . . . You must burn both candles down to the sticky wick . . . Moved out the family this weekend . . . Now I have a bachelor pad worthy of a visit . . .
PeAcE to BuD . . .

Craig

Craig MAN,
Thank you kindly. The management assumes no responsibility for what is found.

B.C. over.

Friday, February 12, 1999
Bud,
Thanks again for helping me with my bags at the airport yesterday. Mimi and I had a swell time sharing a small portion of our journey with you. By the way, I didn't really leave my heart in San Francisco. It was actually a perfectly good and barely used all-cotton handkerchief. I left it at the hotel. I'm going to miss that hanky.

Bill K

Bill,
You may miss the hanky, but you sure won't miss the panky. I got the skinny after dropping you at the South Terminal on a slow and

enlightening ride with Mimi to the North Terminal, but nothing like the ride that lies ahead for you friend. Please do this kid a favor and send me one of the photos you took of her while you were in My Fare City. I will keep it safe and unpublished, cross my aching heart.

B.C. over.

Tuesday, February 16, 1999
Bud,
Happy Chinese New Year . . . It's the Year of the Rabbit . . . I am a fellow cabbie in Milwaukee that entirely enjoys your Chronicles from the Fringe . . . I log onto Captivated weekly to read your groovy, always right-on, translations of the fellow cabbie . . . Talkin' about the Year of the Rabbit, I recently had a fare that I picked up at bar time. They were both brutally drunk, and before I was 2 blocks, they started fuckin' like a bunch of rabbit's . . . It was pure insanity . . . Trippin' the light fantastic . . . I quickly popped in a killer DEAD tape and let them get bizzy . . . Keep up the good work my fellow cabbie . . . P.S. I got a huge tip . . . for the ride . . .

Holy Cow

Holy Cow,
Nothing quite like buns up kneelin' in the ol' rear view mirror. Kinda gives sightseeing and "points of interest" a whole new slant. As to the Chinese New Year, Happiness to you, too, Happy Hack. I celebrated the pre-dawn start of my shift by handing out a firecracker to my fares, doormen on Union Square, and homeless people I thought would enjoy a little civil disobedience. I even did the old trick using a cigarette as a timed fuse and left a delayed bang by a rival cab that cut in front of me to get in a cab line. As I rounded the corner after planting the prank (I was off to greener pastures) I heard it go off. That rude yellow belly musta shit in his already dirty underwear. Hee Haw.

B.C. over.

Wednesday, February 17, 1999
Hey Bud,
It's Mike and Elizabeth from Chicago. Thanks for the tip on that great place to eat. Food was great. We enjoyed the ride with you. We'll be back to see you soon. Oh yeah, how was the rest of your shift?

Mike & Elizabeth

M & E,
It's funny, if you ask any cab driver how his night has been, he will always say it's been lousy. He always has to work you for that tip. Today, though I got out early, I was issued a junker for a car. Instead of this being a minus, I turned it into a plus. The car was a piece of shit, so I told all my passengers that I was saving up money to put towards a new cab. It actually worked. People felt sorry for me and by playing on their emotions, the tips doubled. This didn't take away from the fact I had to drive the piece of crap for ten hours, but I needed the money, which is a common theme for us cabbies. Each time I hit the accelerator, the car wheezed as if it would be its last breath. I thought about the bad gas mileage I was getting, but then I put it out of my mind so it wouldn't get me down. I stayed in the city all night and basically ran around on short trips. I had a fare in the back seat most of the night, which is always good.
After midnight, I took a final radio call. By this time the car sounded pretty bad. However, earlier in the evening, I did call the window guy to see if I could switch cars. He told me to tough it out the last few hours of the night. Later, I would be glad I made this call. Why? Because if you break it, you buy it. It's a tough policy because many a cabbie has lost his job because he was unable to pay the company damages incurred to a cab he drove.
As I took a gal from North Beach to the Upper Haight, the car was sounding horrible, even more so than at the beginning of the night. As I turned onto her block the engine seized. She had to walk the half block to her place, but she did pay me and left me to wait for

a fuckin' tow. Dispatch said it would be a few hours, which was way too long for me. I called the window guy and he said that if it does start to try to limp it back. I waited some more. I was frustrated as hell, but happy that if it had to happen that it happened at the end of the night after I'd made my money. About ten minutes after the engine died I tried it one last time and to my surprise the old beast started! I got on the radio told dispatch to cancel the tow and started to drive back to the garage. At each stoplight I put the transmission in neutral and kept the r.p.m. high enough so the engine would not stall. It sounded real bad and the car was smoking something awful. Fuck my personal safety; I had to get this piece of shit back to the garage. I don't know how, but I made it back, and as I rolled up to the gas pump, the cab gasped out one last breath and then died as inertia inched us forward. After the gas man filled her up, we both pushed her from the pump to the garage.

I'm glad I called the window guy earlier that night because the next day, I came to work and saw the car with its engine hanging from a chain. Had I not called they could have tried to blame the problem on me and I was not gonna buy a new engine for that junker. They're still rebuilding the engine and soon that cab will be in service again. Hell, almost every cab in the fleet has had major engine work done to it. The mechanics at the garage remind me of the TV show M.A.S.H.; remember "meatball surgery?" Same concept with the cabs: Patch 'em up, send 'em out. Gauges and warning lights are a low priority to them. It's the engines and transmissions that matter. Keep them running and on the road.

B.C. over.

Friday, February 19, 1999
Hey Bud!
Didn't want a ride. I've been in a car with you before going to Weeds with beer bottles being hurled at our window and you behind the wheel laughing like a hyena. Say hello to Hemi And Meaups ! See You later.

Greg EDEE

Hey Now Greg!
As I remember it, you were somewhat lit yourself there cowboy.
Cab driver wisdom says if you shut the door on the truth it will
come in the window. The beer bottles hurled at us only were near
misses, unlike the first shot I arched out my window, over our car to
bounce off of the homies' hood. Thankfully we were both stopped at
a red light when they stirred the pot, otherwise it might have ended
up like the Grand Prize Game.

B.C. over.

Friday, February 26, 1999
Howdeee. Didn't know if you knew it yet, but I'm a daddy! Kinda
gives you hope for the future of our great nation. Cassidy Blue
Rodencal, born 2.5.99, 8 lbs., 4 oz. I'm psyched! Just think, Uncle
Bud! P.S. Congratulations on your 10 years of driving cab! Go Cubbies!

Peace, Wild Bill

"If the truth be known—
These good hearts flapped in fibrillation.
They feared the rogue vibrations
From the freaking Acid Graduation
Kesey and the Pranksters planned;
Their freaking Day-Glo last round-up in Winterland."
The Electric Kool-Aid Acid Test
It sure seems like 10 years and time does fly when you're
having fun. But, that would be a serious over-estimation of
my cabbie graduation. Love and happiness for the bright light
shining from Cassidy's soul. I can feel the warmth and positive
energy. Wild Bill, you are the man.

B.C. over.

Saturday, February 27, 1999
Hi Bud,
A couple of weeks ago you drove me to Larkin/Sacramento, I
mentioned downloading a Dave Barry article about dogs watching

television and running behind the TV to find the real thing, Barry's assessment that this was further proof that a dog IQ was equivalent to that of a saltine cracker. The ride ended about then, you gave me a captivated.com card and invited me to give it a try, to which I said thanks, I would do that and so I have, and thanks again.

Cool Runnings, Dennis

Dennis the Menace,
I do so enjoy getting a shout from a local who has actually meandered around the streets of My Fare City with me. As our conversation dwelled on the humor of a saltine cracker, my mind felt like a restaurant-size package of saltines that had been crushed after a morning spent in my back pocket. I picked you up nine hours and fifty minutes into my shift, so thank you for dropping me a line and reminding me that it could be the first, the worst or the last fare of the day that might come back my way.

B.C. over.

Saturday, February 27, 1999
Be careful Bud. Sounds like some bad folks out there. Lets hope they are not the Ted Bundy type. Prayers to all the cabbies.

Anonymous

Hey Sweetheart!
I used to pray when I was a baby bud, and then later when I was in deep shit, and even then I was just praying to God that if I just got out of whatever I got in, I would promise to be good. Thanks for your prayers. Let us pray . . . Now I lay my car in gear, I pray the Lord my rubber smear, If I Lord should run a stop, I pray the Lord you ain't a cop . . . "my way, or the highway" . . . to heaven.

B.C. over.

Thursday, March 4, 1999
Hi Bud,
I really enjoy your website, and your adventures in S.F., and I must say I can relate to you as I'm also a cab driver. I drive a cab in Glasgow, Scotland and most of the things that happen to you, happen

over here too, and in most of the big cities in the world also, I guess. I've been driving a cab now for 25 years, and all that time, there have been two drivers murdered, one male, one female in my city. By my thinking, that's two too many! So Bud, from all the cab drivers in Glasgow, to all you guys over there, be careful on the streets. Our thoughts are with the family and friends of the poor guys who were murdered. From a fellow knight of the road . . .

Billy

Billy,
Thanks for your kind words. It's good to know that you understand how sad this sort of thing is, from the inside out. My heart weighs heavy at the recent crime wave to hit us hacks in My Fare City, death was not part of the job description. Alas, everything not specifically stated in the contract, is stated in the contract. Keep the sunny side up and the greasy side down.

B.C. over.

Thursday, March 11, 1999
Hiya Bud,
I'm all in favour of the idea. I like seeing the pics you post on the site. Interesting to see what is going on around the other side of the world. Cheers dude. Stay safe.

Chris E from Oz

Man from the land of Oz,
So glad to be reaching around the world, See ya on the highway. 1-800-travelbc.

B.C. over.

Tuesday, March 16, 1999
Hi, How are you?
Just got back to work and decided to check out your site. I'm impressed, very professional. Do you do it all by yourself? Anyway you are probably racking your brains thinking who is this email from? We were the fare you picked up at the Gates Hotel to take us to the airport (customers of the week). I rang you on

your cell phone, you sounded confused then as well. I'm still after my 15 minutes of fame so I hope to see our photograph on the site next time. I check it out. Meanwhile, hope things are cool and the people of SF keep giving you plenty to write about, missing the place already. Cheers for the lift (ride).

Tracey Eastwood (and the other guys)

"Tracey and the guys head back across the pond"

Tracy,

So glad you made it home safe and sound. Yes, it was shocking to actually get a call for an airport run on my cell phone, as it's usually my old man checking up on me, or occasionally another driver with a tip. The remainder of my airtime being split between wrong numbers and perhaps a very, very lucky bill collector. A tip from another cabbie can change the specter of your day, for much cash, or a rude arrival into the 4th lot if you take his "open lot" at the airport report from a bit too far away. Cabbies have a few close allies much like any business you choose, though this is the first job where the management thinks being a "team player" is giving 'em five bucks a visit. No degree on the wall though the bulletproof glass speaks for itself. As to your query regarding the "Riders of the week," you Brits made the final cut, and are now archived. (See week 48—Fare Game) Ya all did catch me off guard as the infamous "Gates of Insanity" hotel is one I usually wouldn't get a call from on the day shift. Those airport cops were pissed off about the key to your mums tattooed along the side of their ride.

B.C. over.

Thursday, March 18, 1999
Bud,
Your site is fantastic, always a hoot. I check faithfully every week for updates. The boys in the band (me, too) are all connected and we all love your ramblings. I don't know how or what your acting career is but, damn, you got potential, as maybe, best-selling author or at least one that should be required reading by millions. Hope to see you soon.

All the luck, Lars & Kathy Lizard King!

Lars,
Sure, me and L. Ron Hubbard! "Cabenetics"? First Church of the Last Laugh in My Fare City might take me in?

B.C. over.

Monday, March 29, 1999
Finally!
Someone who knows both; what we go through on a daily basis and how to express it eloquently. I don't have the time to make it through all your stories tonight, but I related to everything I read and will definitely be back. Very good job, sir.

Driver9

Driver9,
Don't call me sir! I work for a living! Seriously, I appreciate the compliment. It means a lot to know that via cyberspace, a trip just by itself, that we were able to connect on a deeper level. Better than ISDN. Personal experience is something I cherish. While often because of communication barriers or just personality, cab drivers tend to isolate. My ability to interact, and become part of my riders' experience is a huge bonus on a job that really is like no other.

Have you had a gander at my A-to-Z cabbie job description? Though the internet is an incredible medium, actually getting out in My Fare City and living whatever reality I choose to make on any given day is what really makes me shine, and even on occasion whine. I love giving it, and living it. Being able to share life that truly plays to the beat of a different drummer, and ain't for just anyone. As I have stated before, the top prerequisites for being a cab driver are thick skin, and an even disposition. To the flood of new drivers My Fare City has thrust on itself due to the 40% increase in medallions issued, and the resulting shortage of drivers, I would add that knowing where the Golden Gate Bridge is wouldn't be a bad idea either. I have had a Mill Valley ride and San Rafael after hapless hacks before me in cab stands around Union Square were unable to take the load, having no knowledge of anything other than the airport and downtown hotels. San Rafael is meter and a half to boot! Have they experienced points north of the Golden Gate Bridge? Well, I have. Not necessarily stoned, but beautiful.

B.C. over.

Tuesday, March 30, 1999

Hey Bud!!

I am STILL reading you all the time, just haven't written lately. Here's a joke I just saw earlier . . . A lady, taking a ride in a cab, suddenly realizes she has no money. "I have no cab fare," she tells the driver, "but will this do?" As the driver glances in his rear view mirror, she spreads her legs. "Oh God lady, don't you have anything smaller?" **LOL.** Have a great day!!!

Sandy Simpson

Sandy!,

Great joke, and not so far from a few times I can remember. Way back in Cab College, you are instructed to bring your raincoat every shift. It is a basic and wise safety measure for when it gets wet, ya know. Did I really even go there? I guess I did.

B.C. over.

Friday, April 2, 1999
Hey Bud!!
I'll be in town this weekend. Do you drive on weekend nights anymore??? If so, fire me that cell phone number and I'll give you all the business I can muster up. Keep up the good work.

Walter

Walter,
Out of the night, into the light.

B.C. over.

Friday, April 2, 1999
Bud . . .
I haven't visited your site for a couple of months . . . I have been visiting since around "Hazy Daze." I just wanted to say that I like the additions of Cabbie of the Month, and Rider(s) of the Month . . . Welcome additions to an already outstanding site. When I visit SF, I hope to end up in your cab . . . Keep on drivin'.

James—Las Vegas, NV

James,
They truly were some hazy daze, and some hazy ways. I find it much more rewarding to dig a little bit during the day for material, rather than the alternative of being suffocated by it at night. Alas, I have lived to tell. Glad to hear the Mug Shots gets a thumbs up, I figured a dash of the virtual would be a nice touch on an already great recipe. Makes me think of meat loaf, one dish I enjoy making. A truly American dish, you can mix and match anything from oatmeal to the kitchen sink. The nice part for you is it is served up fresh, each week. Who knows, you could end up as my rider of the week. Just remember to tip! On a personal and local item to you, I miss those Dead shows at The Silver Bowl. I oh so enjoyed doing a "Hunter S" in Sin City, but it took Jerry to get me there. Fond memories, and some hazy daze in your neck of the wood for sure.

B.C. over.

Tuesday, April 6, 1999
Bud . . .
She's a good actress if being yourself is acting. I think she is a snooty bitch. There is a lot more talent out there, and besides Hole e wood is overrated anyways. She is fake. Blah Blah Blah . . . (Comments on rider Sharon Stone . . . Week 31—I can't drive 55)

Rob

Rob,
Cab driver wisdom say: When you are in New York "fuck you" means hello. When you are in Los Angeles "hello" means fuck you.

B.C. over.

Wednesday, April 7, 1999
Hey bud!
It's always a smile to pull up the Newzflash and see a familiar face as wavy as Davey's. A renaissance man if there ever was one, and well deserving of the full spread on Tales . . . xoxo . . .

Ang

Hey A!
Everyone gets their 15 minutes in the sun, and some of us just continue to have fun. A substitute teacher I had in the fourth grade taught me something beyond the textbook when I told him that I was the smartest one in the class, interrupting him to boot. Mr. Penrose, a very old crow himself, told me, "Mr. Carson, in life you do not want to aspire to be smart, you want to be wise." That old crow is undoubtedly pushing up daisies today, though his words live on. I hope I am as fortunate. Cab driver wisdom say, "Drive for show. Putt for dough." There ya go.

B.C. over.

Tuesday, April 13, 1999
Here's a story from a cab ride I took in Boston. I get into a cab downtown, kind of drunk. The cab driver starts telling me this story about how some woman just held him up at gunpoint and made him drive her all over town. I'm thinking, this guy probably

noticed I'm drunk and is just pulling my chain. Well he kept going on about how scared he was and how crazy this woman with the gun was. I guess I'll never know whether he was telling the truth, but it was a pretty entertaining story.

Nick Hausman

Nick,
For all you do, this buds for you . . .

B.C. over

Monday, April 19, 1999
Bud,
Thanks for publishing the Sharon Stone thing. Natasha Wagner, that's a real woman (she is in that movie with Robert Downey Jr., *Two Girls and a Guy.*) Check her out.

Rob

Rob,
I checked out the movie, and you were right, Natasha is hot. Was not a real good "date" movie though.
Look for Robert Downey to play Bud Carson when the time comes.

B.C. over.

Tuesday, April 20, 1999
Bud,
Glad to read you are alive and well, still cruising the streets of your vibrant existence. Your road has been long, Bud Carson, that is obvious and observed, but oh . . . the many stops you've made along the way. Such pains. Such pleasures. Seek the city and she will show you your self, and introduce you to everybody else. " . . . Here I am, once again. Nighttime skies, black and blue, dogs bark, cars whiz by. Blinking lights. Passersby. I am alone, but not afraid. We all have streets to search." Thanks for sharing, Bud. You are energy. I think about you all the way from chi-town, west town most high. How about I give you a ride? Visit next time? I've just seen a couple of hometown hommies and hammies. All my regards. All my peace.

Ralph

Dearest Ralph,
We have danced some roads, that's for sure. The dust of a thousand galaxies lines the glove box of my 4x4. And all the grease from the window guy to yesteryear, we always turn that motor over, with each time having faith in where we would go when the facts just weren't enough.

B.C. over.

Monday, April 26, 1999
Bud,
Just picked out your site and rode with you through many of the days you have posted. If you think the number of cabs in SF is tough, you should see Montreal, where I live. We have, I heard, the highest number of cabs per person of anywhere in North America. I am a copywriter but definitely not in your moral majority. Well, OK, I do have a partner, 3 kids, 2 cats and a house in the inner burbs of this beautiful city, but I always try to look at and live life a bit outside the box. Maybe the biggest difference between you and me is that I went back to school because my other half was pregnant and I figured that a degree would help us bring up babies with more chances at life than I could give them working in a record store and split shifting as a waiter. I think I look at life the way you do because I traveled a lot when I was younger—as in overland trips bumming across Asia—and have had many jobs in the service industry. So, I have long had a small, secret desire to jump off and just drive a cab. I know it can be tough to make ends meet, and that some of the people, like the Brenda you talked about, can make it kinda hard to keep your humanity, but it also puts you right on the pulse of city life. Oh, and you might like to know that I take a lot of cabs—at least ten per week—but I avoid having a regular because I like variety. In Montreal we have dozens, maybe hundreds of what we call New Canadians driving cabs, mostly from Haiti or from the Middle East, especially Iran and Lebanon. The interesting thing is that many of the Middle Eastern cabbies studied to be doctors, engineers, teachers (and I once drove with a former pilot in the Shah of Iran's

Air Force). Their trouble is that they either had to flee from political violence in their home country without their "papers" or else their degrees aren't recognized here. Okay, have to go—another deadline looming. P.S. I have NEVER written to a website before. Please take that as a very big compliment, Bud. See ya.

Peter Mac

Big Mac,

I take your contacting me with your comments and thoughts as a huge compliment. It is amazing to think that while I bust my hump driving a taxi, I would have never imagined the ability to communicate the experience in such a way that leaves both writer and reader satisfied. Simultaneous orgasm? A matter of perspective, yes definitely. I hear Montreal is a very cool town, I've been told. I'm not sure, but you may have caught me in a recent edition of Simpatico NETLife. What is Simpatico NETLife you ask? I didn't know myself before they contacted Captivated to let us know of the four-star rating they were giving us in their magazine. After receiving a copy, the cover identified the periodical as Canada's Home Internet Life magazine. It was a great honor and right out of left field, as the internet has truly connected the world like never before. I enjoyed your information on the taxi industry in your area as some things differ, though many stay the same taxi driving throughout the world. Tell all the political refugees driving cabs that there are plenty of minimum wage jobs available here in the United States for educated people. Your doctor cabbie could thrive as a Chiropractor. The engineer could make big bucks consulting and the teachers could teach, as we sure need some of them. The guy who claimed to be a former pilot in the Shah of Iran's Air Force could come here and get shot down as many times as he tried to. As far as those hacks not having proper papers or their degrees not being recognized, they never stopped any go-getting American kid. The people that should be doing something better than what they are should just go do it. If you are a victim of circumstance, then tough shit. Been there, done that.

B.C. over.

Monday, April 26, 1999
Dear Bud,
Love yo' site, Especially the crash of the week. But promise me, even if you have to lie, that nobody got hurt. Even better if you won't because I can get some guilt-free laughs for once. Your intro was eerily similar to my life. Never, ever in my wildest dreams, nightmares, or alcohol-induced comas did I ever imagine that I would be driving a cab in the City of Angels, El Lay, Lost Anal-Juice. Of course, I did leave Cleveland looking for a bit more adventure. I even have some education. Went to law school, passed the bar—with a big-assed clang!—and, bug-eyed from the rock and hard place of student loans, and boredom, drove a cab for Valley Cab Co. in the San Fernando Valley, from January to April, 1998. Aside from the money, one reason I went to law school was for more stories, gleaned from practicing the profession. Then, drove a cab, and BOING! Hopped up into the story stratosphere. Four months of hacking yielded many tales for me to tell my grandbabies: the Latex Girls; the Singing Whores and Me; the Nude Man; the Pharmacopian Jew; the Rutters (as in season); Snow White and Prince Charming; the Blood Money Man; and more. Anyway, I was astounded to learn the way those bastards—the owners—treat you guys up in Sam Frank's Disco. A ten-hour shift??? I want my mommy! A 90-buck-per-day lease, for a 10-hour day??? Where's my buttplug? Kickbacks?? Yowza Maria! $135.00 per day in routine costs? EEK! Vile corruption, dinosaurs for management, indeed! How do you stand it? Of course, greed, and desire to pay off my loans early may induce me back into the hacking trade, on the weekends. And, I'm always a ho' for a good story. Fatiguing though it may be, driving a cab is less fatigue than office work. Here in La-la land, we get a 12-hour shift, which, while not effortless, is less sandpaper on the sanity than ten hours in a law office. In any event, keep adding new material, promise me no one gets hurt in the crashes, and God bless.

Dave in La-La Land

Dave,

Glad you enjoy Hacked Up. I'm sorry that I can't lie to you and say that no one ever gets hurt in or out of my photos. Please still enjoy those guilt-free laughs as at least I'm not an attorney, or I would be known as an "ambulance chaser." Oh yeah, I forgot, you said something about being an attorney. Don't be such a tease and submit some of your tales of Los Angeles taxi driving, just giving me the titles borders on being an insult. Then again, if you're saving it all up for a screenplay or something, then forget it, I'll wait until it comes out on video. It's good to know there are others out there with the courage and determination, or possibly a string of failures, which allows them to follow their hearts as hacks. Perspective is a wonderful thing, I'm glad you share it with me.

B.C. over.

Monday, May 3, 1999

Hi Bud,

Enjoy your site. I'll keep checking it out. I drove a taxi in Austin for 15 years, then moved on to more conventional employment but that faded away as soon as they figured out just how rooted I was in the unconventional. Hell, I didn't know myself but it didn't take long to see that I was not an advertising salesman. Today, I'm printing bumper stickers and t-shirts and sometimes, God Help Me, I think of going back to hacking. But not Austin. That's right, I've been thinking about Sin City. I too recall a time when driving a taxi was considered an honorable profession and I'm glad to know there are those out there that still treat it so. Keep up the good work and if possible, tell me where I could find the procedure for getting on as a taxi driver in San Francisco. Any companies you would recommend? Any I should avoid? Of course, there's a good chance I'll never act on this but since I don't have any retirement plan anyway, I may as well live well for the remainder of my time.

Your friend, Les

Les,

David Gilmore said it best "There's no way out of here. When you come in, you're in for good." Should you wish to stop putting off the inevitable, the employment opportunity for cab drivers in My Fare City is very good, the best ever in fact. The city and all their wisdom along with the helpful hand of Da Mayor, Willie Vanilli Brown, figured increasing the fleet of taxi's by 40% would solve the problem. Supply and demand varies considerably at different times of the day, and year. Though I detest math, a rough estimate would be as follows: 400 new medallions issued means two, sometimes three drivers per medallion. A conservative estimate would put at least a thousand new positions as cab driver available, and I'm not even factoring in the oldtimers that would quit. Like the Goldrush of 1849, some people will get fat (the companies), others will work an honest day for some honest pay while the majority will learn a good lesson, the hard way. It's a hard way to make a living, still, every time you hear the band Lynyrd Skynyrd say, "What song is it you wanna hear?" You know.

B.C. over.

Sunday, May 16, 1999

Hey Bud,

I like the new rider of the week pics and stories :>) Did I ever tell you that I live in Southern Illinois???? You know the theme song from "CHEERS" that says, "Where everybody knows your name?" That's where I live. **LOL.** I do have a friend who lives in Antelope, CA and I hope to be visiting there this summer, soooooooooo I am definitely going to come to San Francisco and take a ride in your cab!!!!!!!!!!*smiles.* I will even spring for dinner if you promise to take my pic and make me the rider of the week.

Sandy Simpson

Sandy you little bug-a-boo,

Thank you for your continued support. You are no doubt what I consider a regular rider, and not a bad tipper either. I used to go to my friend Hemi's brother's block party named "Haze Fest" in Carbondale, IL. I think that's the name of the street, but all the beer and mushrooms make some of it indeed, somewhat hazy. Thanks again for your interest. You made me blush and the most bizarre part is you could be a complete lunatic, not to mention hairy armpits. I would at least be able to relate.

B.C. over.

Tuesday, May 18, 1999
Bud,
Wow! Spent a fun morning perusing your mailbag! I'm slow-going on the website, and didn't realize I had so much to catch up on. You (and others) are on the move and groove, Bud—am I surprised?!?? And great news abounding, Bud, thru the grapevine. Endless blessing and endless well wishes . . . As a dear friend always reminded me . . ."You deserve the best!" Happiness to you and yours . . .

Peace, the Meemsters

Hey Now Rider,
They say the universe was born in chaos
hurtling ever since
Toward it's ending entropy
That seems like a pretty Fair Bet
That is more than patience
Higher than acceptance
I will not call it enlightenment
Although I am tempted to

B.C. over.

Thursday, May 20, 1999
Bud,
I've been reading your diary nearly since its inception. I live in Montana and it's interesting to read your stories. Anyways, last weekend I went to a non-work-related convention in Las Vegas. I had to get a cab at five on Sunday morning. The cabbie was nice and I thought, "Hey," or in Montana is it "Hay"? Anyways, this guy

is going out to the airport and the charge is only $5.40. I noticed there was very little traffic and activity at the airport. I got to thinking about you and your stories. So I gave the guy $10. I am by no means rich and just barely middle class and didn't gamble but a few dollars, so it wasn't from any winnings, but if I helped a cabbie crack the nut, that's great!
Thanks!

Bob

Bob,
Glad to hear from a rider in Montana. From the HBO special "Return to Vegas II" on Real Cab Confessions (the show that taped riders secretly), I bet he has a few stories to tell. That was certainly a cheap ride to the airport, as it would not even get you a shuttle bus here. My hat goes off to you for helping the hack during his shift. I wondered if he was a night driver about to finish, having some mean drunks the night before, or just starting out. It's no coincidence that everything is cheap in Vegas, from the 99-cent breakfast to free booze, they keep the focus in the right place, all perspective. Every time I road trip to ski with my pals to Lake Tahoe, we always end up gambling, with the guy who wins the most getting driving duty on the way back. Funny thing, the winner ends up with almost the exact amount the other guys lost. Every time! See ya someday, when I get my act together, move to your state, and fulfill my destiny as a dental floss tycoon.

B.C. over.

Tuesday, May 25, 1999
Bud!,
I am not a weirdo!!!!! *Crossing my eyes and sticking out my tongue at you*. LOL. I am a respectable business owner . . . Duhhhh!!!!!
Giggles

Sandy

Sandy,
I have a feeling you will be doing the same thing someday in my cab, only under different circumstances. I too am a business owner but

respectable would be stretching a bit. In fact, my office (cab) is the most well-organized and cleanest workplace I have had the pleasure of working in. I think being my own boss was in the cards for me, as I can honestly say I am happy doing what I do. In the meantime, I will make sure and slow down, if not completely stop, to smell those beautiful roses. Happyness kiddo.

B.C. over.

Thursday, May 27, 1999
Hi Bud,
Great to see that you're up and running. I missed the updates the last couple of weeks. Hang in there, we all root for the Bud Man!

Lars

LARS,
It ain't easy being me, but I say do the best with the hand you're dealt, and when on duty, follow the Kenny Rogers mantra. "Don't count your money while you sittin' at the table, there be time enough for counting, when the dealings done," or in my case when my shift is over. Like a wise, burnt-out cabbie told me when I was just a green pea, don't rip off drunks, put your twenties in your back pocket as you can't make change with 'em, and never keep your money like a Chinaman (all in a wad). He said to always have my bills in order and without creases or folds in the bills. When I saw the guy on the street the other day, I mentioned to him way back when I gave him a ride and in turn got some words of wisdom. He ended up screwing me out of five bucks, but I think that too was some kind of twisted lesson. He was amazed I remembered, but even more so, I was amazed he remembered.

B.C. over.

Saturday, May 29, 1999
Dear Bud,
I drive a cab in Butte MT and I feel that unless you have driven a cab its hard to understand how this job gets under your skin. I have been driving for three years now and can't see doing anything else! Here in Butte, the job pays $5.15 an hour and all the tips I can

charm off people. The good part is the boss owns everything so he pays for gas, oil, and repairs. I drive the night shift and love it.

Cabbie Daryl

Big D,

Though I suspect Uncle Sam figures into your hand, it sounds like a good deal to me. I have lately been upset due to the large number of bums in My Fare City. People like to be *pc* and use the word homeless, but I see the same ones workin' it for years now. One smelly bum that works the Union Square district has been at it for the ten-plus years I have seen him. With the general assistance the highest in the nation at $380.00 a month, not factoring in social security or the tax-free money they panhandle, these folks have their cake and eat it too. Only new beggars are foolish enough to ask cabbies for any money, since they know we know. When one tries to get something out of my pocket, I let them know to not ask cab drivers. If I am in a real bad mood, or have not gotten laid in a while, I may toss 'em a penny. Their signs say "Anything Helps", and "Will work for food", but ask 'em to rake some leaves, forget it. They are working, and doin' better than I on some days, this is wrong. More and more bums have got the word and they are comin' up like weeds everywhere in town, from Park Presidio blvd. to Union Square, sucking every bleeding heart they come across dry. At least down on Fisherman's Wharf (a.k.a. hell), they qualify as street performance, which is OK by me. If they even had a gimmick bordering on street performance, I could accept their presence, but yet few even try, and some don't even look that bad! The SF Chronicle ran a story on this and focused on a bum who works the Powell St BART station. The guy netted a Franklin ($100) daily to buy his crack. This is wrong. That scam boy did prompt me to dole out my spare change to "The Rock" in hell last weekend, at least he is trying. The mass of mentally ill that Ronald Reagan let out is not an excuse anymore, and I imagine any of them left wandering the streets would have a clean driving record and could become cabbies. A city supervisor is actually trying to train welfare recipients to become cabbies, fat chance. Why would they mess with an already sweet deal to work an honest day's work? I think I need to get laid, I'm feeling a tad resentful. Thank you for checkin' in. I would love to hear about your worst drunk or some tale from the state with no speed limit. (daylight hours, I know).

B.C. over.

Saturday, May 29, 1999
Greetings Bud,
I am a college student who will graduate from Syracuse University in August. I am considering starting an online business, but I don't know if my idea is good enough to succeed. As an experienced internet user, could you please provide me your thoughts on my idea. My idea is to open an online store that allows people to purchase personal items from the privacy of home. I would then ship the items to the customers in discreet packages and maintain strict confidentiality. I think most folks would like to purchase personal items in private. By personal items I mean birth control devices, feminine hygiene products, diet pills, hair treatments for balding, and many other products such as adult diapers. I have always been embarrassed when purchasing some of these items and I figure there has to be many other folks that feel the same way. If you think this is a good idea or you might use a website like this, please reply to this message. If you have ANY suggestions, such as what type of products I should sell, please send me the advice. Thank you for your time.

Lance C

Hey Mr. Wipplehead,
Don't squeeze my Charmin'.

B.C. over.

Friday, June 18, 1999
Hey Bud,
Remember me? Sharon Stone Seagull writer . . . ? I will be heading to My Fare City very soon . . . and I was wondering if you could hook a brother up with a ride? My cousin lives in San Fran and is a

teacher. She grew up in Cocoa Beach (that's where the surfer Kelly Slater is from). It's a kick ass beach town on the east coast of Florida. I like CAPTIVATED because it is very interesting. You should get an Hi8 camera and videotape a typical day in San Fran. Is Cisco "Grape" from San Fran? I wonder. We have a similar BUM ("Lazy Ass") situation in Florida, because the weather is warm they "Gaggle" like Seagulls here . . . It sucks. I'm 22 and I have had a job since I was like 10 years old. No BS. I used to help my Grandpa clean up construction sites. To all the sympathists out there who give BUMS money . . . don't. Go and by them an Egg McMuffin and see if they will take that. I remember in the news some time ago where a camera crew in an undercover van followed a few BUMS around in Orlando. One guy they followed took off his rags and got into a newer Volvo. What a scam. Remember, buy them some food or a Gatorade or something but don't give them money. There are plenty of jobs. Shit I know personally, I had a shit load of them. "Give me the Baby, I'm Hungry, c'mon baby I'm bigger than you and higher on the food chain. GET IN MY BELLY." That's from the new Austin Powers movie . . . Haa haaaa. Hey Bud do you like the movie "Dazed and Confused"? peaceimout.

Rob

Hey There Rob!
Glad to hear from the sunshine state again. Ya know I took an informal survey of fellow cab drivers while waiting at the best place to wait, if you want to wait that is, the airport. I was inquiring to the various uses of Alka Seltzer, other than hangover relief. Nine out of ten cabbies surveyed have been involved or at least admitted to knowledge of this madness. One cat threw the fatal chunks with anchovies wrapped around 'em high in the air, and the birds would eat them in flight, with the same tragic result. It was comforting to know this, especially as most of 'em denied any knowledge of the practice until I confided my tale with Radcliff to them. Each had a similar scenario, though most were from the teen or pre-teen years. This enlightenment also gave me confidence in my sugarless gum as I now believe in their nine out of ten dentists.

Matthew McConaughey's finest hour was *Dazed and Confused* as well as his relationship with Sandra "Speedy" Bullock. Look for an upcoming exposé on My Fare City featuring different bums. No weekly gig for them, though I have oh so been enjoying snapping pics of them, and others. For the seriously mentally ill street people, I will give a buck, or perhaps a 40-oz. I am not without my own sick set of morals too, my nights on the streets of San Francisco assured that. Look for upcoming treats on My Fare City of actual sound. Video is in the works, and specifically on some steep hills . . . There was an old cabbie who lived in a shoe, he had so many tickets, he didn't know what to do. First public service, he blew that chance off, then Willie's amnesty, got abruptly cut off. Round and round the block he did go, to pay for his crime. Whether stopped, or when go. Sometimes I just have to rhyme, though Parking and Moving just did not work on the last line, Shag Baby.

B.C. over.

Thursday, June 24, 1999
Dear Bud,
Am I crazy? I'm considering being a cabbie in your Fare City. Am I crazy, or just desperate? I used to drive in Oakland, but I don't want to be fighting with other cabbies over fares at Bart. Still, I like to drive, and I know the city fairly well. Do you know who's hiring and who/what number I ought to call?

Thanks, Rick

Dear Crazy,
I have been known to say, "I will try anything twice!" I even picked up two times in one shift at Murio's Trophy room, and did not even get a medal. Ho hum. Drive Cab?

B.C. over.

Friday, July 2, 1999
Just checked out your site for the first time and gosh I am so impressed. I enjoyed it immensely. Many thanks and keep up the good works luv!

Sue

Susan,
Rider:
Standing alone
In the corner of a bar
Know I won't make it
To my long lost car
Raising my hand
I'm right for a round
As I await
The bartender sounds
My cab has arrived
And to take it now
Since I know about jail
I take it, and how

Driver:
Do not go gentle into that red light
Nor Yellow
Even green if stale
I've been there
It's rough
Them cops on your tail,

B.C. over.

Sunday, July 4, 1999
Hi Bud,
My wife and I been your guests on our honeymoon. U said we will
find our way to your stories, but we couldn't find it. Please help us.
Remember you dropped us off around Jackson Square.

THx u, Paddy and Kerstin Honey Moonies

Hey Paddy and K,
If you can't stop, at least slow down and smell the pine tree scent.
Try taking a looky loo at "Waiting, Dating, and Mating." I hope the

sparks are still flying, and that I got your information correct, I was feeling a bit dyslexic day that. Lots of legend and mystery surrounds that district in My Fare City. It was the only district to be spared in the great quake and fire of 1906, bizarre, then and now. The then Moral Minority were outraged. See outside the district, the bible thumpers were the minority, but eventually, as with all good things, the government got rid of it. A mantra cried by the locals and stranded seamen at the time became an institution. "If, as they say, God spanked the town for being over-frisky, why did he burn the churches and spare Hotaling's whisky?" A.P. Hotaling owned and ran a lucrative whisky operation in several buildings in the hood. Hee Haw. One alley that remains the same today is Gold alley. A very upscale hot spot is located in the middle of what was once known as "Dead Man's Alley" to the locals. It's a trippy alley to navigate, Bix being dead center, and definitely worth a look. Looking back, it seems to me the process of bringing in large numbers of seamen, some back from work at sea, waiting to get the work that never came, inevitably led to a less-than-zero attitude. This led to the large instance of rape, murder, women on stage with farm animals (for real). For many, these were the best of times as well, perspective, remember? The only real ghost haunting the one area to survive the Great Quake, the place that gave SF the title of Babylon by the Bay (Herb Caen, RIP) is gentrified, but a handful of structures are left. I'll pass the fine recipe on to Radcliff, and I suspect he will have one to send back. Thanks so much for the comprehensive detail on the squab. After the first paragraph, it was easier to deal with it minus the head and feet. I do indeed think the people in cyberspace will dig it. I could have used a tip on how to get one other than with Radcliff. No doubt Chinatown has it. They club your live fish to death in front of you, sell live frogs that really do "taste like chicken", and the funky chickens themselves hang from every other window. I had to go in the back of a Chinatown tourist trap when I purchased my switchblade, next to a Chinatown "petting zoo." I will be on the look for that tasty squab, on the job, no doubt.

                                                              B.C. over.

Monday, July 5, 1999
Hi,
I've been reading your stuff since we met and it's all been good. In fact, when I get back to NZ, I've been seriously considering taking up cab driving as a profession! PS: I see you listen to KUSF, very nice. The company I work for has been streaming for a couple of years now and is unequivocally the best radio station I have ever found, anywhere. Cheers.

Matthew Oram

Hey There Matt,
As I recall, we went from SFO to Oakland airport, and I remember feeling a bit taken back that you had no baggage, at least 'til I dropped you off. Let it stream, live your dream.

B.C. over.

Wednesday, July 14, 1999
Bud,
Your site is really cool. I came upon it quite by accident and enjoyed your stories and cast of characters in your life very much. I had a friend who used to share taxi stories with me and they always made my evening. By the way, this taxi driver had a doctorate in one thing and three masters in another . . . that I know of . . . he was a "different breed of cat" . . . and that is what it takes to be a cab driver . . . especially in San Francisco. I love to write, and I appreciate your creativity here and the way you have "honored" different people along the way by including them and their photographs in your presentation.

Hey There Friend,
I do agree that it takes "a different breed of cat" to thrive and survive on the streets of San Francisco. I have followed my guiding light on many a day and night as being a cab driver does present you with an opportunity to see life and interact as no other occupation hits the same note, nor should try. I have been trying my best to let

folks see what I see, feel what I am feeling. Painting a picture with words is second nature to me, for this I am fortunate. Photographs have been integrated along the trail so I may go a step further beyond the words. As I am a firm believer in ascension, keep your ears and Real Player open as I go beyond sights and work to give you sound in My Fare City.

Happyness,

B.C. over.

Wednesday, July 9, 1999

Bud,

I recently bought a guide book to San Francisco to begin planning my vacation. But after reading a little bit of it, it sounds like a lot of hard work trying to see all those places. **LOL.** I am more of a "fly-by-the-seat-of-my-pants kinda gal!! Maybe you can tell me the best places to visit? At least a couple of "touristy" things and maybe a couple of things that as a tourist I might miss if someone didn't tell me about them? :) And hey . . . if you see a 6ft tall woman with auburn hair standing on the curb????? STOP!!!!!!!!!!!!!!! *GIGGLES*

Sandy

Sandy,

You have found the Golden Ticket to San Francisco.

1. Marin Headlands (Northwest of Golden Gate Bridge)

Just across the Golden Gate you get epic views, and don't forget a picture of yourself with the Golden Gate, and the city as a backdrop. Only cost is the three bucks it takes to get back into the city, bridge toll (transportation not taken into account).

2. Cable Cars (Powell and Market / Hyde and Beach). Ride 'em, hang off 'em, just watch out for that truck mirror as you round a corner and that mirror sticks out all but an unsafe few inches from you, barely knocking you off the car. Remember

when the conductor/brake man yells out, "Right side, suck it up," while a mirror on a parked truck grazes you. Follow the conductor's instructions to avoid road rash.

3. Lombard Street (Between Hyde and Leavenworth). Crooked it is, much like the industry itself. Thought the sign clearly states "No commercial vehicles allowed." No taxicab I have ever heard of has been cited. Gray line and the basic SF tour won't stop here. I can make it from the top to the bottom of the crooked block in 12 seconds, when no other cars are on it. I think it's an industry record, thankfully it's not on mine.

4. Hyde Street Seafood House and Raw Bar (Hyde at Washington St.). Midway on the Hyde St. cable car line lies this little diamond in the rough. The baked, stuffed oysters will make you want to, well . . . have some more! This is the best local flavor seafood place you can experience wearing dress casual clothes, without losing an arm and a leg. The staff is courteous and attentive, and while dining you look around and wonder how you found the place. Take a cab, at least to or from.

5. Specks (Alder Museum Café). Have a pitcher of Bud, after bailing on the somewhat pretentious jazz club next door, don't be shy, as the approach looks like a place you should go with someone who knows about the kind of place, but it's not. Santa still tends bar.

6. Elevators at the Westin Saint Francis (In the hotel of the same name).
They are not going to break through the roof and fly over My Fare City, but they are glass, and free.

7. Sam's restaurant (Tiburon, CA. Find ferry terminal located in hell, tourist hell that is). Take the ferry, or ride your bike there, and ferry back if you are feeling bold. The crab louie is served with such a generous amount of fresh crab it will satisfy even the best of 'em. The outdoor deck is the place to be, sipping a

Mai Tai while you gaze back across the bay at the city. Don't feed the birds. The problem of hungry seagulls is not as bad as the flying rats in My Fare City. The city, and Willie, finally came up with the politically correct decision to control the flying rat population here, the city workers are feeding them birth control, no shit.

8. Elbo Room (18ᵗʰ & Valencia) A cool club in the mission, as live music is at its best in a place like this. Located right across the street from the Mission police station, you even have a sense of security in an otherwise insecure world.

9. Taco Truck (Harrison St., at 18ᵗʰ and 24ᵗʰ) One taco, One buck. I have eaten seven, and have enjoyed two, it's all up to you.

10. Bonfire at Ocean Beach (Take Geary Westbound, 'til the Ocean, then make your way south) Legal, and free. Join one lit, or start your own. Don't sit downwind.

Have, fun, and remember when you get behind the wheel of a rent-a-car to drive fast and take chances . . .

B.C. over.

Friday, July 16, 1999
Hey Bud,
I drive a cab too and I had to pay my company for a parking ticket I got while parked in front of BofA at 2:30 A.M. I never got a ticket in the paper form because I took off when R2D2 appeared behind me. So last night I was taking a nap and I was fourth in line and all this honking woke me up to find the cab in front of me freaking out and the street cleaner coming up. My second ticket so's I chased the DPT lady down to Drumm and asked her why'd she have to give me a ticket and how's it's my job and I can't make 30 bucks in 2 hours at 3 in the morning. I said I woulda moved. She says she's tired of us cabbies lounging out, kicking back all chill in front there. I would've moved and what about postmen, do you give them tickets

and she says she gives everyone tickets except for the black and white. So I peeled out and gave up my cab for a lame shift.

Davey

Davey,
As you know, parking tickets are costly and a waste of our time. My heart goes out to you, I've been there as well. A co-worker got a Bus Zone love note last week for sitting in a bus zone while refueling (coffee), $275.00 I think, and boy was he mad. The backbook looks good in comparison, as at least you can fight, or bribe, or lie your way out of that. I picked up a delivery guy whose truck was towed at 3:01 P.M. on Geary St. between Grant and Stockton, (next to Needless Markup, a.k.a. Neiman Marcus) while making a delivery to the 12th floor. By the time I picked up the disgruntled employee to drive him to the pound (I know it well), he should have checked in on the 13th floor. The heartless Meter Maids are relentless, and like the BORG are not to be fucked with. The driver promised me he was not chatting with any cute secretary and having passed up this opportunity, he became even more incensed. I fueled his fire enough to get paid as I was on his side. His cannon became looser the closer we got to the Tow Yard, conveniently located next to the Hall of Justice (jail, and criminal courts). I told him to keep cool as he steamed off to retrieve his delivery truck. The Bud Carson Award for breaking the law and getting caught in the act goes to a new hack who got a photo ticket for running a red light. The sight of the window guy slipping the ticket under the bulletproof glass, complete with four photos, (cab at yellow, at red, picture of license plate, and best of all the close-up of him, looking a bit dim, no, more then a bit), wins the "better I see what this ticket looks like, as to remind me not to get one." If he loses in court, and most likely will, then his days as a cabbie are numbered. See you on the road Davey, or more likely in court fighting one of these bullshit tickets. Take it all the way to the judge if the pinheads at DPT don't get it that you are working for a living out there. My best-kept parking secret I now submit to you. The law states that it is legal for a vehicle to be

parked in front of a fire hydrant if the driver is in the vehicle. As I have had to brave the lack of parking for over ten years, I know this to be true. Whenever I came home so drunk I could not find a space and did not want to get in an accident or go crazy, I would just park down the street from my place, usually with a six pack, and wait. The few times I fell asleep, I awoke to an open space or a live meter maid alarm. Either way, I was not illegal as I was parked on the fire hydrant and often I got a good buzz waiting. Desperate times require desperate measures. My second-best parking secret would be in North Beach. The block of Kearny between Vallejo and Broadway is pretty fuckin' steep. If you park halfway between the top and bottom, it is impossible to tow you due to the grade of the hill. As a bonus, the lazy people that write the tickets, whether it be cops or meter maids, are too lazy to walk either up or down, then back up the hill to give you a citation. The three wheelers they hum around on would tip over if they even tried. I would also be amazed to find a beat cop who is up to the workout, just to give a parking ticket. This place works 95 percent of the time if your less than an hour with your chances of not getting cited droppin' about ten percent an hour. These are some odds I am willing to work with. DPT can kiss my sweet ass, as they have fucked with me on the job from One Bush to 101 Cal and everywhere in between. As far as your blues go at the BofA, I would think no matter how much competition lies amongst us cabbies that the guy behind you would have honked you out of your slumber and hence the punch below the belt by the meter maid. This is how I move on an early morning at the airport, when I am sleeping, and usually dreaming, I am brought back to consciousness by the horn of the hack behind me. A rude alarm, but I can go back to sleep in the next lot. I try to make sure the guy behind me is right behind me, sometimes even backing up a bit after he parks, to assure he won't just go around me. Otherwise he probably would. Happy hunting in the land of the free (except for parking) and the home of the brave (You gotta be brave if you misbehave). If you snooze you lose, OK. Better yet, just don't get caught

B.C. over.

Friday, July 23, 1999
Bud,
I was just checking out your righteous site and, wow, what a relief to have such raw material from the front lines. I dig riding in cabs on the weekends and your stories are a real turn on. By the way, whose the Cat's Meow with that loco tie? Nice Heine, Baby.

Felicia Humpalot

Felicia,
I think I would need more than bulletproof glass as protection with you steaming up the windows.
Q. Do you know what two all-beef patties, special sauce, lettuce, cheese, pickles, onions, on a sesame seed bum is? A. A Furburger. They are OK if you are really hungry, but otherwise I recommend fresh food.

B.C. over.

Wednesday, July 28, 1999
Hello all! I just wanted to let you know that I linked to you on my web page. Feel free to check it out. Have a great day! (sending a smile)

Heather Rose

Heather,
If you want to know the truth, I don't know what I think about it. I'm sorry I told so many people about it. About all I know is, I sort of miss everybody I told about. Even old Arch and E2, for instance. It's funny. Don't ever tell anybody anything. If you do, you start missing everybody.

B.C. over.

Wednesday, August 11, 1999
Bud, Thanks for responding to my last mess, though I know it violated all manner of etiquette, net-iquette, and don't-you-forgetiquette. I still enjoy hacked up, though I know some people get hurt.

Best—Dave from la la land

Dave from la la land,
Where's the beef? Got milk, etc.? Show me the money. Forget about
hacked up, what about my feelings?

B.C. over.

Friday, August 20, 1999
Bud,
I am a cab driver in Wayne, Mi., and I have had some "lovely"
fares in my day. I have been doing this part time for about 35
years, and I have seen almost everything. I put in 30 years with
GM, and now retired.

Clyde—Belleville, MI

Clyde,
Now I know thick skin and an even disposition are part of the daily
mix, but longevity is much more uncommon, though a part-time
situation would seem to have this attribute in mind. Working
weekends, dead in the morning, tourists in your cab in the afternoon
like flies in a trap, can be stressful to say the least.
Happy trails to you in Wayne, Mi. I'll be up by Traverse City next
month at my pal's parents' place on Torch Lake. I am looking forward
to the break in the action as the ever-changing face of the InSane
Francisco taxi industry policy continues to warp us hacks at every
corner. The theory of the mobius would come in handy. Big meeting
tomorrow to try and get a $75.00 gate cap in force. We will need
the force to be with us on this one. Help me Obe One. Happiness

B.C. over.

Friday, August 23, 1999
Bud,
What you did for the elderly lady going to the Safeway is much
more important than a quick ride and high fare. You can go to
sleep tonight knowing you helped someone who really needed help—
something you also may need someday. Congratulations on being a
true gentleman and a kind human being—we need more people like
you on earth. You made a positive difference in someone's life.

Thank you, Nita Stewart

Nita,

Mobility is a major problem for many folks I drive around, and I appreciate the well wishes from you on a job well done. It is much easier to have a broad perspective on the day shift, as reasons for mobility problems differ greatly from after dark. Health or age seem to be the biggest hurdles for my riders as of late, where intoxication has taken a well-deserved "back seat." Everyone knows Bill W. when the sun goes down, whether he be friend or foe. Thanks again for the good word, Ms. Bonita. Oh yeah, I loved you on Saturday Night Live, but you didn't hear it from me . . . Save a seat for me.

B.C. over.

Wednesday, August 25, 1999
Hi Bud,
I love to read entries on your page from time to time. This was I think the first cab ride I ever took as an adult . . . Me and a woman I met in Yugoslavia flew together to Karachi, Pakistan. We got married five months later, and still are 14 years later. We had no clue what Pakistan was like. We didn't have or read any guidebook. We didn't have hotel reservations and we had flown there on one-way tickets. So we leave customs and immigration, starting to leave the airport at 5 A.M. or so. When we round a corner and see the exit, we can see barricades outside. On the other side of the barricades are dozens of Pakistanis jumping and yelling. On our side are two uniformed men with whips, to keep the crowd back. We go more and more slowly to the exit, and it equally slowly dawns on us that all those people are vying for our attention. We being two of the very few westerners on the flight. Anyway, it turns out all these screaming maniacs are cab drivers wanting to take us, specifically us, to someplace else. We are tired from the all-night flight. Our minds can't even believe what we see before us. So, basically the most persistent of them kinda bundles us into his cab, and puts our luggage on the roof. The cab has no meter. No odometer. No license. He tries to sell us on a five-star hotel, but we had told him we wanted cheap, and we stuck to it. He offers us "nature's gift" (hashish). We finally get to a place, and the

front desk loans us enough money to pay him 200 rupees. No tip, but of course we later learned the correct fare was no more than 50 rupees. I've since taken many taxi rides in many places, but none as memorable as that one.

Ken Riggle

Mr. Riggle,
I bet the "nature's gift" you undoubtedly accepted ran 150 rupees. Here in Northern California, God's Country, "nature's gift" (kind buds) runs four hundred bucks an ounce.

B.C. over.

Tuesday, September 7, 1999
"It's a Lie, It's all a Lie"
•Dispatcher
Good Morning. Day after Labor Day. The way I figure it, I've got four choices on how to get to work. Walk, bicycle, streetcar, cab. I decide as I'm getting ready. I've got lots of stuff to carry. Walking's out. I want to wear a dress 'cuz I've got appointments this afternoon. Bye to the bike. I haven't heard a streetcar trundling West in the last half-hour, which means that they won't be coming back East anytime soon. I decide to opt for a cab.
It's 8:45 A.M. I call. I hold.
It's 9:03 A.M. I place an order. Finish getting ready. Get the trash loaded.
It's 9:30 A.M. Clip my nails, think of Bill, change my jewelry selection.
It's 9:45 A.M. I take the trash down.
It's 9:47 A.M. No cab. I call, dispatcher says, "It's on its way." I go outside. I smoke some kind bud. I talk to my neighbor.
It's 10 A.M. I go to the corner to check to see if a bus is coming. Nada.
It's 10:05 A.M. I call back. I state as throatily and sexily as I can, "The cab you said was on its way hasn't arrived yet." The dispatcher gets a little crazed. He calls the driver. The driver says he was there and I was not. The dispatcher snarls, "Didja hear that?" I retort with the truth, "He's lying." Dispatcher says to the driver,

"Do you hear that? She says 'It's a lie'. It's all a lie." He then asks me, "What do you want us to do?" I say nothing, do nothing, I'll call another cab company. But really, I want to tell him to get a better system, to stop lying, and that I feel stupid for being true to Veterans, for continuing to use them even though my ex drives for them now (or maybe because of it), that I should NEVER have called their lame-o-late asses to let them know when I was sick of waiting and was gonna leave, and that I also WANTED them to send a fucking cab to arrive in three seconds and take me to work for free 'cuz you know what? If he'd have been kind, I would have said, "Send another." Instead, I won't call them anymore. I know, I know, they won't care. But from now on, my tips will probably be a little smaller and my mindset will be a little less tolerant of Veterans. And all for the want of a cab on time. So there you have it Bud. My tale of woe. And also my kudos. Your writing shows much growth and improvement since the start of your journal. Keep passing the open windows and sparkling on our fine city.

Hellen Wheels

Hellen,
Can I get you some cheese with your whine? I would put money down that you are a red-head, or even worse, dye your hair to achieve faux red-head status, which works about as well as a T-shirt and shorts at the end of the cab line in hell (a.k.a. Fisherman's Wharf) at sunset on a Friday night. In the tourists' defense, they don't know any better. A testament to this can be seen throughout the city as I see folks from the Haight to Union Square with the same sweatshirt on. The color may differ, though the print on the front is the same. The print on the front is a sailboat with "San Francisco" written above it, circling around the sailboat abstract. I say abstract because it is done with white lines created with the help of a hot iron. It is made in the USA though the sweatshop in My Fare City's Chinatown District resembles things back in the homeland where making Nike tennis shoes is the highest Man Van Tran will get climbing the ladder of success. The lucky few who make it to land of the free and the home of the brave will labor even lower than manual, with an occasional exception to the rule turning up when you wake up in the middle of

the night to turn the TV off. Before you find the remote, you hear something about no money down, but end up pausing before you go back to sleep to decide whether or not the girls surrounding the geek with a pitch are naturally endowed, or have implants. As you drift off back to dreamland, the point is moot as you will never get a handful, and looking good was all they needed to do on TV. The sweatshirt czar in hell is the only one to sell that cheap print but you still see it everywhere. There are a lot of tourists in this here town, the most stupid being the ones who book a hotel out near Ocean Beach at any time of year and expect the image of California to be the same they saw on the Hertz rental car commercial. Highway 1 may have a lot of curves, along with the babe in the passenger seat, but it's important to remember that the sun don't always shine in My Fare City, or on you moon cake, and that OJ doesn't fly through airports, at least not anymore.

B.C. over.

Monday, September 13, 1999
Bud,
You are truly the ambassador to San Francisco. They could have some big ceremony giving you the keys to the city, but it would not matter because you can go wherever you want. The dispatch is getting better and better.

Smokin Joe

Smokin Joe,
Please open your good book to LUKE 16:1 (the New Testament). The wily manager of another time, he said to his disciples: "A rich man had a manager who was reported to him for dissipating his property. He summoned him and said, 'What is this I hear about you? Give me an account of your service, for it is about to come to an end.' The manager thought to himself, 'What shall I do next? My employer is sure to dismiss me. I cannot dig ditches. I am ashamed to go begging. I have it! Here is a way to make sure that people will take me into their homes when I am let go.'"

B.C. over.

Sunday, September 12, 1999

Bud,

Time flew by and my vacation is drawing near. **Smiles.** I will be flying your way the second week of October. I guess I will just have to flag down every cab that comes my way until you show up? Remember . . . if you see a 6ft. tall woman with auburn hair (I'm sure there aren't that many of us—LOL) STOP!!!!!!!And Bud???? Loved the story of the little old lady and the Safeway :)))) That is exactly the kind of thing I would do too!!!!!!

:) Sandy

Hello Sandy,

I hope you enjoyed your golden ticket that was posted in the mailbag a few weeks ago. It took me some time to get a response as I wanted to give you a head-to-toe variety on the sights and sounds of the capitol of the universe. Unfortunately the only way to guarantee a taxi will stop for you is to have a suitcase at your side, even if it's empty. All of My Fare City's hacks love to go south, and the "keep them wheels turnin', proud Bud keep on burnin'" destination of San Francisco International Airport that 4 out of 5 people with luggage will recommend you take them to. Just make sure the suitcase and yourself are in the vehicle before you disclose where you need to go, wherever that may be. I am curious, for informational purposes of course, when your arrival and departure dates are, exactly. Honestly, I need to do some meditation before your arrival. I will be positioned in the lotus position or the queue at SFO while speaking in tongues, quietly, but audible enough for myself to hear, and also, if I at any point during my transcendental heavy metal should get tape recorded, an extraordinary occurrence would go down. If you played my mellow mantra backwards, memories of Led Zeppelin slowly crashing to earth, you would hear the following, no shit. "So you see!" laughed the cat. "Now your snow is all white! Now your work is all done! Now your house is all right! And you know where my little cats are?" said the cat. That voom blew my little cats back in my hat. And so, if you ever . . . have spots now and then, I will be very happy, to come here again . . .

B.C. over.

Thursday, September 16, 1999
Dear Bud:
Your web page is totally great—my husband and I just came back from
two weeks in San Francisco, and reading your waybills brings back the
whole trip. I love the city, and I'm looking forward to the next time we
can visit. We had a few interesting moments in SF—there was the cab
driver who went into deep and excruciating detail about his recent trip
to Turkey for the eclipse and the Christian sites he saw there. (We
weren't going to say anything, as he was a very nice guy and he hadn't
charged us for waiting when my husband hopped out to drop off
something at a friend's apartment. But I learned **way** more about
alleged appearances of the Virgin Mary in Turkey than I'd expected to
that evening) Oh, and while we were waiting for a bus on Market, an
older lady in a green windbreaker walked past us and slapped my husband
on the ass. He's English, and couldn't quite understand why a complete
stranger would smack him on the bum—I told him it was obviously a
positive reaction to his new beard. :-) I also understand what you were
saying about the homeless problem—we regularly saw a woman sitting
in a wheelchair outside of Lori's on Sutter who would get up occasionally
and wander inside to use the bathroom, her legs seemed to work quite
well when Nature called. However, I loved the guys who provided a little
bit of street theater—the World-Famous Bushman nailed my husband
near Pier 39, and there's a soft-spoken guy on 2nd Street east of Mission
who sells these pretty little café chairs he makes out of old soda cans
and scraps of fabric. Anyone who can create folk art out of stuff other
people throw away is pretty cool in my book.

Best, Melanie Fletcher

Hello Melanie,
I do so love the windy city, blurred memories of visiting Chicago.
The usual suspects would meet for hangover relief at the some
dive, then on to an afternoon at Wrigley, and those 16 oz. Old
Styles that are always difficult to muscle down, the additional 4 oz.
you get over the usual can-o-brew. Still daylight, Cactus or the
Hunt Club was a transitional phase posing for women doing the
same thing, so intensely that nothing but the shoe test might come
of it. Ed Debeviks to inhale the meal, or Centro being the other
choice due to the cute waitresses that at least led us on, better

than our previous stop. The slimelight can rest in peace in my opinion, though the Metro was the venue for a very memorable Ramones show, Ministry too. My friend Ritchie Rich lost his Rolex at that show. X marks the spot, circle gets the square. After midnight, WEEDS on 1555 N Dayton was good for an open mike, and many a free shot from the owner Sergio. Cheers Serg. Late was, and is always great in Chicago, as the point of destination was the mines, The Kingston Mines. With the mines having live reggae 'til 4 A.M. every night of the week, we couldn't go wrong, and never did. My pal from Wicker Park kept us high and happy 'til we made it back to his house. By the time I hit the couch, the drugs had just about worn off, the joint brought the whole event together like a Christmas gift my mom had wrapped, no pun intended. OK, maybe it was. Yes, it was a rude awakening, money stuffed in my pocket in a big ball, like a Chinaman cabbie in My Fare City. Not a joke. You know Chicago is run like a well-oiled machine, and I was not a bit surprised when I found out that the name "The Windy City" was not given on the meteorological angle. It was attributed to the politicians. No shit. It still is windy, too cold, too hot, and patterning my life after the little girl who broke into the three bears' (Chicago?) house and sampled the porridge. The mom and pop bears were too hot (Chicago) and too cold (New York) while the baby bears were just right (My Fare City). It's no coincidence my old man keeps telling me to quit looking for the inner child and to start looking for the inner adult. Thanks again for your thoughts, I was sent on a daydream, and still am basking in the memories, or lack of, that Chicago has served me up. It's been too long since I have had that warm fuzzy feeling, au natural.

B.C. windy over.

Friday, September 17, 1999
Here's another cab story for ya Bud,
Last weekend I was in downtown Boston with my two roommates and a friend. It was about 3 A.M. and we really wanted to get a cab back to our place. Trouble was, everyone else seemed to have the same idea. After waiting for about 30 minutes, we finally managed to get to a cab just as about 6 people who had all been squeezed into the cab piled out. One of them said to us, you don't want this

cab, the driver is crazy! From the look on the guy's face, I believed him, but we really didn't have much choice considering the cab shortage. After my roommate Debbie told the cabbie where we were going, we were off. He was wearing a turban and looked like he might be Middle Eastern. Debbie told the driver to take a left at an upcoming traffic light, and he loudly replied, "Relax baby, I know where the HELL I am going!" in a funny accent. I almost cracked up then and there, but I think we all realized the past occupants of this taxi had not been lying. The driver had no second thoughts about laying on the gas, and weaving around cars. He tried to make some more conversation, asking me about my job, degree, etc. I kept my replies to a minimum, not wanting to egg him on any more than necessary. Later in the ride he tells me, "I got her to shut on, didn't I?" I think he meant that he got Debbie to shut up, but I am thinking he's being pretty damn rude. We did get home fast, and I actually admired the cabbie's driving skills, as he obviously knew all the shortcuts through Boston. I gave him a decent tip, despite his weird confrontational attitude. On the walk from the corner back to our house, my roommates were memorizing his cab number so they could call the company and complain. I chimed in that he did take a cool shortcut that I wouldn't have thought to take, and that he got us back fast. Plus he was good for a laugh. This was one cab driver I won't forget for a while.

Nick Hausman

Nick,
I just love when somebody jumps in the cab and says "get me to the airport (or wherever) and step on it!" It takes away the fare's chance to legitimately complain about the speed and demeanor of my driving. Last time this happened, the guy told me on arrival that I drive like a hooligan. A license to ill, or sometimes thrill, if you will.

B.C. over.

Monday, September 20, 1999
Dear Bud,
When I told my Mom and Dad that my new job was driving a taxicab they didn't cry, only because they knew it wouldn't change my mind.

I needed a job, I had bills, you can't pay for me. Way it goes, Joe. Still, ain't no denying that this can be a dangerous job. I hear that cabbie death rates are higher than cops and convenience store clerks, which is more than average. Night drivers get offered a lot more than day riders; of course, I was a night driver. Way it goes, Joe. One absolute prerequisite to being a cabbie is a nearly psychotic sense of optimism. My best karma is right around the corner; if today sucks, then tomorrow is another better day. Or, the day, week, or month after that. So this decade blows . . . But a cabbie's necessary optimism isn't as psychotic as doom-saying pessimists are inclined to believe. When you think about it, the odds are very much in the driver's favor, in spite of the dangers. There's a lot you can do to make the job a lot less dangerous.

1. Be nice to people, as much as you can. Don't pick fights, and don't let anyone pick a fight with you.

2. Be wary of anyone who is vague about where they are going.

3. Speak good English. Damn, I sure hate to say that, but my observation is that people with immigrant—sounding names populate the death lists a lot more than they should.

4. Above all else, be alert.

That means, little green-pea, heed the words of Sun Tzu, the ancient author of the "The Art of War": Above all else, know as much as you can. Observe to the extent you are able. That means look the fares in the eye when they enter the cab, greet them, then look them all over. A guy who's wearing a trenchcoat on a hot night could be just some flasher on his way to a flashing, but he could also be using it to conceal a piece. Know where all the nearby and far-away cop houses are, so you can pull into the parking lot, bail on the cab, leaving the crook inside. Keep riders in the back seat under observation. I realize that all of this is a lot easier said than done at the end of the night shift when it's about three in the morning and nearly time to go home. The harder it gets, the more important alertness becomes. Some drivers have this more militaristic approach. In Hotel Hell, I once met this Somalian dude from the Horn of Africa. In the '80s, the Americans and Russkies were both trying to get control of the place, each setting up guerrilla warfare schools, and I'll bet this guy graduated at the top of his class in either or both. That's why I got a bit nervous when he told me about his "guardian angel, like you say here." It was a .45 Colt auto, with pearl handles and a bright finish. Gun was worth a good week's fares on the underground market, God only knows how much at a legit gun shop. Trouble with guys like him is that the gun gives them an attitude. Go ahead, try to kill me. Apparently, the thugs do because Somalians are numerous on the death lists hereabouts. The Valley is relatively safe. No cabbies have died here in something like 10 years. Considering the carnage along the coast, that's saying something. Still, being careful never hurts.

LA Dave

Dave my man,
When things go wrong, as they sometimes will,
When the road you're trudging seems all uphill,
When funds are low and debts are high,
And you want to smile, but you have to sigh,
Your work is endless, and meaningless,
Your boss is ready, for a big fat kiss,
On the ass, and all day long,
When harassment and intimidation got you down a bit,
Rest if you must, he won't lest you quit.

Life is queer, with it's twists and turns,
As everyone of us sometimes learns,
And many a failure turns about.
What he might have won if he'd stuck it out,
Stick to your task, though the pace seems slow,
You may succeed with more than one blow.

Success is failure turned inside out,
The silver tint of the clouds of doubt,
And you never tell how close you are,
It may be near when it seems afar,
So stick to the fight when you're hardest hit—
It's when things seem worst that you're unable to quit.

(taxi driver mantra)
Keep 'em comin' L.A. Dave

B.C. over.

Tuesday, September 21, 1999
I was just reading your response to Melanie's letter and you mentioned that someone told you to forget about finding your inner child and instead find your inner adult. My mom found a picture in a magazine once with a picture of kids jumping off of a dock. The caption said "Forget your inner child, find your inner tube." Just something I was reminded of . . .

Brahm Lewandowski

Brahm,
Puff, puff! Chug, chug! Choo, choo! Off they started! Slowly the cars began to move. Slowly they climbed the steep hill. As they climbed, each little steam engine began to sing, "I—think—I—can! I—think—I—can!—I—think—I—can! I—think—I can! I—think—I—can! I—think—I—can! I think I can! I think I can! I think I can I think I can—" My mom inspired me with this passage as a child, in what was to become a mantra of sorts, like no other. When I thought it could get no better, it got better. Resolution came to my world of worries, like a light shining bright. "I—thought—I—could! I—thought—I—could! I—thought—I—could! I—thought—I—could! I thought I could—I thought I could—I thought I could."

Wednesday, September 29, 1999
Bud,
I drive hack in Salt Lake City and love to check out the stories 'n such that you put online. People don't realize how much we see of the human element out there. I probably have 100 stories about this 'n that if I put my mind to it, but wouldn't want to hog all your time with my mental meandering. :) I will attach this small poem I wrote a while back when driving one night. It was Thanksgiving night and I felt compelled to say something about all the homeless we drivers see all the time. If nothing else, for the remainder of

my time on the globe, I will remember how you ended this article. Nights equal the problem people, days equal the solution people. Hope this works because I am kinda computer stupid in some ways (ah hell, in a lot of ways). Let me know if the poem comes along with this email. Keep up the GREAT work. I will try to get more involved as time goes on, if I may be allowed to.

Thanx, inj

Eye Enn Jay,
I do declare, I have never heard the term "mental meandering" ever before and believe me, I have heard most all of 'em. Where I come from it's called mental masturbation and everyone does it, though few will admit to it. Even the few that do would never do this in public, lest exhibitionist and sickos. A trench coat, sneakers with no socks, and an overpowering smell of Old Spice immediately come to mind. Yet, here in San Francisco, not only do people encourage it, they respect it. Cause, it's your thing. Some like myself even do it for an unknown infinity then void themselves of accountability to what comes back from the other side, so as not to influence the spirit in what was intended. I won't descramble your poem to my readers until you free yourself from those chains, mental emancipation I say.

B.C. over.

Thursday, October 21, 1999
Bud,
And now, my own personal tale of terror. One night, I picked up a guy in Pacoima who made me nervous. He had this furtive, weasely quality to him. He had trouble telling me where, exactly, he wanted to go, though he finally gave me an address in Van Nuys. OK, so it was late, about two in the morning. Could just be shitfaced, right? After all the bars were closing. Nevertheless, you had best believe I kept my eye on him. (Where was my guardian angel??) You had also best believe that I got nervous when I noticed that he was looking at me, when he thought I couldn't see him. Cold fisheye in the rearview. And I got really nervous when he slid quietly across the

back seat to where he was directly behind me. We were driving on the 170 freeway, and it was quiet and dark as a tomb outside. That analogy is no accident, friends. What followed wasn't, either. I took a deep breath and swooped the cab over to the side of the highway under one of those pink sodium lamps, flicked on the dome light, stopped and confronted the guy. "You really scare me, mister," I said, "sitting back there, right behind me like that. I think you're trying to rob me." When I said that, his face went absolutely ashen. Like a kid you saw right through, when he was trying to put one over on you. (Do you, like, have eyes on the back of your head?) My heart was racing, but my head was not. I obviously had this guy on the defensive. I was alone, with him. Did he have a gun? I'll never know, and I'm glad. I got out of the cab, and crept on hands and knees around the back, crunch-crunch on the roadside, to back at the trunk. The guy was still in the back. I figured if he was gonna shoot, he'd have to find me first, then go through the cab. The owners could bill me. Plus, there were some nice thick bushes to hide in. Then, along came a car, with headlights blazing. It was a CHP! A cop! Was I glad? I was ecstatic as he SWOOPED gracefully over to the side, then backed up to get near where I was parked. My passenger saw that, then flung open the door, darted across the freeway, bounded over the barrier in the middle, then almost got hit by a southbound car like the mangy Cur dog he was. Chippie was this young guy, who, when I told him what had happened, raced across the highway, almost got hit by another car, like the first guy, then came back. Took a police report. Called dispatch and told them I had a runner. Didn't tell 'em that the first runner was me. Did I do the right thing? Well, I'm here to say, but I debate it often. Drivers I've talked to are divided in their opinions. Most say, right on, buddy! Others say: What if that car hadn't stopped? What if the guy got belligerent and started shooting? Simple, I was out of the cab. What was the guy gonna do? My venerated buddy Sun Tzu basically says to fuck with your enemy, mess with his mind, a good offense is the best defense, which is what I did that night. Turn your weakness into strength. I got away from him while I could, to where he couldn't get an easy shot at me, if he even had a gun. Didn't give him a chance to mess with me. No time to get to the cop house (least I knew where it was). Hand over my heart, swearing on pics of Jesus, Buddha, etc., I think, to my grave, I did the right thing. On the other hand, obviously, if he'd just blasted away in the cab, when he had the chance, he might have hit me. But, maybe not, or at least not fatally. I knew he was there and what he was about. Sun Tzu, I'll hoist a few to ya', old buddy. A few people have even suggested that maybe I was just being a bit paranoid. And, safe at home, fingers wrapped around a beer, reclined in the Barf-A-Lounger, watching Hee-Haw reruns on the tube and listening happily to the radio, I almost buy that. But, I stand behind my belief that the guy was up to no good. It was a combination of things. The vagueness of his directions on where he wanted to go. Some cabbies told me they'd have taken him right to the nearest cop house right then and there. Let him explain, after he's searched for weapons. False alarm, sorry bud, take you home with no fare. But the biggest, most important thing was the way he slid right behind me on the freeway. There was no reason for him to do that, unless he was gonna rob me. There were no signs to read, no nudie/taco/sushi/gay/etc bars to find, no buddies to wave to, just the hacked-off oleanders lining the middle of the highway. Even without his furtiveness, nervousness and cold fisheye in the rearview, that was enough. If you think I did the wrong thing, tell me, 'cause I want to know. If you've been there, done that, tell me what I done wrong. Tell me what you'd do and why. But be prepared to fight. If I get the sense that you're sitting there, sipping wine with no idea of a cabbie's life, be prepared to be eviscerated, humiliated and excoriated. I think what saved me that time was that the guy was at least a bit rational; his plan, if he had one, went awry when I proved to be hip to his tricks. The one nightmare I've never faced was a true, dyed-in-the-wool crazy. The guy who gets in and says he's pissed and wants to hurt or kill you, pulls out his Guardian Angel, points it at choo, then does it before you can say "shit." Went back to the barn, then home to my coffin, closed the lid, opened it and went back on my shift the following night. The cup of life is one-third FULL. So get me a straightjacket. My tennis shoes were tied, and my karma and baseball cap were on straight, for the moment. It was a better day, had nine runs to the Airport, LAX!! a record! plus a couple of others. Mama mia, baby didn't even have the diarrhea, though I did.

DB White

Dave,
It's nice not everyone in your hood is a sellout. You are the man. B.C. over.

Thursday, October 21, 1999
Hey Bud!!
Just got back last week from visiting Sacramento and San Francisco. :>)) I flew into Sacramento to see a friend and then we drove to San Francisco. It was fleet week and I had a great time. I stood on many street corners but you didn't come by . . . or at least I didn't recognize you. **GRINS.** My feet hurt like hell cause I'm not used to walking that much and I needed a taxi and they were all busy! Or at least none of them stopped . . . and I looked pretty damn good! LOL. One thing I didn't like? You can't smoke ANYWHERE OUT THERE! What is with that!? And I was probably the only woman who was walking up all those hills smoking a cigarette! Just cause I was afraid it might be my last. LOL. And BUD? I saw many things that you have written about on here . . . and you are absolutely right . . . IT IS A GREAT CITY!! Your tour is GREAT, but in person was even better! Hope to come back out there soon, it was definitely worth the trip!

XOXO Sandy

Hey Now,
Timing is everything, and sometimes in My Fare City walking is the best option. As far as smoking, it would have been OK in my back seat.

B.C. over.

Tuesday, October 26, 1999
Hello Bud Carson!
I'm Mickey from Japan. I was surfing the net, and I found your homepage. I send this mail because I think that you may be very kind and good personality. Please propagate this message throughout your acquaintances.

Mickey

Mickey Mouse,
You know we have a cookbook here in the states that has literally hundreds of ways to prepare Spam? I think you could benefit greatly from the variety this counterculture bible offers on this fine American dish. Happy trails.

B.C. over.

Monday, November 1, 1999
Hello!
You have been invited by Hyacyn to join the Listed Yahoo! Club

named "Taxicab." To become a member of this club, just go to the Web address below. Yahoo!

Spam man

SM,
I am getting all the YAHOO! I need driving the YAHOO! cab. Every group of guys I chance upon, one of them always yells "YAHOOOOO!" Worth it cause the sleek little NEC touch screen laptop works great and the wireless modem stays connected better than my cell phone, and it's free!

B.C. over.

Wednesday, November 3, 1999
Hey now,
I'm a cabbie in Miami/Ft. Lauderdale area. I've read most of your site up and down—good grief man! I'm cruising nights in a FORD, actually a Mercury Gran Marquis, but 5.0 at any rate. I'm curious. What do you drive usually? I drive for Friendly Checker here and we're less hi-tech than yellow cabs with their pewters and harsh hues, but we dominate the city of Hollywood. I have airport personals and the fares are either round the corner or long hauls to South Beach or Ft. Lauderdale. I really identify with you, your 'tude is similar to mine and I'm one of the rare hacks who lugs a minimum of 30 CDs with me per shift, all beyond eclectic. I also ride a bike to meet my day driver on the waterways. I've been a bartender at numerous jobs, owned a popular coffeehouse with large ashtrays and hung steel construction. Driving a cab is a lot like bartending—you're responsible for your patrons, yet they buy your attention, you pass out the good deeds whenever you can, knowing that it will come back to you someday. Staying out of trouble is job one. Making a buck comes second. I would like to sort out my experiences online much like your site. I'm holding out for a digital camera first. Picture-caption style. I'd rather start like that, since rambling on blank pages is not my forte.

H-Man

Hello H-Man,
I have seized a few engines in my stint as a cab driver, all Ford
Crown Vics as a matter of fact. They were ready to go, I just did a
Kevorkian and put them out of their misery. Like you, I run in a
Mercury Grand Marq which eats up the hills of My Fare City like a
hot knife in to a stick of butter. Getting the overdrive to kick in,
like only an 8 cyl can do, while gunning it up a steep hill gives me
that warm fuzzy feeling. I, like you, take on the service industry
vs. the ever-changing world. It's a constant balancing act with
safety first as you so wisely mentioned. I will put it out there that
it's pretty hard to be prejudicial in my neck of the woods. I have
picked up a night shift here and there but need to keep reminding
myself that chipping will lead to a bad habit, and I got enough
problems as is. Still, it's hard for me not to play after dark once in
a while.

B.C. over.

Wednesday, November 3, 1999
Oy Bud,
I'm a 51-year-old woman from Victoria, Vancouver Island, Canada
and just wanted to let you know that I was indeed Captivated by
your stories. I suppose it doesn't speak well of my own life to say
this, but I read each story with voyeuristic glee. Kind of like a book
you can't put down. It was refreshing too, to read an honest,
unembroidered account of life rather than the usual nicey-nice tripe.
Seems to me you have excellent material for a book . . . perhaps
an ongoing series . . . kinda like Callaghan's Crosstime Saloon,
only it all takes place in a cab and is true rather than imaginary. I
noticed in the reading that you seem to have one foot in each
camp, sort of. I mean on the one hand, most of your observations
about people and events are shown from a counter-culture perspective,
but then you show signs also of having some pretty firm
"establishment" values as well. Guess like all of us, you are the sum
total of your life experiences. So that's about all the pieces of mind I
can spare right now, but just wanted to let you know the work and

communicating you do on Captivated is appreciated and enjoyed by someone . . . probably many someones.
Sincerely,

Divine Madness

Hello North,
I thank you for your kind words. You are correct in the assumption that I see and come from several different perspectives. Bottom line, I am either living in the problem or the solution. My journey through life has not been an easy one, yet I have lived to tell. Having lost count some time ago, I think it's safe to say this cat is on his ninth life. I would like to consider myself kind of an umpire of life, I call 'em as I see 'em. I think what you picked up on is the fact that in my game of life, the rules bend and even change as I most definitely do. In the end, whatever happens, I have learned a lot about myself and about life. I have a much greater respect for life today than I ever imagined possible. What keeps biting me in the ass is responsibility, because respecting life, all life, mandates a certain level of responsibility. I am working on it, and trying to put my best foot forward. I need to remember to live in the now, as one foot in the past and the other in tomorrow just leaves me pissing on today.

B.C. over.

Monday, November 8, 1999
Bud,
I got bored and typed in cab drivers (so many, yikes). I used to drive a cab here in Lexington, KY. I did until some punk shot me in the back!! I thought I hated it, but I really miss it. By the way, nice pics.

Phil Tkacz

Phil,
I am sorry to hear about your untimely departure from the wild world of cab driving. Like women, or even drugs, it's always easier to remember the good times, while blotting out the bad stuff. I

have to remember this everyday, cause when I don't, I get a dose of reality that is about as subtle as getting hit over the head with a ton of bricks. Hence, I stay away from things that have hurt me in the past, with both women and drugs topping the list. I think maybe cab driving was not your problem, but the wingnut with the gun. Some things can't be avoided, and to try and balance out the random acts of violence in My Fare City, I have been rescuing people from MUNI bus stops and letting 'em have a free ride, and every one of my comp riders say it is their first free cab ride. With the odds against 'em, I don't mention it will also probably be the only one they would get. Without mental-health days, I would not keep one step ahead of the men in the white suits, who are waiting for me to fuck up.

B.C. over.

Monday, November 8, 1999
Bud,
I found your site a few days ago, and since have read a few articles. For a person having no "Formal Education," you sure have a TALENT for writing. Your dialog is interesting, captivating, and quite enjoyable to read. Just wanted to tell you that. I look forward to reading more in your site. One other thing, you make references to 12-step lingo. I know this is none of my business, but inquiring minds want to know. I am recovering. And a lot of recovering people have been through so much. So after they get their shit together, seeing people who don't is quite interesting.

Andrea

Andrea,
Attraction, not promotion, eh? The fact I am here to tell should indicate where I am, and how I got here. Funny thing, having traveled on both sides of the tracks, I can honestly say that I would wish on no one what I have had to go through. I tend to learn things the hard way, but having learned a lot, some might say that's the only way I can get it. Sometimes medicine that's good for you can taste real bad.

B.C. over.

Wednesday, November 24, 1999
Waybill? You keep a waybill? If EVERYONE traveled by taxicab EVERYDAY you think the police could make us keep track of where EVERYONE goes? :-) Fourth Amendment violation. At least that is what I plan to tell the police if they ever try to make me keep a waybill. I don't think they will want to chance losing the power to make EVERYONE keep a waybill if I take them to federal court just to force LITTLE OLD ME to do their bidding. :-)

Denis Drew DeSoto (when I winter in S.F.)

Dear DD,
A wise man once told me a story about a lady who went and got her foot run over by a taxi, in the financial district. She reported a yellow cab and the cab #. Apparently she got the cab number wrong. The cab driver who had the unlucky number was stopped, and detained (nice way of saying brought to jail) for questioning. A waybill supporting his alibi prevented an innocent man from having to pay large legal fees and of course jail, other than the complimentary cooling off period initially. Cab College 101. As far as big brother, he is popping up faster than panhandlers on a sunny day in the Upper Haight. Thirty more intersections will be added to the existing seven, equipped with cameras to bust red-light runners, via a ticket by mail. They need four pictures to get ya, and they do, as some sad sack new driver got handed one under the bulletproof glass from the window guy. It had pictures of the cab at yellow, and red. Finally, a close up of the license plate and a headshot of the driver sealed the state's case airtight. Keep an eye on the mail. Should you ever get caught behind someone in any of the photo light intersections, utilize your waybill by flipping down the visor to check it. The headless cabbie does not get mailed any tickets.

B.C. over.

Wednesday, December 1, 1999
Bud,
Feeling sort of down, I clicked on personal journal and what do I

find, but a cab driver who writes. I started as a cab driver after four years in the Coast Guard and got through college and law school while driving and dispatching. After reading your journal, a little, I remembered how tough it was—out on the streets till 2 or 3 A.M., the smell of the engine and the people—yeah, the people—sometimes they smelled a hell of a lot worse than the engine. I thought, at times, of writing but could come up with nothing but short stories. Then, I saw a movie about cabs and driving around the world. It was a series of vignettes, which occurred in a cab at the same hour, but around the world. Someone had done it—they had taken the series of short stories and stuck them into a movie that worked. Well, I'm no longer feeling down. Instead of starting a journal, I wrote it out right here. So, I ended up as a lawyer in Boston, representing cab drivers who suffered personal injuries—until they took Worker's Comp benefits away from Boston cabbies. Do you have them? The class of people who are most vulnerable to injuries, and what do our great pols do—take away benefits and give the profit to the owners. We no longer really have waybills. Just rentals. Strange missive. Why don't you put your intelligent life to good use and start organizing the drivers for wages and benefits.

Good luck! WP

WP,

As I watched the local news the other morning, Ross McGowan, a local newscaster, was interviewing a man who had successfully defended himself against felony charges including burglary and receiving stolen property. You would think that the interesting part about this is that he represented himself. But then, jailhouse lawyers aren't news by themselves. The real story is that the man had two strikes against him (felony convictions). The District Attorney offered four years as a plea bargain, not a bad deal considering the other option is life in prison if he loses. Three strikes, and you're out. He didn't take the deal and with the DA threatening life in prison if found guilty, this guy's credit limit was maxed. He demanded a jury trial and after one and half days of deliberation, he was found not guilty. The newscaster asked the rather clean-cut felon what his plans are now. No, not Disneyland. He said he's going to start driving a taxi here in San Francisco. Should make for some interesting material.

B.C. over

Wednesday, December 1, 1999
Hi there Bud,
I have a trip coming up to your Fare City this Saturday and I'll be depending on my legs and taxis to get around. Been reading your writing for a while and I get the feeling that I have to start from the airport anytime I want to go anywhere . . . hmmmm. So here's the real thing . . . for some reason, going to SF makes me want to do things I don't ordinarily do . . . by temperament or by availability. I'm reading the web and I see this show called "In Bed with Fairy Butch" at the Coco Club . . . sounds like a blast. Now, it's not like I've led a completely sheltered life, but I bet if I walked in there alone, I'd be like Dorothy in Oz. Is it possible to say, take a cab to a place and ask the driver to come back in an hour or two? Would they? How could I be sure to get someone like you? I guess I'm looking to be taken care of in a big city. In the end, I may just play it safe, but it sure would be fun to do something different for a change. You know, going somewhere else always makes me stretch a little and fantasize . . .

Just a girl from NC

Just a girl,
This letter isn't getting posted 'til after your visit, so let me say it was a night to remember. I wondered why you turned on the meter after we parked, first time I've done the math in some time. $13.30 and I hadn't even put the car in gear. I take you around the block, you take me around the world.

B.C. were not in Kansas, or ever were, over.

Wednesday, December 22, 1999
Hi Bud,
I rode with you last week from the airport to the Mark Hopkin's. I

got a chance to read your column today as I'm home for the holidays. I enjoyed it and thanks for the great service.

Write on, Duke Gillingham

Duke of Earl,
During the chariot scene in *Ben Hur,* a small red car can be seen in the distance. The same little red car can be seen driving down cable car tracks, going the wrong way down one-ways, cutting in front of you only to stop in the street to check the garage prices, cause they can't be that much, can they? It's not aliens, which are back by popular demand, it's worse. Seemed like that going up Nob Hill to the Mark, eh? I promise to get that seatbelt fixed.

B.C. over

Wednesday, December 11, 1999
Bud,
I am tired of Big Brother telling us what to do and how to do it. Please run for President this upcoming election.

Pac Man

Pac Man,
Thank you for your words of support. I will immediately start planning the first of several "Benefits for Bud." I will admit, the opportunity for good campaign slogans is there. A few that come to mind; I LIKE BUD. BUD IS FOR THE PEOPLE. BET ON BUD! MORE BUD, LESS TAXES. BUD IS ON YOUR SIDE. Etc.

B.C. over.

Sunday, December 12th, 1999
Hey Bud,
Thanks for the tip to Skinny. I gave you the credit for directing me there so maybe you'll get a half point for the PR. Thought I'd give you that info again, re: Peter Rowan and David Grisman, in case you lost that little slip of paper I wrote it on. The band they had was called Earth Opera (typical late sixties huh?) and they did two albums on Elektra, although the first was better I think. Peter went on to play with a group called Seatrain for a while which had

some interesting personnel, including Peter Greene who basically was the first to play electric rock violin, and a flute player from the old Blues Project group (another name you might like to check out) and of course yours truly on drums (for a while). Anyway, the first album Chris (Peter Rowans' younger brother) and I did was called *The Rowan Brothers on Columbia*, which of course I told you David Grisman produced. That was the group I was with (we all, Rowans, and I, group up in a small suburb of Boston called Wayland actually) but the album also had Jerry Garcia on it, and a whole host of what were the hottest session players around at that time including Russ Kunkle, Jim Gordon and etc. That album is still around too. Anyway, if you run across somebody who was in San Francisco around 71-72 and into all this, drop our name, you'll freak 'em. We were just about the house band at a place called The Boarding House for a long time. Meanwhile, I enjoyed your piece (yes, I did read it). You've got a good style, hope you keep at it.

Take it easy, Sandy Douglas

Sandy,
Thank you for taking the time to email me. I'm never sure who'll actually check out my column, much less give me their two cents. People going to the airport will always get one of my cards, while allowing me to think that the word is being spread. Networking does make the world go round. I thought I saw you at the Radiators show at the Great American Music Hall on Saturday night. I was hangin' out with the usual suspects, and even a fare from earlier that day tagged along. I was working security down by the dressing rooms, and the story goes an angry lesbian security chief started brawling with me and used her authority to have me removed from the building. I did get the boot, but was a victim of circumstance, don't ya know. When Travis Bickle was asked about his driving record, his reply was, "Clean, real clean. Like my conscience." Anyway, the Radiators provided safe passage back to one of the most visually delightful venues in My Fare City.

B.C. over.

Wednesday, December 29, 1999
Happy Y2K,
Has your meter been calibrated Bud Man? Keep up the fine work and don't trust those traffic lights 'round midnight.

Peace from Grand Rapids, Rain Man

Rain Man,
All is well but the blues are about, as we are all still here. As to the meter question, yes, physically. Metaphorically, been a while.

B.C. over.

Saturday, January 2, 2000
Hey you,
It was nice to meet you the other day. A very appropriate welcome home. Felt good. Thank you. I got a little performance anxiety though. Quite funny. I am a taxi kind of girl. Muni too. Ha. You know. Cross between Mary Tyler Moore and who knows what all. Have many stories. Love to share sometime, but oh well. Loved the picture, you wanting 1221 Jones in there, and well Gordon, we have been friends a long time. Stories about him. Well stories everywhere and always. As you know. Happy New Year. Yes, the lights stayed on.

Lorelle P.

Lorelle,
Did ya know 40% of McDonalds profits come from Happy Meals?

B.C. over.

Wednesday, January 19, 2000
Bud!!!
Thanks for coming back to Fiddler's Green . . . No hard feelings. We had a great time hanging with you! Thanks for the ride. Are we the typical tourists or what! Do you still have some pictures for us to see, with a nice long excuse for why you didn't return? Ha Ha. At the least, a nice hello will do. Thanks again tough guy.

A 'n B, your DC girlies

AnBnDC,
For all you did, this bud's your kid!

B.C. over.

Tuesday, January 18, 2000
Bud,
You are one handsome man . . . Love all the new letters . . . I love
the Slogan "LET BUD RULE."

Peaceout, Aimee

Hi Aimee,
Thank you very much. When I was still experiencing growing pains,
people used to call me Skywalker, Bud Skywalker. Help me Obe
One. "Tell two friends . . ." "And so on . . ."

B.C. over.

Sunday, January 23, 2000
Dear Bud,
I have two new rules to live by that I think may help carry me safely
into the next millennium:
1) Never write Bud Carson while drinking Miller Lite.
2) Edit, edit, edit . . .
Thanks for the happy meal tip, however, I prefer Burger King—the
Van Ness drive thru . . .

Lorelle

Lorelle,
Special orders don't upset me. You can have it your way, or any
other. My rules to live by would be my old stand by: 1) drive fast 2)
take chances . . . and since you don't drive . . .

B.C. over

Saturday, February 5, 2000

Hi Bud,

My name's John and I come from London. Compliments on a genuinely interesting website. Trouble is with the internet, even if this may be the ultimate form of freedom of speech there is so much crap. It takes courage for a man to sort the wheat from the chaff! It's good to hear about the philosophy of the ordinary man. A lot of people walk through life without purpose and it's good to hear some thing that helps a little. Anyway, just wanted you to know that you've got another mate who's put you on his favorites list. Keep it up man, you're doing a great, worthy job.

John

John,

Thanks for writing in. Ya know we hear a lot about those famed London cabbies, and the hard test they have to pass. The only thing I got out of My Fare City's test was the quickest way to the jail. It was a point A to point B question where you had to write out the street to street directions (and the only one that was not multiple choice). I had to laugh as they, coincidentally or not, started it near my residence. I got the question right, and was literally off to the races. Still, all the skills to be a good taxi driver in San Francisco could not be taught or tested in any way. At least not until we get the equivalent of the Kobiashi Moreau test. For those of you unfamiliar with this, it is a training program for Star Fleet cadets. It was featured in Star Trek, The Wrath of Khan. Kind of a no-win scenario. See it's the stress, as well as the guns, that can kill ya. Anyway, I would love if extreme cab driving could be part of next year's X-Games. I would personally take any visiting cabbies out for a spot o' tea, Bud Carson style. Cheers.

B.C. over.

February 18, 2000
Hi Bud,
Cool to see what you do. This city has so many stories to tell, and as you mentioned, so many wired things are going on in the night you wouldn't believe if you didn't experience it by yourself. And even more, it's real and priceless. Maybe one of the tougher jobs in this life but also one you love more. I'd like to ask you for some advice: how can I get behind the wheel of a cab in SF, actually to do the same as you do. You know, to get started and not to hit the wall after the first corner you take. I'm from the Swiss Alps and some things go a little bit different even if you assume being a city afficionado doesn't make a big difference in this world. Maybe the city talks are somehow the same, but the little tricks to get around and to survive, that's another story. And for the rest: my background is somehow similar to yours, you know, little cities, various jobs and moving around. And a bunch of stories to tell. So in this point I'd be very pleased if you could give me some information. I know the city pretty well, some secret corners, but as I told you, for the rest, that's another story. And last but not least: I met a fellow who's driving a cab in Santa Barbara after having driven his cab in NY. The poor guy was nearly going to freak out because there's just one main street, slow traffic, many cops and empty streets at night. You see, being in a nice place doesn't improve your health condition. He must be the only street maniac in this town . . . He freaks out when anyone asks him how his night has been!

Sincerely, Tom

Tom,

Thanks for your kind words. It's not just a job, it's an adventure. Here is how you can become a San Francisco Taxicab owner, a much better gig than the high gates and no rights that most drivers, including myself, suffer through. If you wait until you come up on the list you will still have drive a bit before they issue your medallion to you, but not much. Here is how to get on the Regular/Ramp Medallion Waiting List. I am on it, and you should be too. Most guys don't have the extra cash when they start driving, or don't intend on driving that long. Funny thing is, you don't even need to be a cab driver to get on this list! Sure, you need a letter from a company that says they will hire you, but any company will give you one of those if you tell them you want to drive a cab for them. Just fail to mention that you want to start driving in 15-18 years when your name comes up on the Medallion list. LOL. OK, complete the Application for Convenience and Necessity for Motor Vehicle for Hire Permit at SFPD Taxi Detail, 850 Bryant Street, Room 458, San Francisco, CA. Application Fee $340.00+s/c. A letter will be sent from the Taxi Detail when the applicant from the Medallion Waiting List becomes eligible for either a ramp or regular medallion and a medallion is available. You are then required to advise the Taxi Detail when you have fulfilled the full-time driving requirement at which time you are sent a Medallion Applicant Packet. Current Taxicab Commission guidelines for a full-time driver are defined as someone who has driven a minimum of 156 shifts of at least four hours in length during a one year period. Upon completion of the application and obtaining the additional information required (medical examination, DMV printout and minimum of 156 original waybills), you then call the Taxi Detail (415) 553-9844, to schedule an examination date. Your application is then accepted for review, and then the exam is administered while the waybills are checked and counted. Your file is forwarded for review and checked for completeness. Upon approval the applicant is put on the next Taxicab Commission hearing agenda for notice and approved on the next hearing date pending any objections. The current application fee is $559.25. When you get called up for the Taxi Medallion is the time to then go get your A-card and start driving.

Here is that process as described in Section 1089 (d) of the Municipal Police Code. First, you must be a resident of the United States, of good moral character. (No proof required on the moral part). Second, you must be 21 years or older to start driving, no age requirement to get on the medallion list, partly why the list is made up of the children and relatives of cops, meter maids, and other city folk "in the know". Third, be of sound physique, with good eyesight and not subject to any disease, condition, infirmity, or addiction to the use of alcohol or any controlled substance, which might render you unfit for the safe operation of a taxicab. It also might not, which would allow you to work sick, drunk, stoned, fat, and in a bad mood cause you lost your glasses. Fourth, be able to read and write the English language. Barely. You will need to be able to read and write the numbers on the meter as well as the address, time, and number of passengers on your waybill, and nothing more. As an owner and Medallion holder this is very important. If you are not an owner like most drivers, then all you need to write is your name and cab number on your waybill, that's it. The window guy will accept your gate fee, and waybill at the end of each shift. If you are not an owner, but fulfilling the driving requirement to receive your Taxi Medallion, make sure your waybills are accurate and complete, as they will be checked out by the Taxi Detail. Fifth, be clean in dress and person. In San Francisco you are by law able to wear any type of headdress, while driving your cab. At Cab College our teacher said you can even wear a ski mask, if that strikes your fancy. If you're a guy who wishes to wear a dress, that's fine too, personally I dress up as a clown every Halloween. No matter how bad or aggressive I drive, people who would flip me off start to, then see me, smile and LOL. I even bring candy to give to strangers and children throughout My Fare City. Sixth, have a valid California Driver's License of a class sufficient for the lawful operation of the motor vehicle to be driven. This is just the normal driver's license. In 1989 when I was issued mine, all I had to do was surrender my driver's license from the state I moved from (Colorado) and take a vision, and knowledge test. I almost flunked the vision test, it came down to the final question, "Is the red ball inside or outside of the box?". If I miss this one question, I would then fail the vision test and not receive my license until I came back with glasses and passed it. As I slowly started to say inside the box the guy administering the test stretched his arm out wide and gave a fake yawn that sounded like owwww. I quickly said, "OUTSIDE!". He smiled and said, "Congratulations Mr Carson, you passed." I love random acts of kindness. Since 1989 all I have had to do is pay to renew it each year, either on line or by mail, no re testing of any kind. You then need to attend and complete a certified and approved Cab College, and obtain a Certificate of Completion and ADA Certificate at Cab College. Pick a company then have them give you a letter of intent to hire, if you don't first succeed, try again. Usually any company will give you one provided you can give them a printout of your driving record from Department of Motor Vehicles, dated within 30 days of application. Then get yourself a passport size color or black and white, full face photograph, some companies will take the picture for you. You can't wear a hat, scarf, or sunglasses in the photo, only on duty. Then bring all of the above to SFPD Permits, 850 Bryant Street, Room 458 (Monday–Friday, 9:00 a.m. to 12 noon, 1:00 p.m. to 3:00 p.m.), to submit an application for Driver Public Vehicle for Hire permit plus $74.00 (seventy-four dollars) in cash for Application Filing Fee and $42.00 (forty-two dollars) in cash for Fingerprinting Fee. The application process takes approximately one week, after which you will be scheduled for taxicab class on Thursday of the following week. Upon completion of the class and passing of the test, a temporary permit is issued. The test is all multiple choice except for one question. The one essay question requires you to write down, street to street, the quickest way to the jail from Broadway and Octavia in Pacific Heights. Though my first thought was just becoming a cab driver must be the quickest way, I then realized they were asking about literal and short term directions. I figure most new drivers have been to 850 Bryant before, whether it be from a criminal court date, or spending the preceding night in the drunk tank. Once the temporary permit is issued, you may begin to work as a San Francisco Taxicab Driver, and ride off in to the sunset, like your humble narrator. You will have to pick-up your permanent permit, official Taxi Driver Badge and A-Card at the Tax Collector's Office at City Hall, Room 140 (Monday–Friday, 8:00 a.m. to 5:00

p.m.). Allow 8 weeks for the city to process it. The Tax Collector will charge a fee of $60.00 (sixty dollars).The fee breakdown is: License Fee $45.00, Badge Fee $10.00 and Identification Card Fee $5.00. Now Tom, the fact that you are from the Swiss Alps means first work on the residency, maybe your acceptance into Cab College might get you a student visa; they do it for Beauty College, so why not Cab College? As to your friend in Santa Barbara, sounds like he would do better up here in Northern California. You also hit the nail on the head seeing the possibilities for a storyteller, and yes it certainly is real and priceless. As far as driver safety I've developed this theory that it seems that all the really weird things that happen to cab drivers happen to them the first couple of months that they drive cab. They're kind of like prey in the jungle, like a newborn or something saying "victimize me". People pick up that energy, and will see you as a crime of opportunity. It takes experience and experience alone to know how to differentiate between fares that will be a problem and fares that won't. I have never been robbed but did have one guy try once, with a Kentucky Fried Chicken Drumstick! I threw his drunken ass out of my cab and in to the gutter from which he came. If I ever had a real gun in my back, I would not, and you should not, resist, as life is worth more than a pocketful of small bills. Good luck to you on your journey Tom.

B.C. over.

March 20, 2000
Budman!
I don't think I can go on much longer without your stuff. Where the ?=**&% are you? You got writer's block or something?
Yours truly,

B. Cabbie in Bergen, Norway

Hey Baard,
Yeah, hit a few roadblocks. My old 486DX2 finally died along with another attempt at normality. I am not going to fight it anymore. I gave the PC a proper burial, similar to the television at the beginning of SCTV (Canadian comedy program) and returned to driving nights.

I have never been happier. Remember friend, old cabbies never die, they just need to lie low once in a while. Thank you for your support, and stay tuned.

B.C. over.

April 3, 2000
Bud,
What ever happened to Debbie Boone? I once rolled my window up on the hand of a cigar-chompin' 'bigshot' the night before he was to play an amateur golf tourney with his other cigar-chompin' friends. I might have added a stroke or two to his game. I slap myself for not checkin' in on your wit and charm more often. I hope you keep it up.

Jim in Monterey

Captain Jim,
Keep on riding that mystery ship . . .

B.C. over.

May 16, 2000
Hi,
I am an on-again-off-again S.F. cab driver (Veterans), currently exiled in Chicago. I read online, last week, that the city is going to add 100 more cabs to the approximately 1300 (according to the story) that are already on the street, when the meter goes up to $2.00 a mile. But, I have heard from another source that the city would add 300 last year, 300 this year and, then, maybe 100 more. So that could add up to about 1400 or as many as 1800 (!). I wish I could rely on the newspaper story (probably *Examiner*). Do you know what the final figure will be (or how many there are now)? I e-mailed Gavin about this but he did not answer me this time—which makes me worry, a lot. He answered before, twice, on my opinion that the waybill is a clear Fourth Amendment violation (if everybody took a taxi everyday, could the police make us keep track of where everybody goes?; in a couple of years somebody has got to come up with a GPS to keep the trip sheet for a hundred dollars: with 500,000

rides a week downloaded into a police computer every week in a city of only 750,000).

Denis Drew

Hey Denis,
More important than the cabs would be the upcoming proposition to start issuing medallions to the cab companies instead of to the individual drivers. Prop M. At this moment, it stands for mellow.

B.C. over.

June 5, 2000
Bud,
Well, cab drivers are scum bags. Now I know you're a scum bag. Worse. You're a whore. A pimp and a whore under one roof. And you're a fucking little sociopath. These credentials are impressive, but won't necessarily make you a good cabby. You do look the part, if you weren't so goddamn cute. A few more years of drink and drugs will take care of that. Anyway . . . Cab drivers are scum bags. They lust only for whores and gambling. They like to fight. They like to kick jerks out of their cab. They are jerks. They're not nice to women and children, even if they are women and children. Arty types don't make the grade. They're sheep in cab driver clothing. A real cab driver is a full time son of a bitch. He may or may not know how to speak English, but you can bet he's a talking asshole in any language. The son of a bitches will never grow up. They don't want real jobs. They're eternal boys, which is to say your average American fellah, except they do it for a living. Have a beer . . . Cabbies take the worse shit a man can take and get paid for it. Mercenary killers are higher on the ladder. So are whores when it comes to selling your ass. A cabby is a legal criminal. Something like a lawyer, same branch of pedestrianism. Know what they call a cabby without a hangover? A nonsequitur. No such animal. You'd fit in there pretty well. Drugs too. You gotta take lots of drugs to be a cabby. But know how to handle them, combine them like an alchemist. The best cabbies can shoot a goofball in their neck going sixty in heavy traffic and the passengers won't even notice. You'd do alright there too. Where was I? . . . Oh, yeah. The most important part—and I don't know if you fill the bill

here. We'll see—a cabby's gotta know how to push a hack. If you can't pass a hack through the eye of a needle, you ain't no cabby. The cab's gotta be an integral part of you. It has to fit like a glove, hang like a genital, bounce like a tit, shit like an eagle, fly like a demon, burrow through the city like a rat in a garbage heap and come out shining. You gotta be able to sneak up on a fare like a pickpocket. You gotta squeeze through double parked cars like toothpaste. There can't be more than the distance between the hem of a whore's skirt and her snatch between you and sleepwalking pedestrians. You gotta have nerves of steel and the patience of a toad. Otherwise you'll crack up. You'll get fired or end up in a fireball on the freeway. Cab driving is magic and you gotta master the automatic pilot. If you're the type of pedestrian who bumps into other people on the street, probably you won't make a cabby. Got it? . . . Now's for the passenger. You gotta put meat in the back seat. That meter's gotta be running or you ain't going to make it. You're going to sweat blood to find the bastards and eat shit when you do. They'll put you through the ringer. "Driver, where you taking us? This isn't the right way. I'm taking your number. The police will hear about this!" They'll get out after chewing your ear off and stiff you. The ones you've given the best service to. The insult cuts like a knife and the stiff knows it. It's hard out there these days. People make their little power plays wherever they can. You got to shrug your shoulders. Keep your armor shining. Keep the meter running. You'll be a true blue misanthrope in no time. Just take a few hundred of the bastards around on Saturday night and you'll see what I mean. They get in smelling of toothpaste, deodorant, perfume, and mouthwash. You'll pick them up a few hours later reeking of garlic, alcohol, digesting food. A rich nauseating stink of momentary happiness. They'll scream in your ear and tell bad jokes. The assholes will test your patience. They'll spill drinks, vomit, ejaculate and fight like cats and dogs. You'll get real familiar with the hose and the rag. You pick them up overflowing with gaiety at the beginning of the evening and drop them off at the end angry, depressed, gibbering drunk. You'll hear the same selfish, petty, narrow-minded, ignorant, misinformed, vicious conversation repeated over and over. Every one of the bastards thinking their situation is unique. Planning kids, marriages, and careers before they know how to tie their shoes. It's the same everywhere. The big muddled blueprint of the herd. Now you'll have some fine human experiences, the kind that flood you from head to toe with a warm sense of beatitude. You'll pick up the father who's just watched his wife give birth. You'll pick up the widow who's just watched her husband die. You'll pick up the ones that have been stabbed and shot and raped and take them to the hospital. You'll take them home later bandaged from head to toe. You'll pick up the guy on his way to the bridge to jump. You'll pick up the young lovers and you'll wipe off the back seat when they get out. You'll pick up a thousand sob stories and broken hearts. You'll pick them up by the tens of thousands and they'll all give you the same corny lines. The hopeless banality of it all will sicken you like the smell of rotten meat. But the cab driver has to put up with it. He gets the big picture. He gets the whole stinking overview. It's okay for the passenger who experiences reality from one point of view. But a cabby sees it like the Buddha. He's got to cultivate the sewer. Another beer? Sure, sure. Go ahead. Have a line. That's what it's there for. Don't interrupt. I keep losing my train of thought. Everybody's desperate. Everybody's got guns. They'll shoot you in the back and ask questions later. You gotta have your radar on. A map of the city's gotta light up in your brain. You gotta see not only where the fare is when I call it, but the fare that ain't called. You'll see a fuzzy area where the danger is. It'll come as a stink or a bad taste in your mouth. You gotta size up a killer from several blocks away before you can see his eyes. Gotta see how he's standing. How he's dressed. How he signals you. If he's hiding something, it'll show. A sick light will burn a hole through the map. You'll pass him at sixty. Only then will you see the ozone in his eyes. The blank hole, which is the enemy. Hermes won't fail you here. Take my word for it. That's why I don't put no fucking cage between you and the back seat. If you're stupid enough to pick up a cemetery run, you shouldn't be driving in the first place. There's something else. You gotta be a good Christian. You gotta be nice. A real sweetheart. You gotta be kind as a bloodthirsty bat at a prayer meeting. Clever as a praying mantis in some rich matron's crab salad. Somebody different for every asshole that gets in your cab. Oldest trick in the world. All holymen are hip to it. You gotta be what they want you to be. Then you'll succeed. I mean you gotta be nasty when it's necessary. But not lowbrow nasty. You gotta score. And you don't score with cheap shots. Another thing you should keep in mind: Cab driving is contagious. Once you're addicted, it'll eat you inside out and spit out the pit. You won't ever want to go back to a regular job, that is—if you're a true hack. Of course I know you're a whore. You already know the business from one angle. It's like religion. Eat at some holy trough while the head monk sticks it to you. Anyway, as I was saying, the virus is lethal. You'll find you can't function without the cab. You'll hate it. Take a day or two off and you'll be longing for your ride. It's like drugs that way. Cab driving will eat your soul and there won't be anything else for you. Guess that about covers the details. Only thing you have to do now is get out there and get to work bud.

Ken Waino

Ken,
You dispatchers think you know it all. Thank you very little.

B.C. over

June 22, 2000
Hi Bud,
I hope you will remember me. I am the girl from Austin, Texas who rode in your cab way back in February. You were the cooooolest person! Remember? I was dating a guy who has your same birthday? (Operative word there is WAS) You took me to the Haight to make last-minute, tie-dye purchases before my trip to the airport. We stopped and had a beer before my flight, too. What was the name of that bar? Then in my haste, when you dropped me at SFO, I forgot my goods in your cab and you were kind enough to circle the airport and return it all to me. Your parting words were something about packing yourself into my suitcase. Anyway, I immediately checked out Skinny.com and have been enjoying it ever since. I've been disappointed that I've never seen an e-mail I sent to you. Did you ever receive it? Well, just wanted to let you know I'm still checking you out and still remember the kindness you showed me

that day in February. Hope all is well! It sure is boilin' hot here in Texas so enjoy that cool SF weather. I'm jealous!

Laurie

Hi Laurie,
I wish I could meet a positive significant other, but for now my parrot will have to do. She doesn't mind that I work nights. keep that wheel turnin', I'll keep my tires burnin', until we see each other next time . . . (the card you sent was so, it was . . . it gave me that "warm, fuzzy feeling") . . .

B.C. over.

July 1, 2000
So, what happened to Bud Carson? No updates on his site. His is head, shoulders, chest, hips and ankles above the other cabbie sites out there. Miss his missives. Hope he's not "in the care of the state." If he is, lemme' know where and I'll send him a snail mail, wishing him well. Maybe he's gone on to bigger and better. Whatever that could be. An answer, please?

Dave from LA, CA, USA

Dave,
I am back in the diamond lane, looking for that diamond in the rough.

B.C. over.

August 9, 2000
Hi Bud,
I guess you must either be away, or as I found when I operated my website for a few years, you may be buried in email, or possibly just buried. I sent you a note a week or more back wondering if you might still have an email address for Sandy Douglas. I found his note to you, and your reply on your website, and was hoping you might be able to either forward my note to him, or send me the address he sent his message to you from. Sandy was an old best friend of mine. I'd really appreciate it if you would just send me a brief reply letting

me know you've received this note. If you don't have the time to search for his address right away, I surely understand.

Thanks kindly, Shel Ritter

Shel,
Tap you heels together three times and say there's no place like my fare city . . .

B.C. over

September 14, 2000
Bud,
Hey I am the guy that you gave the ride to from San Francisco to almost Mountain View. Bro! I look forward to reading your stories and thanks for the great company. Take care of yourself and be safe!

Mark President, SumoStyle

Hey Mark,
Next time bring enough money to make it past Burlingame.

B.C. over.

September 28, 2000
Dear Bud,
In my community (Albuquerque), the yellow belly cabs lease their cars and do the cell phone trick with the doormen at most of the larger hotels. This includes the Hyatt, Crowne Regency (hoity toity Holiday Inn) and the Sheraton. We turn in our money at the end of the shift for a commission. There is very little left for a kickback so we don't get many of the calls except when yellow is tied up so I can empathize with you on this issue. A royal pain in the a—to say the least.

Keep the Cab Rollin', Tony

Tony,
Ahh, kickbacks, they kinda remind me of the preview channel. I figure at the end of my life, when I take that meter-and-a-half ride to the stars, I will be enlightened. Everything will make sense, to

me and my maker. Except for one thing. How the hell did I spend close to a year (added together) watching the preview channel? I dunno. Same goes for kickbacks, I don't know and don't want to. The lion's share of kickbacks were given to the hard ass behind the bulletproof glass. The doormen are a mixed bag. The Hyatt Regency doormen, the worst offenders, deal out the airports to the limo guys, and then gouge cabbies when an airport does come up. On the flipside, the Westin St. Francis will not accept a tip from a cabbie even if offered. Lately I have not found myself in any hotel line. I am back to my random systematic order of traversing the famed cobblestone hills, letting fate, skill, and as always, a bit o' luck light my way.

B.C. over.

"bud waits for his next fare"

Cabbie Lingo

A-card: Hack License.

Bartertown: Central waiting lot (queue) of cabbies at San Francisco International Airport.

Backbook: When you have missed a workday and your shift did not get filled, you then owe the company the cab fee for that evening. The company deducts money from your next few shifts in order to cover the fee.

Boneyard: Place where you pick up the cab.

Bingo: Response given to affirm or confirm a dispatch call to a specific address. The dispatcher calls out the cross streets (California & Kearney) and if a cabbie is there he/she responds by saying, "Cab#007 Bingo Cal/Kearney." The dispatcher then gives the cab the exact address, which the driver repeats to confirm the order.

Bud Carson: The next best thing to a bingo!

Concrete Jungle: Part of cabbie queue in parking structure at SFO, G-33 to be exact.

Crack the Nut: To make enough money to cover cab fees, gas and kickbacks.

Deadheading: Driving empty down to the airport to get a fare.

Dispatcher: The person who receives all incoming calls from customers, calls out all radio calls to the cabbies and handles any miscellaneous questions drivers may have while on the road.

Dropping: As the driver drops off a fare at a given cross street, he/she gives dispatch the location they are at to try to grab a nearby fare.

Irie: Feelin' good, Rastafarian saying.

En route: To be on the way to an area with unfilled orders, with a fare in the cab.

Franklin: A hundred-dollar bill. Also known as a "Ben Franklin."

Front Office: A virtual cash cow, (aka the grafters).

Kickback ("tip"): A kickback to the dispatcher by the cabbie insures fast and accurate delivery of radio calls. It is not required but is highly recommended especially if the cabbie wants an airport run. A kickback given to the window guy helps gets the cabbie a good cab if you don't have one assigned and insures that gate fee, gas and vouchers are added correctly when you turn in. Kickbacks need to be made at the beginning and end of the cabbie's shift because the dispatcher's and window guy's shifts change conveniently midway through the night shift.

Meter: Self-explanatory.

Meter an a Half: Any ride fifteen miles beyond the San Francisco city limits is charged the fare on the meter plus an additional fifty percent of the fare (i.e. A $50.00 meter value would be a fare of $75.00 outside the city limits).

No Go: What a cabbie reports to the dispatcher if they get to a radio call and nobody is there. The dispatcher will give that cab the next order that comes up in their area, sometimes right away.

Possible: Pedestrians trying to hail a cab without a call in to the dispatcher. The cabbie calls the dispatcher, "Possibles at 5th & Mission." The dispatcher calls out the location "We have possibles at 5th and Mission" and if a cabbie is in the area he/she will respond. This comes in handy on slow nights.

Regular Rider: A customer who regularly rides with the cab company on a daily or weekly basis. A regular rider is a consistent fare and usually a good tipper because they get priority service.

Runner: A person who ditches the cabbie for a fare.

Script: Looking strangely like monopoly money, the city issues "Para

Transit Script" to people that qualify for ten cents on the dollar. Issued to everyone from the little old lady going to the grocery store on a midnight run for sugar, to a working girl on her way to a trick, the runs are short and sweet as people find it easier to tip more if it isn't their money. Not all companies accept script, though I haven't found a hack yet that won't buy a thirty-dollar book for ten bucks . . .

Short: (Reference to San Francisco Airport.) If a cabbie can pick up a fare from the airport, drop the fare off, and make it back to the airport within thirty minutes, he is referred to as a "short." To avoid a long wait for another fare, that cabbie will then go to the front of the line to insure another fare immediately.

Short Shift: Instead of a full shift, the cabbie only works for a couple of hours and then turns the vehicle over to another driver. The cabbie pays a per-hour charge for the vehicle use instead of the regular gate charge.

Spare Cab: A cab identified by four numbers, rather than three on the outside of the cab (starting with a two, "2xxx"). A spare cab is legally operated by using a medallion out of a regular (three-numbered) cab, usually when the regular cab is being repaired. The mileage on a "spare" cab is almost sure to be over 500,000 miles but with most the odometer is broken before this and never repaired. A cab becomes a spare when the medallion number is upgraded to a newer cab. This leaves the former cab still operable, but very old and prone to constant breakdowns. If a spare cab gets you through your shift without breaking down, it's a good spare.

Stretching: Falsifying the cab's location to appear closer to a possible pick-up address and bingo the order. This practice is widely used but frowned upon by dispatch and other cabbies that may actually be closer.

Tweeker: Reference to amphetamine user.

Voucher: A statement, card, or receipt provided to a rider by his/her company, which pays the rider's fare same as cash. Also, term used to describe a rider whose company pays the fare; usually a good tipper (i.e. Cab #491 voucher at 6th and Folsom).

Waybill: The written record of all fares for the shift. Documents pick-up address, time of pick up and drop off, drop-off address, number of riders, and fare charged. Rarely does a cabbie record all of his fares.

Window Guy: Issues the cabbies their waybill before they leave, calculates the cab fee upon arrival (i.e. gas, gates, etc.). Like Danny DeVito from the TV show *Taxi*, he never smiles.

Zone: Something cabbies get into on occasion.

Sometimes It's Better To Be Lucky Than Good . . .

Taxicab Regulations Section XVII, Part C, subset 18
www.penderislandstaxiandtours.com

"bud, lorelle, aimee, and daisy"

I picked up my future wife Lorelle from San Francisco International

Airport, while working a day shift in one of the YAHOO! netcabs, December 30th 1999. Aimee was born March 27th 2002. I am now living the American Dream, on Pender Island, British Columbia, Canada.